Values in Youth Sport and Physical Education

As sport has become more intense, professional and commercialized so have the debates grown about what constitutes acceptable behaviour and fair play, and how to encourage and develop 'good' sporting behaviour, particularly in children and young people. This book explores the nature and function of *values* in youth sport and establishes a framework through which coaches, teachers and researchers can develop an understanding of the decision-making processes of young athletes and how they choose between playing fairly or cheating to win.

The traditional view of sport participation is that it has a beneficial effect on the social and moral development of children and young people and that it intrinsically promotes cultural values. This book argues that the research evidence is more subtle and nuanced. It examines the concept of values as central organizing constructs of human behaviour that determine our priorities, guide our choices, and transfer across situations, and considers the value priorities and conflicts that are so useful in helping us to understand behaviour in sport. The book argues that teachers and professionals working with children in sport are centrally important agents for value transmission and change and therefore need to develop a deeper understanding of how sport can be used to encourage pro-social values, and offers suggestions for developing a curriculum for teaching values through sport in differing social contexts.

Spanning some of the fundamental areas of sport practice and research, including sport psychology, sport pedagogy, practice ethics and positive youth development through sport, and including useful values and attitudes questionnaires and guidance on their use and interpretation, this book is important reading for any student, researcher, coach or teacher with an interest in youth sport or physical education.

Jean Whitehead was an international long jumper and physical education teacher. She led sport psychology and coordinated the academic disciplines in human movement studies at Bedford College of Higher Education, UK. In research at the University of Brighton, UK, she focused on achievement goal perspectives and measuring values.

Hamish Telfer was course leader at the University of Cumbria, UK, for the postgraduate degree in Sports Coaching. Now retired, he is still actively involved in research and publication in sports coaching, particularly practice ethics and reflective practice. He has been a Great Britain Team Coach for Cross Country.

John Lambert is a Senior Lecturer in Sport Coaching and Physical Education at the University of Brighton, UK. He works in talent ID for a Premier League football club. His main research interest is teaching values through sport having worked on a major international sport for development project for over ten years.

Values in Youth Sport and Physical Education

Edited by Jean Whitehead, Hamish Telfer and John Lambert

LONDON AND NEW YORK

First published 2013
by Routledge
2 Park Square, Milton Park, Abingdon, Oxon OX14 4RN

and by Routledge
711 Third Avenue, New York, NY 10017

Routledge is an imprint of the Taylor & Francis Group, an informa business

British Library Cataloguing in Publication Data
A catalogue record for this book is available from the British Library

Library of Congress Cataloging in Publication Data
Values in youth sport and physical education / edited by Jean Whitehead, Hamish Telfer and John Lambert.
pages cm
ISBN 978-0-415-53306-5 (hardback) — ISBN 978-0-203-11415-5 (ebk)
1. Sports for children—Moral and ethical aspects. 2. Physical education for children. I. Whitehead, Jean.
GV709.2.V35 2014
796.083—dc23
2013027163

ISBN: 978-0-415-53306-5 (hbk)
ISBN: 978-0-203-11415-5 (ebk)

Typeset in Times New Roman
by FiSH Books Ltd, Enfield

MIX
Paper from
responsible sources
FSC
www.fsc.org   FSC® C013604

Printed and bound by CPI Group (UK) Ltd, Croydon, CR0 4YY

This book is dedicated to Martin Lee

Contents

Illustrations

Contributors

Editors

John Lambert, University of Brighton; School of Sport and Service Management

Hamish Telfer, formerly of the University of Cumbria; School of Sport

Jean Whitehead, University of Brighton; School of Sport and Service Management

Authors

Isabel Balaguer, University of Valencia, Spain; Department of Social Psychology

Nick Balchin, Falkirk Council Educational Psychology Service

Anat Bardi, Royal Holloway University of London; Department of Psychology

Isabel Castillo, University of Valencia, Spain; Department of Social Psychology

Mike Cockman of the former Bedford College of Higher Education

Cathy Devine, University of Cumbria; School of Sport

Joan L. Duda, University of Birmingham; School of Sport and Exercise Sciences

Paul Freeman, University of Exeter; College of Life and Environmental Sciences

Carlos E. Gonçalves, University of Coimbra, Portugal; Faculty of Sport Sciences

Antonis Hatzigeorgiadis, University of Thessally, Greece; Department of Physical Education and Sport Science

Don Hellison, University of Illinois at Chicago, USA; Professor Emeritus, College of Education,

Zoe Knowles, Liverpool John Moores University; School of Sport and Exercise Sciences

Hannah Leger, University of Exeter; College of Life and Environmental Sciences

Martin J. Lee, Deceased; formerly at the University of Brighton (see 'Martin Lee's work on values', page xvi).

Alec Leslie, University of Exeter; College of Life and Environmental Sciences

Nikos Ntoumanis, University of Birmingham; School of Sport and Exercise Sciences

Eleanor Quested, University of Birmingham; School of Sport and Exercise Sciences

Shalom H. Schwartz, The Hebrew University, Jerusalem, Israel; and National Research University, Higher School of Economics, Moscow; Professor Emeritus of Psychology

Craig Williams, University of Exeter, UK; College of Life and Environmental Sciences

Foreword

Several years ago I learned about John Lambert's work in the University of Brighton's Football 4 Peace initiative, a programme that promotes peace in contested and often violent territories such as Northern Ireland and Israel. Participants are taught guidelines for working and playing with each other such as neutrality, equity, inclusion, respect, trust, and responsibility. I found his ideas compelling, especially since my own work since about 1972 has used physical activity to promote life skills and values in low-income, mostly minority neighbourhoods.

In recent years, my colleague Tom Martinek and I have been advocating our own version of values education in our work with urban kids. These activities reminded me of my early discussions with John, so when he invited me to write a foreword for a book he and his colleagues Jean Whitehead and Hamish Telfer had edited, called *Values in Youth Sport and Physical Education*, I immediately said yes, despite having just returned from nine months out of state teaching and consulting.

Values in Youth Sport and Physical Education is a blend of theory, research, experience and practice that should appeal to a wide audience (e.g. researchers, practitioners, parents, and others concerned with the direction of youth sport). It draws on some of the major contributors to the youth sport literature, especially Martin Lee, who played a pivotal role in the ethical development of this field.

The idea of values raises the question of *whose* values. Winston Churchill had values, but so did Hitler! Values are broader and more stable than attitudes, yet they can be more or less stable, neutral or not, and conflicting or not. Value theory is not neutral. It is instead pro-social, and requires compatible values in practice.

Although the book's style is intended to raise questions rather than give definitive answers, theoretical and empirical models are discussed, and a case is made for several specific theories and approaches, among them selective sport psychology concepts such as task-ego and achievement goal theory, a coaching model for the transmission of core values to promote peace, and value theory as a new overarching research paradigm intended to highlight motivational criteria for personal decision-making in sport. Issues include whether values can be taught through sport, how to deal with value conflict, what constitutes fair play, and how youth sport professionals can be agents of change.

In the United States, strong evidence supports the view that youth sport has been politicized and professionalized in recent years, leading to a quest for 'suitable' interventions that focus on pro-social values. One effort, led by Martin Lee and others, is the development and implementation of the Youth Sport Values Questionnaire. Using this tool, data showed that kids aged 12–15 ranked enjoyment and personal achievement in sport highest, and winning lowest. Similar findings have also been reported in the United States.

Value transfer in youth sport has been problematic, yet claims of automatic transfer by some youth sport and physical education practitioners continue. However, in the United States, some progress has been made thanks to the creative work on transfer by Tom Martinek, David Walsh, and others. These efforts need to continue until automatic transfer is put to rest.

Don Hellison
University of Illinois at Chicago

Martin Lee's work on values

Martin Lee pioneered the study of youth sport values in the UK using the conceptual frameworks of Rokeach (1973) and Schwartz (1992) from social psychology. He was a post-graduate student of Rokeach at Washington State University, and his 1976 MSc thesis applied the Rokeach Value Survey (RVS) to study sport values of varsity, and recreational footballers and non-footballers. Back in the UK, at Bedford College of Higher Education, he had a series of research commissions from the English Sports Council in 1987–9, to (1) review the literature on fair play, (2) identify issues related to fair play, (3) propose the development of an instrument to measure sport values, and (4) identify emergent values in young soccer and tennis players. From 1990 to 1993 he was the UK representative and leader of the Committee of Experts of the Council of Europe Committee for the Development of Sport (CDDS), and worked on a European project on Ethics in Sport and Young People. In 1994, at the University of Brighton, he had a Sports Council grant to study Young People, Sport and Ethics: an Examination of Fairplay in Youth Sport, and in 1998–9 he led a grant from the Economic and Social Research Council (ESRC), with Jean Whitehead, on The Effect of Values, Achievement Goals, and Perceived Ability on Moral Attitudes in Youth Sport. The research reported in Part I of this book was conducted under these grants.

Martin's work on values was set in the context of his deep concern for the welfare of children in sport and the need to see sport and physical education from their perspective. He founded the Institute for the Study of Children in Sport (ISCiS) in Bedford, wrote courses on coaching children for the National Coaching Foundation and the UK Government, and a book on Coaching Children in Sport (Lee, 1993). Despite retirement and the diagnosis in 2000 of a terminal illness, Martin continued to publish his work and, as a Fellow of the Physical Education Association, he gave their Fellow's Lecture in 2003 on values in physical education and sport. His last chapter (Lee, 2007) summarised current challenges to sport, education and society. Martin died in 2009, and his professional papers can be read in a Special Collection at the University of Exeter Library where he was both student and lecturer in his early career in physical education and sport.

References

Lee, M. (ed.) (1993) *Coaching Children in Sport: Principles and Practice*. London E. & F. Spon.

Lee, M.J. (2007) Sport, education and society: The challenge. In C.E. Gonçalves, S.P. Cumming, M.J.C Silva and R. Malina (eds) *Sport and Education: Tribute to Martin Lee*. Coimbra: University of Coimbra, pp. 197–207.

Rokeach, M. (1973) *The Nature of Human Values*. New York: Free Press.

Schwartz, S. (1992) Universals in the content and structure of values: Theoretical advances and empirical tests in 20 countries. In M.P. Zanna (ed.) *Advances in Experimental Social Psychology*, 25, 1–65. London: Academic Press.

Acknowledgements

Abridged reprints

Chapter 2: Martin J. Lee, Michael Cockman (1995). Values in children's sport: Spontaneously expressed values among young athletes. *International Review for Sociology of Sport*, 30(3/4), 337–350. Copyright © Sage Publications Ltd. Reprinted by Permission of Sage.

Chapter 3: Martin J. Lee, Jean Whitehead, and Nick Balchin (2000). The measurement of values in youth sport: Development of the Youth Sport Values Questionnaire. *Journal of Sport and Exercise Psychology*, 22, 307–326. Copyright © Human Kinetics. Adpated with permission from Human Kinetics.

Chapter 4: Martin J. Lee, Jean Whitehead, and Nikos Ntoumanis (2007). Development of the Attitudes to Moral Decision-making in Youth Sport Questionnaire (AMDYSQ). *Psychology of Sport and Exercise*, 8, 369–392. Copyright © Elsevier Publications. Reprinted by Permission of Elsevier.

Chapter 5: Martin J. Lee, Jean Whitehead, Nikos Ntoumanis, and Antonis Hatzigeorgiadis (2008). Relationships among values, achievement orientations, and attitudes in youth sport. *Journal of Sport and Exercise Psychology*, 30, 585–610. Copyright © Human Kinetics. Adapted with permission from Human Kinetics.

Appendix 3: Extracts from Martin Lee (ed.) (1993). Why are you coaching children? In *Coaching Children in Sport: Principles and Practice*, pp. 27–38. Copyright © Taylor & Francis. London: E. & F. N. Spon. Reprinted by permission of Taylor & Francis.

Funding

Research in Chapter 2 was commissioned by The Sports Council Research Unit, London WCIH 9RA

Studies 1 to 4 in Chapter 3, and Studies 1 to 4 in Chapter 4, were funded by a commission to Martin Lee by the English Sports Council (now Sport England)

Study 5 in Chapter 4 and both studies in Chapter 5 were supported by grant R000222219 awarded by the Economic and Social Research Council (ESRC), UK, to Martin Lee and Jean Whitehead.

In Chapter 8 the work of Shalom H. Schwartz was partly supported by the HSE Basic Research Program (International Laboratory of Sociocultural Research)

Preface

This book develops from a series of studies by Martin Lee on youth sport values. It was first suggested by Hamish Telfer, in conversation with Jean Whitehead, to fill an important gap in the literature. As a researcher, Martin was concerned about unethical behaviour in sport and saw value theory as a new paradigm that could explain children's moral decision-making in situations of value conflict. As a teacher and coach he cared about the development and well-being of children and that they should not be put into an adult sport model. His philosophy was 'sport for kids', not 'kids for sport'. As a pioneering thinker he challenged assumptions and conventional wisdom. This book reports and extends his research to provide a resource on values for the sport and physical education communities and a foundation for further research and practice.

Jean worked alongside Martin while studying achievement goal orientations. She collaborated in developing his values and attitude questionnaires and in research about relations between values, attitude and achievement goals. Her perspective has been to clarify how the youth sport questionnaires can be used internationally in exploration of other issues, how they integrate with life values, and how values and achievement goals interact.

Hamish's perspective as an international performance coach and practitioner academic in coaching practice has been to develop an understanding of the professional context in which youth sport and physical education take place, and the dilemmas encountered by practitioners. As coaches engage with wider agendas than performance sport, this area of values is of particular importance in orienting practice appropriately.

John's approach as teacher and coach has been in exploring the development of value based coaching in divided societies. As a practitioner–researcher he has contributed a contrasting action research perspective leading to a coaching model for teaching values, accompanied by a coach education system, which has been widely used in international interventions and is underpinned by value and learning theories.

None of the editors is an expert on value theory or the wider moral context in which Martin wrote. We are most grateful to Anat Bardi and Shalom Schwartz for their chapter, which demonstrates how the Schwartz value structure, which has dominated values research for three decades, provides a framework for under-standing value conflict and intervening effectively to reduce it.

We are also grateful to Anat Bardi of Royal Holloway College for updates on value theory; to Richard Fisher of St Mary's College, Twickenham, for help in developing the rationale and introduction; to Nikos Ntoumanis at the University of Birmingham for reviewing some chapters; to Simon Whitmore and Joshua Wells at Routledge for guidance and patience as many diverse issues caused delays in publication; to Alastair Lee for his support of the book and permission to reprint some of his father's material; and to all our contributors who have brought the book to life.

John Lambert
Hamish Telfer
Jean Whitehead
May 2013

Introduction

Exploring youth sport values

Editorial team

This introduction is being written shortly after the London 2012 Olympic and Paralympic Games. The Olympic creed refers to taking part rather than winning, and the struggle rather than the triumph, which brings into sharp relief the often conflicting nature of values.

As sport has become more professional and commercialised there is increasing pressure to win rather than simply to take part. The conflict often becomes a moral one between cheating to win and playing fairly. In the light of widespread examples of unethical behaviour in adult sport there is a need to mimimize the permeation of such behaviour into youth sport.

One purpose of this book is to present value theory as a new paradigm that is particularly appropriate for studying fair play and children's moral decision-making in youth sport. Two inherent characteristics of values are particularly pertinent to the understanding of conflicts and dilemmas. First, whether or not young competitors will cheat is influenced by their *value system* – the relative priorities they give to different values. Is winning or fairness more important to them, or are both equally important? Second, an understanding of *value structure* – the extent to which different values are naturally compatible or conflicting – helps to identify those situations in which values are most likely to conflict, and also the particular values that can be promoted to reduce conflict. Such information is needed by researchers and by an increasing range of sport professionals who are agents for value transmission and change.

Across the social sciences, human values are regarded as the most important psychological variables. They are central beliefs about what is desirable in life. They guide decisions and behaviour by prioritising choices and providing standards for our judgements and evaluations. They transfer across situations. They influence commitment and performance yet their study has been relatively neglected in sport. This book seeks to fill the gap by publishing initial information in this new field as a resource for others to build on. Thus we include a range of perspectives and sometimes refer to unpublished or ongoing studies to show how the field is developing. Given current debates regarding ethical behaviour in sport and a need to develop the notion of 'good' sporting behaviours early in the lives of children and young people, this seems a good time to publish work on a new paradigm.

Alongside the consideration of the values of sport participants, attention must be given to the values of youth sport and physical education providers and policy-makers who set the context for engagement. These claims for values are not new, since they have been debated by providers as long as there has been organised sport and physical education. Sport is considered to be intrinsically important in the form-ative experiences of children and young people and most nations and cultures, in some way or other, spend considerable time and resources exposing children to sport and associated physical activities. Sport is often regarded as possessing inherent qualities that shape and influence children and young people. To some extent notions of 'fairness', 'trying hard', learning to 'work with others', being able to accept both 'winning' and 'losing', and of course the intrinsic qualities of developing an 'active healthy lifestyle' are all recognised as what sport participation can provide for child-ren and young people. However, it is also important that sport providers seek to understand the value priorities of children, who do not think like adults.

The use of sport and physical activity to reduce anti-social behaviour and promote prosocial behaviour has often been ill-informed. For example, it has been traditionally assumed that sport participation *per se* has a beneficial effect on social and moral development and will promote cultural values, but this position is not in accord with research evidence which is more subtle and nuanced. In a review of sport morality research Shields and Bredemeier (2007) reported a nega-tive relationship between moral reasoning and some team sport participation but also consider that positive outcomes might occur under the right conditions. In his foreword to this book, and from four decades of experience in promoting values and life skills to young people, Don Hellison robustly rejects the notion that values transfer automatically. The effective promotion of socially desirable values requires understanding and sustained targeted intervention. The growing commer-cialisation of sport with its attendant 'problems' relating to antisocial behaviour in adult sport and a concern that unethical practices will permeate into youth sport is now a major concern. Clifford and Feezell (2010) argued that principles of sports-manship are no longer demonstrated to young players and that there is a need to reclaim moral language and respect for others and for the game itself.

It is against this backdrop that we present some conceptual background and conclude with an interactionist model to guide the organisation of the book. Each chapter, then, poses a question about values – but we cannot provide all the answers.

Historical background to the study of human values

Clarifying the constructs: values and attitudes

The study of values emerged from the study of attitudes. Allport (1968: 59) described the attitude concept as 'the most distinctive and indispensable concept in American social psychology'. In social psychology an attitude is commonly defined as a predisposition to respond in a positive or negative way to some specific stimulus, or attitude object (Fishbein and Ajzen, 1975). Attitudes have cognitive, affective, and behavioural components, thus someone who has a positive attitude to a particular sport team may keep track of their performance, feel elated when they win, and go to see them play. People have attitudes to very many 'attitude objects' which in physical education and sport could include a particular teacher, activity, uniform, or type of behaviour (cheating or teamwork).

Rokeach (1973) distinguished between values and attitudes, as described below, and between two conceptions of values. He noted that values were interpreted both as criteria that people hold to guide their decisions, and as properties of objects (e.g. this object has a value). He considered it more productive for the social sciences to regard values as criteria. He thus defined a value as 'an enduring belief that a specific mode of conduct or end state of existence is personally or socially preferable to an opposite or converse mode of conduct or end state of existence' (Rokeach, 1973: 5). This simply means that people apply their values to decide how to behave (mode of conduct) as they strive for a long term goal (end state.) In Rokeach's terms, it may be important to someone to behave in a self-controlled manner to reach a state of social recognition. In sport this could mean it is important to play fairly in order to win.

This definition reflects Kluckhohn's (1951) view of values as 'conceptions of the desirable' and distinguishes between instrumental values (conduct) and terminal values (end states). Rokeach also distinguished between intrapersonal values (e.g. competence) and inter-personal values (e.g. equality). Appendix 3 includes a short questionnaire, based on the work of Rokeach, for students and coaches to consider the consistency of their own values in sport and in general life.

The most important characteristic of values, for the purposes of this book, is that people and groups regard some values as more desirable than others and give more attention to them, thus creating subjectively ranked hierarchical *value systems*. Rokeach defined a *value system* as 'an enduring organisation of beliefs concerning preferable modes of conduct or end states of existence arranged along a continuum of relative importance' (Rokeach, 1973: 5). Thus, it is not enough to know which values a person holds. Many young competitors value both winning and fairness because each is desirable. What is more useful is to know which value holds the greater importance in governing their decisions and behaviour.

We can now distinguish values from attitudes by their higher level of abstraction. That is, people have very many attitudes and each one applies to a specific situation, but they have very few values and each one is quite abstract and so generalises across many situations. People who value fairness will try to be fair at home, at school and in sport. Moreover, values are always 'desirable' whereas attitudes can be both positive and negative. Most importantly, values are hierarchically ordered and attitudes are not.

Why values matter

Centrality

Rokeach argued that 'the value concept, more than any other, should occupy a central position across all the social sciences – sociology, anthropology, psychology, psychiatry, political science, education, economics, and history' as it is 'able to unify the apparently diverse interests of all the sciences concerned with human behaviour' (Rokeach, 1973: 3). He drew his conclusions from five assumptions about human values:

1   the total number of values that a person possesses is relatively small;
2   [people] everywhere possess the same values to different degrees;
3   values are organised into systems;
4   the antecedents of human values can be traced to culture, society and its institutions, and personality;
5   the consequences of human values will be manifested in virtually all phenomena that social scientists consider worth investigating and understanding.

Antecedents and consequences

An advantage of the centrality of values is that in a research design they can be considered as *dependent variables*, depending on cultural, institutional, or personal forces, or as *independent variables* influencing cognitions, emotions and behaviour of all kinds (Rokeach, 1973: 23).

Value systems and value structure

A major contribution of Rokeach (1967) was the Rokeach Value Survey (RVS) to measure the rank order of short lists of terminal and instrumental values and thus identify the *value systems* of individuals or groups. Although this instrument has been criticised for its sampling of content and use of single items, it pioneered the study of human values. A prime reason for exploring values is to discover which ones are given the greatest importance and consequently the most influence in human decision-making. Transferring the questions to physical education and sport it is important to know how young participants prioritise such values as enjoyment, fairness, excitement, winning, team cohesion, tolerance, conformity, and how these values relate to those of their coaches, teachers, and peer group.

Subsequently Schwartz (1992) built on the work of Rokeach and developed the Schwartz Values Survey (SVS) which includes independent ratings of each value. The ratings allowed him to explore the commonality of values around the world and use data from over 60 nations to develop a circular *value structure* in the form of a continuum of values based on their motivational content and the correlations between them. Values based on similar motives are adjacent, while those based on conflicting motives are diametrically opposed. Within this circle, 10 basic values were identified: self-direction, stimulation, hedonism, achievement, power, security, tradition, conformity, benevolence, and universalism.

The structure can also be described by two orthogonal bi-polar axes, one running from values of *self-enhancement* to values of *self-transcendence* (concern for self versus concern for others) and the other from *openness to change* to values of *conservation and stability*. This structure shows natural compatibilities and conflicts among the values and underpins the dynamics of value conflict. It is fully described by Bardi and Schwartz in Chapter 8 to show how it can be used as a basis for intervention to reduce conflict between fairness and winning. Thus the study of *value structure* complements the study of *value systems* by identifying those values which may conflict.

A feature of the natural *value structure* discovered by Schwartz (1992) is that it is based on values which have the same meaning around the world and which rest on the survival needs of humans as biological organisms, engaged in social interaction, and needing group maintenance and survival skills. The individual values are so well integrated that a relationship with one value implies reciprocal relationships with other values in the system. Thus, if the value of winning increases as a result of external pressures, the value of fairness is likely to decrease.

Schwartz (2007) shared the concepts of Rokeach, and regarded values as (1) beliefs linked to affect, (2) desirable goals that motivate action, (3) beliefs that transcend specific actions and situations, (4) standards or criteria for evaluation, (5) ordered by relative importance, and thus (6) guides to attitudes and behaviours.

The alternative conception of values

Rokeach's second conception of values as properties of objects is examined in Chapter 1 which asks the question Why are sport and physical education valuable?

Values in youth sport and physical education

Early research in sport psychology mirrored the mainstream confusion between values and attitudes. For example, Webb's (1969) 'attitude' scale was effectively a values scale as it assessed personal priorities for winning, playing well, and playing fairly. Moreover, there was not a suitable instrument to measure values as personal criteria based on a comprehensive set of values drawn from young participants. Braithwaite and Law (1985) critiqued Rokeach's (1967) RVS and recommended that value items be drawn from the population of interest. Lee subsequently led a Council of Europe initiative in 1990–1993 in which 12 countries piloted a common protocol to identify the values expressed in discussions with young competitors about moral dilemmas in their sport. When international funding to complete the work evaporated Lee and his co-workers continued in the UK. They constructed three research instruments: the 18-item Youth Sport Value Questionnaire (YSVQ) to assess the *value systems* of young competitors, the Youth Sport Values Questionnaire–2 (YSVQ-2) to assess higher order moral, competence and status values and the Attitudes to Moral Decision-making in Youth Sport Questionnaire (AMDYSQ) to assess acceptance of cheating, acceptance of gamesmanship, and keeping winning in proportion (see Chapters 2–5).

The influence of values, as personal criteria, on behaviour has also been central in a range of intervention projects which have developed to promote values of social responsibility and other life skills in value education or community youth development programmes (e.g. Hellison, 2003). Since 2001 value promotion has been explored from an action research perspective in a project initiated by the University of Brighton to teach values through soccer to Jewish and Arab children in Israel and subsequently in other divided societies. The Football 4 Peace project uses value-based coaching to promote values of respect, trust, responsibility, equality and inclusion, and neutrality (see Chapters 9 and 10).

The alternative approach which focuses on the value of objects or, in this case, types of activities has explored the values of sport and physical education to society (see Chapter 1). Within this approach some attention has also been given to 'task value' within the expectancy-value model of achievement motivation (e.g. Eccles and Harold, 1991). Here the intrinsic, utility, and attainment values and perceived cost of an achievement task are evaluated to determine engagement or persistence with the activity. Since these task evaluations influence participation motives it is important to distinguish such motives from values, which are criteria for self-evaluation related to the self concept. For example, the values of playing fairly or being tolerant or compassionate are not participation motives. However, there is scope for exploring interactions between the subjective values of activities and the value priorities of individuals.

Moral development and children's values

A book titled *Values in Youth Sport and Physical Education* which draws attention to encouraging fair play requires some reference to the wider moral context and alternative explanations for the development of moral reasoning. Two major approaches will be summarised before presenting an alternative values-based model, using the arguments of Lee (1993).

Social learning theory rests on two processes. First, behaviour is considered to change as a result of reinforcement patterns, such that actions which are reinforced become more likely, while actions which are punished become less likely. Second, in the process of modelling, the behaviour of other people is observed and copied. Thus social influences lead to an internalisation of moral standards. This implies that practitioners should (a) reward good behaviour, (b) ignore, or perhaps punish, undesirable behaviour, and (c) model good behaviour.

Structural-development theories, which have been widely used in sport, rest on the principle that moral development follows cognitive development, as illustrated by Piaget ([1932] 1972). Kohlberg (1976) proposed three levels of moral reasoning: (a) egocentric morality, (b) social responsibility, and (c) independent morality. Each level has two stages. This approach has been criticised on invariance of the stages, structural wholeness, and the implication that only clever people can make mature moral decisions. Haan (1978) criticised Kohlberg's work for a reliance on unrealistic moral dilemmas. She argued that moral decisions are made on the basis of moral balance between the parties involved and moral dialogue to resolve disagreements. She further proposed that the basis of the dialogue is developmental and passes through a series of five levels characterised by three processes: assimilation, accommodation, and equilibration. Lee (1997: 549) illustrated the mature equilibration process among children in a middle school who, without adult intervention, organised a soccer league in their recreational breaks, with fouls adjudicated jointly by team captains, players selected to create equal teams, and a rule that the team judged to be weaker should play down the slope of their playground.

In sport, the structural development approach was adopted by Shields and Bredemeier (e.g. 1994, 2007) for studies of sport, character and morality. They found lower levels of moral reasoning for dilemmas in sport than in daily life after about 12 years of age and also proposed a theory of 'game reasoning' in which egocentricism has legitimacy in the discrete sport context where decisions on rule breaking may be delegated to officials. However, they also report that children can develop moral reasoning through a sports situation when this outcome is specifically planned and worked for. For example, in a summer camp where three groups were treated differently there were improvements in moral reasoning in both the social learning group and the structural development group but not in a traditional physical education group.

As a student of Rokeach, Lee learned that values provide an alternative approach to studying how people make moral decisions, because they force them to examine their priorities in what they want to achieve (terminal values) and how they go about this (instrumental values). The notion of a value as a central personal belief, related to self concept, emphasises personal choice and accords more autonomy to the individual than a response to social reinforcement or automatic passage through developmental stages. Moreover, value theory provides an understanding of universal principles of moral judgement, rather than situationally specific behaviours, and does not require definition of complex terms such as character. Thus Lee adopted a values-based approach to understand children's moral decision-making in youth sport.

A tentative research model

A reliance on structural development theories gives only a minor role to the influence of others. Shields and Bredemeier (1994) proposed a model which takes account of contextual influences but Lee (1995) argued that questions remain about the social influence processes by which young people come to a consistent view of the appropriateness of particular forms of behaviour in sport, and who is influential at different stages of development. In the context of Vallerand and Losier's (1994) social psychological approach to sportsmanship Lee offered a tentative social psychological model for values research (Figure 0.1) based on an interactionist perspective. This was intended to pose questions about the processes which account for particular behaviour patterns and to generate hypotheses about relationships between individual and environmental influences at different developmental stages and career points.

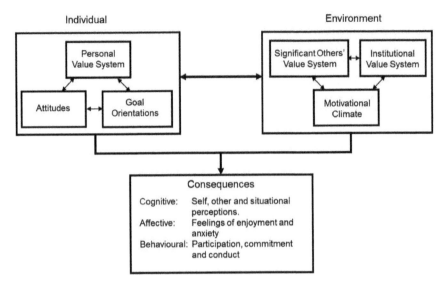

Figure 0.1 An interactionist model for research development
Source: adapted from Lee (1995)

This model was the conclusion to a paper that argued for an integration of value theory and achievement goal theory to develop an understanding of how best to promote sport to children and ensure positive outcomes (Lee, 1995). Thus the top line of small boxes relates to components of value theory and, in the original model, the other small boxes related to achievement goal theory. We use this model as a broad framework for the development of the book, but have replaced perceived ability with attitudes, to better represent the chapters in Part I.

While personal values are important in themselves in any examination of sport engagement they are also part of the larger sport milieu. There is in an important interface between the values of those who engage in sport and the institutional value system seen in the values of youth sport providers and the wider national policies and assumptions which drive them.

This book focuses predominantly on youth sport, rather than physical education, because that is where the research based on the Schwartz (1992) value theory has been done. To the extent that sport is a component of physical education programmes the information should have specific relevance for physical education teachers. Moreover, since values are central beliefs which transcend situations, the basic information about how values influence behaviour through the dynamic interplay between *value systems* and *value structure* has applications for general life beyond the youth sport or physical education contexts.

Organisation of the book

The book is organised in two main parts, focused on the *Individual* and *Environment* boxes of Lee's model, with an opening chapter and a final chapter that take wider perspectives.

Chapter 1 (by Devine and Telfer) asks why physical education and sport are valuable. It describes objectives of different 'providers' in education, the voluntary sector, and local authorities, then discusses a range of values attributed to physical education and the various forms of sport and physical activity provision. In unpicking where children and young people engage in sport, it becomes easier to identify the interface between the values being espoused by providers and those which children report. It raises the issue of potential dissonance in values between providers and participants, thus setting a broad context for the book and why an examination of children's values is important. This chapter takes Rokeach's (1973) conception of values as properties of objects, whereas subsequent chapters take his view of values as personal criteria for decision-making.

Part I relates to *individual differences* and to *value systems*. Chapters focus on the nature and measurement of personal values, their relationships with attitudes and motives, and their stability across cultures. The section opens with four abridged articles by Lee and his co-workers which describe initial stages in exploring youth sport values. We have removed some material which duplicates the introduction. To enhance readability for the non-specialist we have also removed some statistical material and added a link box at the end of each chapter to relate it to the next one with material that is not in either. Collectively, these link boxes provide a brief overview of this section.

Chapter 2 (by Lee and Cockman) asks what sport values young people hold. It explores the values that are spontaneously expressed by young players when discussing moral dilemmas in their own sport then identifies and describes 18 independent values which guide personal conduct in youth sport.

Chapter 3 (by Lee, Whitehead, and Balchin) asks which sport values are most important. Through focus groups it clarifies the meaning to young participants of the 18 values identified in Chapter 2, then describes the construction of the Youth Sport Values Questionnaire (YSVQ) to assess their relative importance. The *value systems* of young competitors are shown to be consistent across age, gender, type of sport, and level of competition. Enjoyment ranked first followed by personal achievement and socio-moral values. Winning ranked last.

Chapter 4 (by Lee, Whitehead, and Ntoumanis) asks how important ethical attitudes are. It differentiates values and attitudes, identifies three categories of unethical behaviour (professional fouls, cheating and gamesmanship) and draws on youth sport experts and focus groups of young competitors to construct the Attitudes to Moral Decision-making in Youth Sport Questionnaire (AMDYSQ). This measures keeping winning in proportion, acceptance of gamesmanship, and acceptance of cheating. A survey shows the attitudes ranked in the foregoing order, with females having higher ethical positions.

Chapter 5 (by Lee, Whitehead, Ntoumanis, and Hatzigeorgiadis) asks how values influence attitudes and achievement goals. It first develops the YSVQ-2 to measure higher-order moral, competence and status values, then shows how these values predict prosocial and antisocial attitudes via the mediating role of goal orientations.

Chapter 6 (by Whitehead and Gonçalves) asks how similar youth sport values are in other nations, and presents data from five continents. It compares a preliminary international youth sport *value system* with a global hierarchy of human values derived by Schwartz and Bardi (2001) using the Schwartz Values Survey (SVS), and reports the use of the SVS to explore cultural differences in Australian and Singaporean swimmers.

Chapter 7 (by Balaguer, Castillo, Quested, and Duda) asks how values relate to motivation. It uses the SVS to extend Chapter 5 by exploring how values relate to achievement goal orientations and also to motivational regulators described by self-determination theory. Values of self-transcendence and self-enhancement related to task and ego orientation respectively, and also to intrinsic motivation and external regulation respectively.

PART II relates to *environmental influences* and to *value structure*. Chapters focus on the role of significant others (coaches and teachers) and institutions (state and independent schools and a sport camp), and the resultant learning environment. It opens with a key chapter that provides a structural framework for intervention and change, and also integrates *value systems* and *value structure*. Part 2 then continues with practical applications in the field which relate to issues of value transmission and behaviour change.

Chapter 8 (by Bardi and Schwartz) asks how *value structure* underlies value conflict. It describes the conceptual framework of the Schwartz (1992) *value structure* with inherent compatibilities and conflict among values, and integrates Lee's youth sport values within the structure as specific exemplars of universal human values. It uses the framework to select a suitable value for an intervention to reduce the conflict between fairness and winning. This chapter also outlines mechanisms for value change.

Chapter 9 (by Lambert) asks how we can teach values through sport. It describes the Football 4 Peace intervention programme to teach values of respect, responsibility, trust, equity and inclusion, and neutrality through a soccer camp for Jewish and Arab children in Israel. The coaching methods develop from an action research perspective and the Sport Plus model of Beedy (1997) and use a *facilitate–observe–reflect* approach. The promoted values are located in the Schwartz *value structure* in opposition to values of power and security and are appropriate to reduce conflict in divided societies.

Chapter 10 (by Lambert) asks how coach behaviour creates a motivational climate. It describes the selection and training of F4P coaches and the need for them to modify their traditional technocratic approach, which focuses on enhancing physical skill and reflects values of power and security, to a democratic approach which reflects values of equality and transfers responsibility to the children through a climate in which 'everyone is a winner'.

Chapter 11 (by Freeman, Leslie, Leger, and Williams) asks how important the values of significant others are. Using the YSVQ it finds high similarity between the values of high school pupils and their physical education teachers, and that the pupils' perceptions of their teachers' values mediates this relationship. The value systems of pupils in state and independent schools differ.

Chapter 12 (by Telfer and Knowles) asks how sport practitioners can balance conflicting values. It uses reflective practice through an auto-ethnographic approach to present a fictional dialogue between a coach and his mentor regarding a coaching practice dilemma. This demonstrates how issues relating to coaching dilemmas between the overt outcomes and values of the sport and those of the children (and possibly coaches) can often be at odds. It highlights issues inherent in the distinction between the value placed on 'winning' and on 'doing one's best' while also attending to the development of the young performer.

Part III (Chapter 13) asks what questions remain. It presents supplementary material to extend some key issues, integrates findings from youth sport questionnaires with those from adult life questionnaires, discuss relationships between value theory and achievement goal theory which has been a dominant motivational paradigm in sport psychology, reviews the role of values and attitudes in understanding fair play, integrates findings about value transmission and change, and illustrates the consequences of interactions between individual and environmental influences for values associated with commitment and performance in young swimmers.

The appendices present supplementary material. Appendix 1 describes the cross-cultural validity of YSVQ-2 and its relationship with other variables. Appendix 2 describes the development of an AMDYSQ-2 which refocuses one scale on preference for fairness over winning. Appendix 3 provides short questionnaires to prompt discussion among students and coaches about their own values. Appendix 4 presents research questionnaires for youth sport values and attitudes with brief guidance on administration and scoring. These questionnaires have been submitted to the PsycTESTS database of the APA (American Psychological Association). Supplementary information will be added as it becomes available.

References

Allport, G.W. (1968) The historical background to modern social psychology. In G. Lindzey and E. Aronson (eds) *The Handbook of Social Psychology*, 1, 1–80. Reading, MA: Addison-Wesley.

Beedy, J.P. (1997) *Sports Plus: Positive Learning Using Sports*. Hamilton: Project Adventure.

Braithwaite, V.A. and Law, H.G. (1985) Structure of human values: Testing the adequacy of the Rokeach Value Survey. *Journal of Personality and Social Psychology*, 49(1), 250–63.

Clifford, C. and Feezell, .M. (2010) *Sport and Character: Reclaiming the Principles of Sportsmanship*. Champaign, IL: Human Kinetics.

Eccles, J. S. and Harold, R.D. (1991) Gender differences in sport involvement: Applying the Eccles' expectancy-value model. *Journal of Applied Sport Psychology*, 3, 7–35.

Fishbein, M. and Ajzen, I. (1975) *Belief, Attitude, Intention, and Behavior: An Introduction to Theory and Research*. Reading, MA: Addison-Wesley.

Haan, N. (1978) Two moralities in action contexts: Relationships to thought, ego regulation, and development. *Journal of Personality and Social Psychology*, 36(3), 286–305.

Hellison, D. (2003) *Teaching Social Responsibility through Physical Activity*, 2nd edn. Champaign, IL: Human Kinetics.

Kluckhohn, C. (1951) Value and value-orientations in the theory of action: An exploration in definition and classification. In T. Parsons and E. Shils (eds) *Towards a General Theory of Action*. Cambridge, MA: Harvard University Press, pp. 388–433.

Kohlberg, L. (1976) Moral stages and moralization: the structural-developmental approach. In T. Likona (ed.) *Moral Development and Behavior*. New York: Holt, Rinehart and Winston.

Lee, M.J. (1993) Moral development and children's sporting values. In J. Whitehead (ed.) *Developmental Issues in Children's Sport and Physical Education*. Bedford: Institute for the Study of Children in Sport, pp. 30–42.

Lee, M.J. (1995) Relationships between values and motives in sport. Paper presented at the 9th European Congress in Sport Psychology, Brussels, Belgium, 4–9 July.

Lee, M.J. (1997) Moral Well-being: The role of physical education and sport. In N. Armstrong, B. Kitty and J. Welsman (eds) *Children and Exercise XIX*. London: Spon, pp. 542–62.

Piaget, J. ([1932] 1972) *The Moral Judgment of the Child*. London: Macmillan, excerpted in *Social Psychology: Experimentation, Theory, Research* (ed. W.S. Shakian). Scranton, PA: Intext, pp. 604–7.

Rokeach, M. (1967) *Value Survey*. Sunnyvale, CA: Halgren Tests.

Rokeach, M. (1973) *The Nature of Human Values*. New York: Free Press.

Schwartz, S. (1992) Universals in the content and structure of values: Theoretical advances and empirical tests in 20 countries. In M. P. Zanna (ed.) *Advances in Experimental Social Psychology*, 25, 1–65. London: Academic Press.

Schwartz, S.H. (2007) Value orientations: measurement, antecedents and consequences across nations. In R. Jowell, C. Robert, R. Fitzgerald and G. Eva (eds) *Measuring Attitudes Cross-Nationally: Lessons from the European Social Survey*. London: Sage, pp. 169–203.

Schwartz, S.H. and Bardi, A. (2001) Value hierarchies across cultures: Taking a similarities perspective. *Journal of Cross-Cultural Psychology*, 32, 268–90.

Shields, D.L.L. and Bredemeier, B.J.L. (1994) *Character Development and Physical Activity*. Champaign, IL: Human Kinetics.

Shields, D.L.L. and Bredemeier, B.J.L. (2007) Advances in sport morality research. In G. Tenenbaum and R.C. Ecklund (eds) *Handbook of Sport Psychology*, 3rd edn. Hoboken, NJ: Wiley & Son, pp. 662–84.

Vallerand, R.J. and Losier, G.F. (1994) Self-determined motivation and sportsmanship orientations: An assessment of their temporal relationship. *Journal of Sport and Exercise Psychology*, 16, 229–45.

Webb, H. (1969) Professionalisation of attitudes towards play among adolescents. In G. S. Kenyon (ed.) *Aspects of Contemporary Sport Sociology*. Chicago, IL: The Athletic Institute, pp. 161–78.

1 Why are sport and physical education valuable?

Values, sport, and physical education

Cathy Devine and Hamish Telfer

This chapter examines the nature of sport, physical education, and physical activity provision within which children's experiences are located. The relationship between the professed and assumed values inherent within such provision and those which children and young people report, is important to understand if teaching and coaching is to be of relevance. Research indicates a potential dissonance between the values of children and young people, and the values and benefits claimed for sport and PE programmes. This leaves practitioners with potentially difficult decisions in terms of practice orientation to match competing demands and assumptions 'for' and 'about' their practice.

Understanding the nature of provision of the various agencies charged with responsibility for the delivery of sport, physical education and physical activity is therefore central to understanding the reported values of children within these programmes. To this end the various, but particular 'value systems' may be both explicit and implicit. An exploration of these systems with their various ideological claims and values is necessary in setting the scene for a more detailed examination of children's values in sport. An understanding of this philosophically contested area should therefore lead to a better and more productive experience for both practitioner and the young participant.

Introduction

The idea that sport in all its varying forms and contexts has a set or sets of values attached to it, is not new. The fact that these values, however intangible, tend to be seen as positive, bestows upon sport the cachet that sport is 'a good thing'. This in turn confers upon those who engage in sport as participants, coaches or volunteers, a certain 'virtuosity' by society more generally. However, the notion of exactly what these values are, who determines them, and in what seemingly rapidly changing contexts they are demonstrated, is slippery terrain.

Lee (2004a) asked the central question of why we provide sport for children. He considered the balance between children's experiences and reasons for participation, and those of the coach or volunteer, as well as the roles and functions sport and physical education fulfil in society. In outlining such inter-relationships, Lee argued that it was essential to understand the varying nature of provision as a prerequisite to examining the reported values of children involved in sport. This is important. Without an understanding of the aims and nature of sport provision (with the potentially concomitant variation in explicit and implicit value systems at work), it becomes difficult to position the reported values of children within these systems and structures. Put simply, examination of children's values needs to be understood within the context in which they are experienced. The situational context of club sport may determine the nature of the value system, which in turn, may be different from that of the physical education lesson. This sporting and educational landscape therefore becomes an important factor in setting the scene for any examination of children's values in sport when set against the aims and objectives of the provision. This is especially so when there may be a dissonance between the values of the provider or provision and those the children report in that the priorities within their value systems differ.

Lee (2004b) also considered the impact of modern sport development policies and strategies as well as the nature of changes in physical education within education policy. He recognised the influence of these strategies in terms of how sport and physical education were being 'used' and commented upon a concomitant blurring of boundaries, arguing that sport and physical education frequently involved many of the same activities to different ends. Often achievement goals usually more associated with sport, overtake the more universal and altruistic ends claimed by physical education with boundaries therefore becoming difficult to identify. These boundaries are examined later in this chapter.

Sport and local government sport provision are often subject to rapid revision following changes in government policy in education. There is no doubt, for example, that the nature and impact of sport development policies and practices has altered in relation to shifts in education policy, with attempts made to broaden the way in which young people engage with sport and physical activity. In addition, social policy changes have often led to changes in the raison d'être for physical education in schools, and more importantly, what is taught, why and how.

The sport provision landscape

Children's experiences of sport may be considered to be drawn from three broad areas of provision: from physical education programmes delivered through school, voluntary sector opportunities involving local clubs that tend to be sport specific, and provision by local authorities (sport development). Each of these has a different primary focus at the heart of their provision. Thus what constitutes sporting 'experience' is contested ground. Increasingly however, the objectives of all three merge as attempts are made to address multiple social objectives through co-ordinated social policy influences. For example, attempts to engage children and young people in physical activity as part of a health agenda often involve sport. Indeed 'multi-agency approaches' are frequently encouraged as a means of cost reduction as well as reducing duplication of resource. Thus local authority sport provision may serve both health and social policy agendas as well as that of encouraging sport participation with a performance sport objective.

This sport provision 'trialectic' of education, voluntary sector, and local authority settings therefore needs examination in relation to the various professed objectives, outcomes, and systems of engagement. Of especial importance is the experience of children and young people in a sport development system geared towards performance as distinct from an education setting with a focus on the development of the physical literacy of the young person. Central in this debate is the nature and scope of involvement by central and local governments in determining rationales. Varying social policy initiatives, including sport and physical activity, have attendant ideological underpinning. Thus attempts to get the nation more active using sport as a vehicle for this aspiration means that the purpose of sport in this context is often far removed from that of sport performance and the demands of competitive sport.

Some mapping of the potential sporting experience of children and young people is consequently needed in order that their reported values relating to their engagement are better understood in the context of the location of that experience. Indeed some initial discussion of what is meant by values may be pertinent.

Values

It is important at the outset to understand that what is meant by values in sport and physical education is contested rather than consensual terrain. The perceived value of sport and physical education differs according to who is doing the valuing and the outcomes being sought. Prior to any examination of the reported values of children and young people, it is important that the professed values attached to the provision of sport and physical education are considered through the lenses of the various stakeholders. These include: academics, policy-makers, government, and of course the general public. However, even in representative democracies, although children and their parents may be stakeholders to a greater or lesser degree, depending on the compulsory or voluntary nature of the activity, their involvement in decision-making within sporting and physical education infrastructures, may be minimal.

Philosophical interest in values includes attempts to account for which things have value or are valuable, and this is closely related to concerns with the nature of 'good'. It is useful to distinguish between intrinsic value, things that are valuable or good *in themselves,* and extrinsic value, things that *lead* to good or valuable things. Thus, something considered to have extrinsic (means) value is a means to an end and has relational or instrumental value. In contrast, something with intrinsic (end) value is considered to be an end in itself, and possesses inherent value and internal goods. Frankena (1973) argued that values which are good in themselves are considered to be superior values. Thus those values which depend for their value on what they lead to (extrinsic) are deemed less 'good'. Philosophers tend to consider intrinsic value in universal terms. Aristotle (1968) saw it in terms of truth; for Kant (1967) it was good will; and for Mill (1962) it was 'general happiness'. Wright (2004) identified three overarching intrinsic values as being truth, morality and happiness, but regarded happiness as being the most important value in physical education (PE). Kretchmar (1994) ranked the 'prime intrinsic values' in sport, with pleasure ('personal embodied wisdom') first, closely followed by skill ('practical wisdom'). Third was (theoretical) knowledge and finally health (which, in contrast, he considers the most important extrinsic value). For these authors, the primary value in both sport and PE is pleasure.

Valuing sport and PE extrinsically means using them as a tool to produce something else considered valuable. For governments or policy-makers this may be educational attainment, health (or reducing the cost to the state of ill health), regeneration, social inclusion, social control, employment, economic growth, discipline, patriotism, or ideology (e.g. naturalising: competition, winning and losing, or hegemonic masculinity). For individuals, perceived extrinsic values may be: money, fame, celebrity, medals, fitness, weight loss, or appearance (as 'technologies of femininity or masculinity').

Thus the value *of* sport and values reported *through* experiences of sport are complex. It is in this contested terrain that those who participate construct meaning out of sport and physical activity experiences. Therefore sport, physical education, and physical activity become ideologically important tools for social policy in shaping attitudes and values of those who engage at all levels. A degree of scrutiny of the relationship between society and social policy is useful in order to unlock the various motives for the promotion of sport and PE.

Society and social policy

In Lee's (2004b) critique and commentary on the 'functions of sport' within society he acknowledged the relationship between society, policy-makers and governments in attempting to fulfil a number of different functions through sport and PE. These include developing a coherent sense of identity for individuals, and socio-political positioning as well as national and commercial success for nations. Furthermore, broader contextual influences on sport and PE policy include political ideology and the differing core political values of, for example, social democracies (equality and collective responsibility) and conservative or neoliberal governments (competition and individual responsibility). Sport and physical education policy does not stand outside of these belief systems and is therefore shaped according to the prevailing social and political climate and values of societies and governments. In addition, evidence-based policy- and decision-making might appear to be of obvious importance, but evidence may be used to a greater or lesser extent, and may be interpreted partially or differently.

Physical education

In general, PE is considered a compulsory component of the education of children. As a consequence, there has been a significant tradition in most democracies of advocating intrinsic values relating to the education of children. However, the most dominant position with regard to PE has more often been to regard it as extrinsically valuable in relation to, for example, the dualistic training of bodies and the naturalisation of competition. Thus, given the hegemony of competitive sport, PE could be considered to be only partially egalitarian, and possibly to some degree coercive rather than inclusive. Further, the nature of its intrinsic value is contested, with the main contenders being either movement pleasure or moral value. Nevertheless, as Lee (2004b) conceptualised, it can be broadly considered to have an egalitarian process orientation.

Hardman and Marshall (2005) reported in their study of PE worldwide that a majority of countries have legal requirements for physical education in schools. There are only a small number of countries, mainly on the African continent and Middle East, where physical education is not compulsory and may be denied especially to girls. Furthermore, they comment that:

> there is a predisposition to a competitive sport discourse dominated by games, track and field athletics and gymnastics, which account for 77 per cent and 79 per cent of physical education curriculum content in primary and secondary schools respectively. Such sustained orientation raises issues surrounding meaning and relevance as well as quality of programmes provided and delivered.
>
> (Hardman and Marshall, 2005: 7)

Contemporary issues facing PE can be identified as the following: what is it and why is it valuable? Given its compulsory nature, is it meaningful and relevant to both girls and boys? It is fair to say that although there may be historically and geographically contextualised dominant positions, there is no consensus of opinion in relation to any of these questions. As Pringle puts it:

> it is clear that debate about the aims and outcomes of PE is ongoing. In contemporary times this debate has been concerned with various issues including: the relationships between PE and competitive sport, PE and health/anti-obesity activities, the gendering effect of PE, the (mis)appropriation of indigenous knowledge, and, more broadly, the relevancy of PE within the era of late-capitalism.
>
> (Pringle, 2010: 119)

This historically contextualised role and therefore value (whether explicit or implicit) of PE has been documented by a range of authors. Kirk (2011) gives an overview of PE for state school pupils in Britain over the past century and outlines the progression from military drill through Swedish and educational gymnastics to sport-based forms. He also noted the general trend towards co-educational programmes from those which previously segregated the sexes, as well as a continued widening of the range of activities on offer.

The underpinning values associated with these shifts in the manifestation of PE were often perceived as extremes. Extrinsically valued outcomes of 'discipline' and dualistic 'physical training' of bodies (for both war and work) central to the militaristic drill and physical training for the male working classes in the early 1900s, were juxtaposed with the intrinsically valued, child centred, Laban-influenced, holistic or embodied 'movement' of educational gymnastics in the 1950s. This is fundamental to understanding how values attached to the teaching of physical education have developed.

Evans and Penney (2008) highlight the profoundly child centred narratives associated with PE in the UK outlined in 'Moving and Growing' (MoE, 1952) which was to impact on policy in the UK for some considerable time. They note the range of activities (which included dance with an emphasis on 'movement as an art') as an attempt to realise the ambition that 'Every child was considered to have an equal right to a 'movement education'. Every child's physical development was to be leavened through a pedagogy emphasising creativity, spontaneity and risk taking' (MoE, 1952: 36).

They argue that by the late 1970s a culture of 'performativity' across all education began to take hold in national politics and school governance. What dominated the discourses in defining school curricula was the 'vision of learning... predicated on the development of ability hierarchies and of principled differentiation; on measuring "performances" in a range of activities according to pre-given criteria of what each pupil can or should display' (Evans and Penney, 2008: 40). Further, 'in effect this pedagogy predicates a social order characterised by 'vertical hierarchies', in which individuals are ascribed positional status by virtue of how well they can perform' which is 'profoundly a-social and disembodied in its separation of body and mind' (Evans and Penney, 2008: 42).

These examples of discourses of and within PE over the years, need to be understood in relation to the democratisation of education more generally, both in relation to class and gender. The general democratisation of education as a fundamental right 'for all' is now clearly established if not always afforded in all countries. However, education 'for all' (not just a male elite) might still be differentially interpreted and more crucially, valued. It too often comprises an academic or liberal education for a minority (usually a privileged and hegemonic group) and prioritises activities considered to be intrinsically valuable such as sport and outdoor and adventurous activities. However, the majority may still receive a vocational and technical education which utilises PE instrumentally for perceived extrinsic benefits such as exercise or fitness activities as technologies of health, masculinity or femininity. In Britain's elite private schools moreover, sport has always been the more dominant force for (mainly) upper class boys for at least the last two centuries. As such it has been used to inculcate ideologies associated with the British class system of leadership and character-building, making it ideologically distinct from state sector provision.

Gendered agendas have been woven through PE curriculums over many years, and Kirk (2011) outlines the different forms of PE that have historically been valued by physical educators, with men emphasising a sport skills approach based on the developing disciplines of sport science serving sport competition, and women emphasising creativity, flexibility and aesthetics. However, more recent developments have seen a synthesis of male and female activities, with Kretchmar (1994: 230) arguing for 'activities that can be enjoyed for their own sake, that have intrinsic value'. This is important when considering the extensive critiques of gendered curricula with their associated gender stereotyping and exclusivity, undertaken by the likes of Hargreaves (1994) and Evans *et al.* (1996).

In examining the contemporary position, Pringle (2010: 119) states that 'the dominant justifications for PE rests on instrumental and developmental goals'. These are powerful given the important role that PE appears to play in contemporary schooling worldwide. Physical education programmes are increasingly laying claim to a role in preparing young people for life with its associated social and moral challenges including the development of self-esteem and coping with stress. Pringle (2010: 125) argues that 'attempts to legitimate or secure the place of PE within education have been typically associated with aiming to achieve broader social goals, such as the production of socially responsible, healthy, active, and critically informed individuals'.

Penney *et al.* (2002: 15) assert that 'internationally, physical education remains firmly associated with the wider world of sport', and that, 'more specifically, physical education is regarded as a key foundation for ongoing involvement in sport'. In relation to the UK, Houlihan and Green have commented:

> it appears that part of the explanation for the rise in salience at central government level of school sport and PE lies in the redefinition of the role of PE, such that it is seen as playing an important role in achieving broader educational objectives such as whole school improvement, community development and effecting personal behavioural and attitudinal change among pupils.
>
> (Houlihan and Green, 2006: 82)

Notwithstanding the dominance of extrinsic justifications for the importance of PE within the curriculum, there is an extensive literature relating to its intrinsic value. Understanding these differing justifications for and of PE, helps in determining the value systems at play in their competing claims. The debate is perhaps best summed up by Kretchmar, who reminds us that 'Whenever sport, dance and games are made to do work for other values, instructors risk deflating them, removing a degree of their charm, making them less enjoyable…they snuff out freedom, exploration, play and much of the meaning and fun that can be found there' (Kretchmar, 1994: 121).

Recent advocates of the primacy of the intrinsic value of play, pleasure and meaning include Burrows (2005), Morgan (2006), Hawkins (2008), Booth (2009), Rintala (2009), Pringle (2010), Smith (2011) and Wright (2004: 149) who identifies three distinct sources of intrinsic value in PE as being 'an obligation to truth, moral values and the desire for happiness'. In a similar vein, Pringle (2010: 119) argues for movement pleasure as the prime intrinsic value and contends that 'many sport pedagogues recognise the value of movement pleasure in PE but few overtly accept that the promotion of such pleasure is of legitimate educative value'.

Burrows (2005: 14) is concerned that a biomedical approach could lead to impoverished PE programmes extrinsically and dualistically justified so that 'physical activity for its own sake, the pleasure of moving is replaced with the notion that you move because it's good for you or it will make you less "obese," or "thin"'. She contends that developing an intrinsic love of movement should be prioritised over the extrinsic and dualistic medicalisation and disciplining of the body. Finally, Smith argues that 'in *physical education as education in, through, and about movement,* we find the essence that allows us to capture the diverse and complex practices that are, or have been physical education' (Smith, 2011: 27) and further that, 'a compulsory school physical education programme has the potential to address matters of physical literacy, the sensations of pleasure, and those social justice issues that can be addressed through children's engagement in play' (Smith, 2011: 31).

Kretchmar (1994) advocates the use of the term 'movement' as opposed to 'physical' in relation to the subject matter of PE. Movement is an holistic or embodied term which does not separate people into minds and bodies and therefore avoids the dualistic linkage of PE with the 'lesser' body and academic subjects with the 'superior' mind. This then leads to the notion of 'movement intelligence' which can be argued to be an essential component of 'the good life' for people, as opposed to technocratic physical training or education directed at bodies as just one component of people.

For similar reasons, Whitehead (2007: 296) advocates the term 'physical literacy' and describes it as 'the ability and motivation to capitalise on our motile potential to make a significant contribution to the quality of life' and further, that 'we are as we are because we are embodied, and to respect this human characteristic in all young people is a right for every pupil'. She also notes 'that several countries have adopted this concept (physical literacy) as an integral part of their work in the field of physical education' and that physical literary is central to Sport Canada's and Sport Northern Ireland's aims and policies' (Whitehead, 2007: 287).

In sum, therefore, while policy-makers and politicians may be primarily interested in PE because of its perceived extrinsic benefits or outcomes, many PE academics make the case for its inclusion based on its intrinsic value, which is essentially an anti-dualistic argument based on children as embodied entities and the notion of personhood. The nature of this intrinsic value tends to be conceptualised as movement pleasure and/or moral value and, depending on the weight accorded to these two 'essences', different movement activities will be privileged. In addition, 'meaning' is linked to personhood and should more accurately be the plural 'meanings'. If movement pleasure or happiness is considered the prime intrinsic value and meanings are democratised to include both traditionally male and female physical culture, then the subject matter of PE is much broader than sport. Conversely, if the prime intrinsic value of PE is considered to be moral development, and meaning is seen to relate primarily to male physical culture, competitive sport will be privileged.

Sport provision and sporting opportunity

The following sections examine two broad areas of sport provision that are common in most developed countries, namely provision by the voluntary sector and provision by local and central government for sport and physical activity (but notionally separate from physical education).

The voluntary sector (or civil society) can be regarded as falling into two distinct traditions comprising sport specific national governing bodies (NGBs) of sport and sport-specific clubs, as well as non-sport-specific organisations and clubs (NSSCs), such as youth clubs and multi-activity clubs. The former operate primarily within a 'grassroots sport' or 'sport for sport's sake' tradition with a performance and excellence outcome orientation. This naturally aligns with extrinsic values that privilege 'talent', competition and winning. It feeds a small number of performers (in relative terms) into elite sport which is commercialised or professionalised to a greater or lesser extent. In contrast, NSSCs are more likely to be concerned with 'sport for all' with its egalitarian participation, process orientation and the intrinsic value of happiness relating to embodiment.

In contrast, in some countries particularly those with social democratic values, sport has become part of the welfare state. As such it is seen as a valuable component of leisure which may be subsidised by the state in order to achieve social objectives or redistribute common wealth. In this instance, the prevailing values may be to do with sport development to promote either social inclusion and equal opportunity, or social control and surveillance. In this context, sport is about participation rather than performance and has been termed 'sport for good' (Collins and Kay, 2003; Coalter, 2007; Collins, 2010) or 'sport for all'. The value of sport can often be construed as extrinsic and instrumental in relation to the common good, and may be to a greater or lesser degree either inclusive or coercive. Conversely, 'sport for social good', at best is sometimes linked to the intrinsic values associated with well-being and happiness, defined crucially in an egalitarian democratic sense, as 'sport for all'.

Sport and its associated values

Sport is often considered to have an interest of its own with internal goods and intrinsic value. This raises a number of questions. In particular, as Devine (2012: 5) puts it, 'what do we mean by sport, and can such a thing as sport be considered to have an interest independent or otherwise of the interests of people? Further, if we argue that sport (however we define it) has goods of its own, what are these and should we value them?'

To understand the contested views surrounding the value of sport and the commonly held view that sport is a 'good thing', we need to unpack the meaning of sport and its mythopoeic nature (Coalter, 2007). In order to do this it is useful to consider the three differing concepts of: 'sport for sport's sake', 'sport for good' and 'sport for all' in more detail. In brief, 'sport for sport's sake' refers 'to participation in sport as an end in itself' while 'sport for good' refers 'to the use of sport to achieve greater social objectives' (DCMS, 2002: 43). 'Sport for all' however, in its broadest sense, relates to 'popular movement culture' (Eichberg, 2009: 446). Eichberg summarises the three sport forms as: 'sport of competition and achievement; sport of discipline and integration; and sport of meeting and relation' (Eichberg, 2009: 457).

Thus, sport governing bodies and clubs can be considered to engage in 'sport for sport's sake', state agencies in 'sport for good' and perhaps less of a neat fit, PE in 'popular movement culture'. This offers a succinct if uneasy fit in terms of separating the various ways in which engagement is met. Finding a legitimate and agreed sense of the nature of sporting practice has been the subject of historical and current discourse regarding the dominant sport form. Attempts to privilege one of the three (often 'sport for sport's sake'), particularly at the boundaries between the three different areas of sport provision and PE contexts is often the case. It is therefore important to examine the values, both implicit and explicit in each of the three sport forms.

Sport for sport's sake

In general, 'sport for sport's sake' (i.e. intrinsically valuable *to* sport) tends to refer to a traditional conservative view of sport which, within the literature of the philosophy of sport, is often referred to as 'a rule governed activity that is about excellence, an understanding of how to play the game, and, in competitive sports, winning' (Abad, 2010: 27). This sport concept tends to be the one evident in NGBs of sport and sport specific clubs. As Collins (2010: 368) explains, in the UK up until the 1980s, 'voluntary governing body business (was) intended primarily to support elite athletes and provide new facilities for the growing interest in sport which came mainly from the middle classes. At this time NGB concern could be clearly defined as 'sport for sport's sake'. Coakley (1998) elaborates on this sport form and specifically refers to the intrinsic and extrinsic values of sport defined as 'institutionalized competitive activities that involve vigorous physical exertion or the use of relatively complex physical skills by individuals whose participation is motivated by a combination of personal enjoyment and external rewards' (Coakley, 1998: 19). The value system here is notionally a combination of intrinsic (personal enjoyment and moral development) and extrinsic (performance hierarchies and winning). However, it is important to note that extrinsic value is considered essential to these activities.

Collins (2010: 374) notes, 'increasing participation has been a role of some NGBs, but for many their *raison d'être* has been to win matches and develop performance athletes'. In general then, even the *participation* activities of NGBs and sports clubs tend to be 'for sport's sake' in relation to 'grassroots sport', which refers to the base of the performance ladder of 'sport for sport's sake', rather than the two alternative conceptions of sport. Consequently, NGBs and sports clubs also act as part of the supply chain which produces athletes for the commercial sector, including some professional sports clubs or businesses.

The intrinsic values of 'sport for sport's sake' are often deemed to be twofold: personal enjoyment, and moral development via competition (relating to 'fair play', the 'level playing field', 'winning and losing' and 'excellence'). In relation to personal enjoyment, Butcher and Schneider (2001: 35) contend that 'for many, perhaps most, participants in sport, its activities are intrinsically rewarding. They bring a feeling of pleasure and provide experiences that are enjoyable and worthwhile'. However, empirical evidence shows that personal enjoyment of sport is by no means universal and also, moral development is not a 'good' exclusive to sport. Indeed, moral development via sport is often not supported by the evidence (see, for example, Collins and Kay, 2003; Coalter, 2007).

There is a further twist to the intrinsic value claims for competitive performance sport, in that its intrinsic value is often advocated not directly in relation to people, embodied or otherwise, but *for its own sake*. Thus, as Devine points out, 'the "sport for sport's sake" policy purpose rests on the implicit assumption that sport can be considered to have an interest of its own, internal goods and intrinsic value' (Devine, 2012: 5), and 'this carries an implicit justification of *competitive* sport as an obvious good' (Devine, 2012: 3). Within the philosophy of sport literature, MacIntyre's (1981) notion of practices as operations which have value contingent on their value to people, is extensively accepted. Thus Butcher and Schneider (2001: 32) contend that 'sports are practices and... practices are the sort of things that can have interests. Respect for the game will thus entail respect for the interests of the game (or sport) as a practice'. However, it is important to note that in a later work MacIntyre makes explicit that:

> When some local community embodying networks of giving and receiving is in good order, it is generally and characteristically because its judgements, standards, relationships, and institutions have been periodically the subject of communal debate and enquiry and have taken their present form in part as a result of such debate and enquiry.
>
> (MacIntyre, 1999: 157)

If 'sport for sport's sake' is to become or perhaps remain the legitimate primary sport form, particularly if it has a reach over and beyond the voluntary performance sport sector and the commercial business and entertainment sectors, all stakeholders must be represented and recognised in that debate and enquiry. This is of critical importance, *within universal and compulsory settings* including all government provision, particularly PE. Loland (2002) emphasises this shared ethos of the nature of the internal goods of sport and McFee (2004: 77) extends this notion to point out that 'if this is right, we can criticise the practice if the ethos is not *shared*, not *just*, and so on'. Otherwise, as Devine (2012: 6) argues, an over-interpretation of 'sport for sport's sake' runs the risk of 'presenting sport uncritically as autotelic and elevating it to the status of an ideal or embodied subject in its own right with people as subordinate objects of instrumental value to service the interests or "sake" of sport'; especially since, as Butcher and Schneider (2001: 46) note, 'a practice takes on a life of its own'.

Sport for good

'Sport for good' (i.e. extrinsically valuable *to society*) usually refers to the place of sport in social democratic welfare as part of what Coalter *et al.* (1988: 10) call 'recreational welfare'. As such, it can be considered to be a social 'good' with intrinsic value, that should be more widely and progressively distributed ('sport for good' as equality, the early form of 'sport for all'). Alternatively, it can be viewed instrumentally as a tool with extrinsic value, to achieve social inclusion (but not necessarily economic inclusion) or indeed, for social control (safety net or coercive 'sport for good'). As Coalter (2007: 23) puts it, 'historically, public investment in sport has been characterized by a dual purpose: to extend social rights of citizenship and to use sport to address a wide range of social issues'. The hegemonic 'sport for good' form at the beginning of the twenty-first century tends to be that of social inclusion and social control. Loland points out that:

> Instrumentalism has a certain commonsense appeal. It provides ready and concrete answers to questions such as 'What is sport good for?' Moreover, instrumentalist views challenge idealist conceptions of sport as a politically neutral and ideal sphere of universal value, views not uncommon in the traditional rhetoric of sport leaders and politicians.
>
> (Loland, 2004: 112)

Loland also comments that 'sport for good' policies tend to stress 'a wide menu of external economic and social benefits from social programmes including sport, such as: adding to social cohesion; improving health; encouraging lifelong learning; combating social exclusion; and helping economic, physical and social regeneration' (Loland, 2004: 369). These instrumental concerns are extensively evident within international and national sport policy documentation such as the European Commission's White Paper on Sport which claims that 'as a tool for health enhancing physical activity, the sport movement has a greater influence than any other social movement' (European Commission, 2007: 3) and that 'sport makes an important contribution to economic and social cohesion and more integrated societies' (European Commission, 2007: 7). It also states that, 'The Commission will promote the use of sport as a tool in its development policy' and 'sport has a considerable potential as a tool to promote education, health, intercultural dialogue, development and peace' (European Commission, 2007: 9). However, as Devine argues:

> sport for social good as a policy justification in these new public management times, with an emphasis on centralised technocratic executive governance rather than devolved bottom up representative government (Grix 2009; Green 2009), runs the risk of descending into a reductionist instrumentalism, survivalism, rationalism and healthism within a hegemonic audit culture.
>
> (Devine, 2012: 8)

Sport for all

McDonald's (1995) seminal paper on sport for all (i.e. intrinsically valuable *to people*) argued that 'a yawning chasm separates ["sport for sport's sake"] from the social philosophy of *Sport for All*' and that 'for sport to relate to every 'individual' it has to be defined universally' (McDonald, 1995: 73). He further elaborates that 'the "sport" in "*Sport for All*" is a loose term for such disparate activities as informal recreation, leisure pursuits, play, health promotion activities as well as formal organised sport' (McDonald, 1995, p.73). In a similar vein, Kretchmar (1994: xviii) has used the term sport more 'broadly and generically to refer to many movement activities', that is 'human movement with a focus on five of its intentional or purposeful forms: sport, dance, exercise, games, and play'.

It is important to draw on the empirical evidence which consistently shows that far more people are interested in 'sport for all' than 'sport for sport's sake' activities and that this is particularly the case for girls and women. Accordingly, Van Tuyckom *et al.* (2010) showed, using the Eurobarometer Survey 62.0 (TNS Opinion and Social, 2004: 1077), that 'For the majority of countries the occurrence of regular sporting activity "sport for sport's sake" was less than 40 per cent'. However, the White Paper on Sport (European Commission, 2007: 2) using the same data, claims that 'approximately 60 per cent of European citizens participate in sporting activities "sport for all" on a regular basis'. Further, findings from the most recent Eurobarometer Survey (TNS Opinion and Social, 2010)[Q1] are summarised below:

- 40 per cent of EU citizens play sport at least once a week (p. 8);
- far more people get 'informal' physical exercise (in such forms as cycling, walking, dancing or gardening) than play organised sport (p. 14);
- men and women generally do very similar amounts of physical activity (p. 17);
- men in the EU play more sports than women and this is particularly marked in the 15–24 age group (p. 8);
- two-thirds of respondents (67 per cent) are not members of any sports clubs or centres (p. 24);
- among those who say that they do sport or physical exercise, most activity is in informal settings, such as parks or other outdoor environments (48 per cent), or simply on the journey to and from work, school or the shops (31 per cent) (p. 19);
- fitness centres (11 per cent), clubs (11 per cent) and sports centres (8 per cent) are less popular, also 8 per cent exercise at work and 4 per cent exercise at school or university (p. 19).

Henning Eichberg's (2009) 'philosophy of moving people' is of increasing importance in the debate on the function and purpose of sport and PE in wider society. This outlines a philosophy of 'sport for all' which he terms 'the other sport' and bases this on what he terms 'bodily democracy.' He explains that 'the philosophy of sport has...kept a strange distance from...complex empirical reality' and has 'remained to a large extent captured by the ideas of competitive elite sport' (Eichberg, 2009: 116). He develops this further in that 'the turn from sport for the few to body cultural practice of the popular masses can thus help the philosophy of sport to overcome its traditionally narrow focus on the mythology of achievement and the normative moral philosophy of fairness' (Eichberg, 2009: 116). Eichberg argues for a more bottom-up, plural definition of sport given that large 'parts of what nowadays is called "sport for all" are non-competitive and are derived from traditions of gymnastics, dance, festivity, outdoor activities, rambling and games, rather than from classical modern sports' (Eichberg, 2009: 115). Consequently, Devine argues that 'sport for all' can be considered 'to focus on sport for peoples (individuals, communities, and societies) sakes in relation to the intrinsic value of movement pleasure, or sport for wellbeing, joy, happiness' (Devine, 2012: 8). She further argues that this combines the original social democratic recreational welfare approach to 'sport for all' as extending 'the recognition and distribution of the individual, shared and common goods ... which constitute movement and sport' (Devine, 2012: 8), with Eichberg's bottom-up, plural, inductive, definition of 'sport for all' as popular sport.

The value of sport, therefore, depends on which sport concept is being referred to. Lee's work tended to primarily critique hegemonic 'sport for sport's sake' which is why the value contrast with PE is so evident. However, if the sport in sport education encompasses 'sport for all' and even 'sport for good' then the value gap may not be as large. Lee (2004b) showed empirically that in sport, of 18 values, children rank the intrinsic goods of enjoyment (ranked 1), personal achievement (ranked 2) and 'sportsmanship' (ranked 3) much more highly than the extrinsic good of winning (ranked 18, i.e. bottom). This ranking is even more pronounced for girls. Consequently, as Coalter (2007: 7) suggests, 'If research is to inform policy, then it is essential to seek to explore the question of sufficient conditions – which sports, in which conditions, have what effects for which participants'. It can therefore be argued that 'sport for all' with its emphasis on intrinsic value and bodily democracy should be the preferred universal form. In this vein Devine (2012) argues that 'the realisation of ... the IOC's aspiration to sport as a human right ... for all, and consequent democratic sporting accountability, necessitates a 'sport for all' rather than 'competitive sport for sport's sake' policy direction' (Devine, 2012: 1).

As Coalter (2007: 7) makes clear:

> if sports policy and practice are to mature and their interventions to become less ambitious and more effective, there is a need to 'demythologise' or 'decentre' sport. In a sense *sport* is a collective noun which hides much more than it reveals – perhaps this simplifying function is part of its political attraction.

The physical education and sport debate

Given the preceding analysis, those advocating the primacy of the intrinsic value of movement pleasure within PE are understandably concerned with the further 'sportification' of PE. The wisdom of privileging sport, generally meaning 'sport for sport's sake' as opposed to 'sport for all' within PE is an ongoing discourse within the physical education profession. The move (some may say lurch) towards 'sportification', may be as a result of either the perceived intrinsic (moral development, pleasure, 'meaning' *for some*) or, more likely, perceived extrinsic (talent identification, 'for sport's sake', discipline, competition) value of sport. An example of the 'moral development' approach is Siedentop's (1994) concept of sport education in which 'the biggest lesson is to play hard, play fair, honor your opponent, and accept that when the contest is over, it is over. What matters most is taking part fairly and honorably, not which individual or team wins or loses' (Siedentop, 1994: 13). Similarly, although Kirk (2006: 255) argued 'that if we work to experience activities that are inherently pleasurable and intrinsically satisfying, then there is a possible future for activities such as sport', he then draws upon the 'moral development' argument and concludes 'that school physical education is well placed to take up this challenge of sustaining sport *as a moral practice*' (Kirk, 2006: 263; emphasis added).

Concern regarding the possible (re)signification of PE as competitive (team) sport or 'sport for sport's sake' is evident in the literature. Thus, Kay (2003: 8) argues that there is an increasing emphasis in PE teaching on 'skill-based, performance-improving . . . coaching . . . [rather than on] physical education teaching [which] embodies a pupil-centred rationale'. Wright (2004: 151) reports 'many writers, for example, Capel (2000), Houlihan (2000), Mountakis (2002), Penney (1998, 2000), Penney and Chandler (2000), have argued that if competitive games are seen as the mainstay of physical education, they fail to do justice to all its other aspects'. Further, Wright (2004), citing Capel (2000), comments that:

> physical education should benefit every pupil regardless of ability or enthusiasm for the subject, and therefore an emphasis on sport and with it an emphasis on competitive success can result in finite resources being used for a few elite performers rather than being available to encourage participation for all.
>
> (Wright, 2004: 139)

Lee (2004b) identified the potential for a conflict of values between PE and sport, by which he meant 'sport for sport's sake'. He explained that as a teacher he was 'concerned with helping all students find an activity that would engage them and perhaps provide an interest during adult life, a universalist process orientation' as distinct from his orientation as a coach which was with 'helping those with talent to excel' (Lee, 2004b: 7). In adapting Schwartz's (1992) structure and contents of values and applying these to sport (as 'sport for sport's sake'), he argued that the values of PE align more with concern for others while the values of sport align more with self interest. The key orientations of concern for others, resulting in benevolence and universalism, and that of self interest resulting in achievement, power and status, arise from this position. This bifurcation is the crux of the possible conflict of interest between sport and PE elaborated so persuasively by him.

It is clear that Lee therefore contrasted PE with the 'sport for sport's sake' form rather than, for example, 'sport for all'.

Wright arrived at the same conclusion as Lee in that 'the development of the person, *qua* person, is key in any educational process' (Wright, 2004: 151). Wright is also clearly of the view that intrinsic values:

> are best safeguarded by the primary school teacher who knows the children holistically, and, who, because she teaches all aspects of the national curriculum (NC) can enable children to see physical education as an integral part of the primary school curriculum.
>
> (Wright, 2004: 149)

This raises critical issues regarding the delivery of PE by specialists and indeed by coaches. This careful distinction between PE and sport is maintained in some of the recent sport and coaching pedagogy texts for example Armour (2011) is clear about the central role of the professionally trained physical educator within an education setting.

Conclusions

Lee's seminal work on children's values within the discipline of social psychology has been of immense importance in attempting to bridge evidence-policy-practice divides and crucially, in articulating how children value sport and physical activity. This work could not be of more importance in the current climate where in some, even most, countries, 'sport for sport's sake' and coaching are either firmly embedded or encroaching further into the physical education landscape with NGBs of sport being given the remit to increase participation via 'grassroots sport' rather than 'sport for all'.

This has significant implications for PE. PE and sport practitioners may well have competing sets of values and priorities and with schools outsourcing both the curriculum and extended curriculum to NGB's, then 'sport for sport's sake' rather than physical education or 'sport for all' will be the order of the day. This is especially the case given that coaches are still trained via the NGB coach development systems with their primary focus on performance and elite sport. Even if coach education is refocused to relate to 'other' population groups, this still tends to be within the context of 'grassroots sport' and a performance ladder, which relates to sport for sport's sake rather than 'sport for all'. The shifting of these tectonic plates therefore logically requires that coaching is pulled closer to teaching and that the process of coach education will need to be significantly revised.

Sport is also being written into international policy documents and sometimes even framed as a *human right* (by definition, universal). The International Olympic Committee (IOC, 2010: 11) claims that 'the practice of sport is a human right', but outlines role 12 of the IOC as being 'to encourage and support the development of *sport for all* (our emphasis)' (IOC, 2010: 15). The European Union's Lisbon Treaty states that:

Union action shall be aimed at . . . developing the European dimension in sport, by promoting fairness and openness in sporting competitions and cooperation between bodies responsible for sports, and by protecting the physical and moral integrity of sportsmen and sportswomen, especially the youngest sportsmen and sportswomen.

(European Union, 2008: 158)

Also, enshrined within UK sport's coaches' Code of Practice (Sportscoach UK, 2005) is the requirement that 'coaches must respect and champion the rights of every individual to participate in sport' and should 'assist in the creation of an environment where every individual has the opportunity to participate in a sport or activity of their choice' (para. 1). Thus, *universalist* claims are increasingly being made about sport.

In this context, it is important to question whether this 'right' relates to Lee's 'universalist process orientation' ('sport for all') or 'elitist outcome orientation' ('sport for sport's sake'). Further, we can ask, do all individuals/ children want to participate in sport and which sport is this? Lee's research relating to children's values and sport is also prescient in relation to the status of children in society. As David (2005) argues, there has been a shift from a needs-based to a rights-based approach to children. Thus, if children are seen as passive objects, meeting their needs is based on reactive, paternally motivated charity and protection. Alternatively, children can be seen as the subject of rights with consequent legal obligations under domestic and international law, and attendant non-discriminatory and equality-directed guarantees and entitlements.

The Convention on the Rights of the Child (United Nations, 1989) has been ratified by all but two countries (USA and Somalia) and a number of the articles therein can be related both to the sport provision 'trialectic' and the current research on children and values. Thus, while articles 2, 3, 12 and 13 relate to the rights: not to be discriminated against, to have their best interests considered as a primary concern, to express views that should be given due weight, and to freedom of expression, it is to article 31 that we turn to find the right to rest and leisure and to freely participate in cultural life. In sum, then, a combination of these articles points towards a universalist process orientation/'sport for all' approach to sport provision for children, rather than an elitist outcome orientation/'sport for sport's sake'.

Finally in relation to sport and values, it is useful to ask questions about who, what, why and where. First, *who* is sport for? We might assume for both men and women, and boys and girls as participants, performers and athletes as well as for society at large, including both public and private sectors. However, it is important to ask whether all individuals want to participate in sport and is sport a universal right and/or a compulsory duty? Second, *what* is sport? 'Sport for sport's sake' (including 'grassroots sport'), 'sport for good', or 'sport for all'? Thirdly, *why* value sport, for intrinsic and/or extrinsic reasons? Intrinsic values could be pleasure, joy, happiness or moral development or they could be pleasure, skill, knowledge or health. Extrinsic values might be to contribute to social cohesion, improving health, encouraging lifelong learning, combating social exclusion and economic, physical and social regeneration. Or they could be related to performance ranking and winning. Finally, *where* should sport be practiced? The issue here is one of public or private ownership of recreational facilities, schools and parks, in addition to the natural landscape of open spaces, nature reserves, rivers, forests, coasts and mountains, and access to them.

The purpose of investigating the values reported by children and young people participating in sport and physical education is perhaps best summarised by Patriksson (1995: 128; cited by Coalter, 2007: 23):

> The futility of arguing whether sport is good or bad has been observed by several authors. Sport, like most activities, is not a priori good or bad, but has the potential of producing both positive and negative outcomes. Questions like 'what conditions are necessary for sport to have beneficial outcomes?' must be asked more often.

References

Abad, D. (2010) Sportsmanship. *Sport, Ethics and Philosophy*, 4(1), 27–42.

Aristotle (1968) *Nichomachean Ethics*. Book X. London: Heinemann.

Armour, K. (2011) *Sport Pedagogy: An Introduction forTeaching and Coaching*. London: Prentice Hall.

Booth, D. (2009) Politics and pleasure: The philosophy of physical education revisited. *Quest*, 61, 133–53.

Burrows, L. (2005) Do the 'right' thing: Chewing the fat in physical education. *Journal of Physical Education New Zealand*, 33(1), 7–16.

Butcher, R., and Schneider, A. (2001) Fair play as respect for the game. In Morgan, W.J., Meier, K.V. and A.J. Schneider, A.J. (eds) *Ethics in Sport*. Champaign, IL: Human Kinetics, pp. 21–48.

Capel, S. (2000) Physical education and sport. In Capel, S. and Piotrowski, S. (eds) *Issues in Physical Education*. London: Routledge Falmer, pp. 131–43.

Coakley, J. (1998) *Sport in Society: Issues and Controversies*. Boston, MA: McGraw-Hill.

Coalter, F. (2007) *A Wider Role for Sport: Who's Keeping the Score?* London: Routledge.

Coalter, F., Long, J. and Duffield, B. (1988) *Recreational Welfare: The Rationale for Public Sector Investment in Leisure*. Aldershot: Gower/Avebury.

Collins, M. (2010). From 'sport for good' to 'sport for sport's sake'-not a good move for sports development in England? *International Journal of Sport Policy and Politics*, 2(3), 367–79.

Collins, M. and Kay, T. (2003) *Sport and Social Exclusion*. London: Routledge.

David, P. (2005) *Human Rights in Youth Sport*. London: Routledge.

DCMS (2002) *Game Plan, a Strategy for Delivering Government's Sport and Physical Activity Objectives*. London: Department for Culture, Media and Sport.

Devine, C. (2012) London 2012 Olympic legacy: a big sporting society? *International Journal of Sport Policy and Politics*, 5(2), 257–79.

Eichberg, H. (2009) Bodily democracy: Towards a philosophy of sport for all. *Sport, Ethics and Philosophy*, 3(3), 441–61.

European Commission, (2007) *White Paper on Sport*. Brussels: European Commission. Retrieved from http://ec.europa.eu/sport/white-paper/whitepaper8_en.htm#1.

European Union (2008) *Consolidated Versions of the Treaty on European Union and the Treaty on the Functioning of the European Union.* Brussels: Council of the European Union. Retrieved from http://register.consilium.europa.eu/pdf/en/08/st06/st06655.en08.pdf.

Evans, J. and Penney, D. (2008) Levels on the playing field: the social construction of physical 'ability' in the physical education curriculum. *Physical Education and Sport Pedagogy,* 1 (13 January), 31–47.

Evans, J., Penney, D. and Davies, B. (1996) Back to the Future: Education Policy and Physical Education. In Armstrong, N. (ed.) *New Directions in Physical Education.* London: Cassell.

Frankena, W. (1973) *Ethics,* 2nd edn. Englewood Cliffs, NJ: Prentice Wood Hall.

Green, M. (2009) Podium or participation? Analysing policy priorities under changing modes of sport governance in the United Kingdom. *International Journal of Sport Policy,* 1(2), 121–44.

Grix, J. (2009) The impact of UK sport policy on the governance of athletics. *International Journal of Sport Policy,* 1(1), 31–49.

Hardman, K. and Marshall, J. (2005) Update on the state and status of physical education world-wide. *International Council of Sport Science and Physical Education.* Retrieved from http://www.icsspe.org/documente/Status_PE_Hardman_and_Marshall.pdf.

Hargreaves, J. (1994) *Sporting Females: critical issues in the history and sociology of women's sports.* London: Routledge.

Hawkins, A. (2008) Pragmatism, purpose, and play: Struggle for the soul of physical education. *Quest,* 60, 345–56.

Houlihan, B. (2000) Sporting excellence, schools and sport development: the politics of public policy spaces. *European Review in Physical Education,* 6(2), 171–92.

Houlihan, B. and Green, K. (2006) The changing status of school sport and physical education: explaining policy change. *Sport, Education and Society* 1 (11 February), 73–92.

IOC (2010) *Olympic Charter.* Lausanne: International Olympic Committee. Retrieved from www.olympic.org/Documents/Olympic%20Charter/Charter_en_2010.pdf.

Kant, I (1967) *Critique of Practical Reason.* London: Longman.

Kay, W. (2003) Physical education, RIP?, *British Journal of Teaching Physical Education,* 34(4), 6–9.

Kirk, D. (2006) Sport education, critical pedagogy,and learning theory: toward an intrinsic justification for physical education and youth sport. *Quest,* 58, 255–64.

Kirk, D. (2011) Children learning in physical education: a historical overview. In Armour, K. (ed.) *Sport Pedagogy: An Introduction for Teaching and Coaching.* London: Prentice Hall.

Kretchmar, R. S. (1994) *Practical Philosophy of Sport.* Champaign, IL: Human Kinetics.

Lee, M.J. (2004a) The importance of values in the coaching process. In Silva, M. and Malina, R. (eds) *Children and Youth in Organized Sports.* Coimbra: Coimbra University Press, pp. 82–94.

Lee, M. (2004b) Values in physical education and sport: A conflict of interests? *The British Journal of Teaching Physical Education,* 35(1), 6–10.

Loland, S. (2002) *Fair Play in Sport: A Moral Norm System.* London: Routledge.

Loland, S. (2004) Normative theories of sport: A critical review. *Journal of the Philosophy of Sport,* XXXI, 101–21.

MacIntyre, A. (1981) *After Virtue.* London: Duckworth.

MacIntyre, A. (1999) *Dependent Rational Animals.* London: Duckworth.

McDonald, I. (1995) Sport for all–RIP. A political critique of the relationship between national sport policy and local authority sports development in London. In Flemming, S., Talbot, M. and Tomlinson, A. (eds) *Policy and Politics in Sport, Physical Education and Leisure*. Eastbourne: Leisure Studies Association.

McFee, G. (2004) *Sport, Rules and Values.* London: Routledge.

Mill, J.S. (1962) *Utilitarianism*. London: Collins.

MoE (1952) *Physical Education in the Primary School, Part One: Moving and Growing.* Ministry of Education Pamphlet No 24. London: Her Majesty's Stationery Office (HMSO).

Morgan, W. (2006) Philosophy and physical education. In Kirk, D., O'Sullivan, M. and Macdonald, D. (eds) *The Handbook of Research in Sport and Physical Education*. Thousand Oaks, CA: Sage.

Mountakis, C. (2000) The differences between PE and top level sport. *European Physical Education Review*, 3(1), 21–32.

Patriksson, M. (1995) Scientific review part 2. In *The Significance of Sport for Society – Health, Socialisation, Economy: A Scientific Review*. 8th Conference of European Ministers Responsible for Sport, Lisbon, 17–18 May 1995. Strasbourg: Council of Europe Press.

Penney, D. (1998) Positioning and defining sport and health in the curriculum. *European Physical Education Review*, 4(2), 117–26.

Penney, D. (2000) Physical education, sporting excellence and educational excellence, *European Physical Education Review*, 6(2), 135–50.

Penney, D. and Chandler, T. (2000) Physical education: What future(s)? *Sport Education and Society*, 5(1), 71–87.

Penney, D., Clarke, G. and Kinchin, G. (2002) Developing physical education as a 'connective specialism': Is sport education the answer? *Sport, Education and Society,* 7(1), 55–64.

Pringle, R. (2010) Finding pleasure in physical education: A critical examination of the educative value of positive movement affects. *Quest*, 62, 119–34.

Rintala, J. (2009) It's all about the –ing. *Quest*, 61, 279–88.

Schwartz, S. H. (1992) Universals in the content and structure of values: Theory and empirical tests in 20 countries. In Zanna, M. (ed.) *Advances in Experimental Social Psychology*, 25, 1–65. New York: Academic Press.

Siedentop, D. (1994) *Sport Education: Quality PE through Positive Sport Experiences* : Champaigne, IL: Human Kinetics.

Smith, W. (2011) An alternative to Kirk's idea of the idea and a future for Physical Education. *Asia-Pacific Journal of Health, Sport and Physical Education*, 2(2), 23–33.

Sportscoach UK (2005) *Code of Practice for Sports Coaches*. Leeds: National Coaching Foundation.

TNS Opinion and Social (2004) *The Citizens of the European Union and Sport Special Eurobarometer 213, Wave 62.0*. Brussels: European Commission. Retrieved from http://ec.europa.eu/sport/documents/publications/ebs_213_report_en.pdf.

TNS Opinion and Social (2010) *The Citizens of the European Union and Sport Special Eurobarometer 334, Sport and Physical Activity*. Brussels: European Commission.

United Nations (1989) *Convention on the Rights of the Child*. New York: UN Office of Public Information. Retrieved from http://www2.ohchr.org/english/law/crc.htm.

Van Tuyckom, C., Scheerder, J. and Bracke, P. (2010) Gender and age inequalities in regular sports participation: A cross-national study of 25 European countries. *Journal of Sport Sciences*, 28, 10.

Whitehead, M. (2007) Physical literacy: Philosophical considerations in relation to developing a sense of self, universality and propositional knowledge. *Sport, Ethics and Philosophy*, 3 (1 December), 281–98.

Wright, L. (2004) Preserving the value of happiness in primary school physical education. *Physical Education and Sport Pedagogy*, 9(2), 149–63.

Part I

Values, attitudes and achievement goals

2 What sport values do young people hold?

Values in children's sport: Spontaneously expressed values among young athletes

Martin J. Lee and Michael Cockman

Considerable concern has been voiced in recent years over the conduct of participants in sport; it has spread to include behaviour in children's sport. The objects of this concern include, most commonly, forms of cheating, aggressive or violent behaviour, and lack of respect for opponents and officials. It is not restricted to particular nations or sports but appears to be worldwide and is reflected in a considerable literature concerned with the nature of fair play and moral development in sport (see Bredemeier and Shields, 1993). While the most public occurrences, which are the sources of concern and attract media attention, are in adult professional sport, it is the extent to which such behaviour may be found in the lower level of sport for children which has most recently attracted the attention of researchers (Bredemeier, 1994).

Fair play and its related term 'sportsmanship' appear to refer to patterns of behaviour in sport which are characterised by justice, equity, benevolence, and good manners while striving for athletic superiority. The behaviour which defines fair play may be considered to be a manifestation of prevailing attitudes, and of values. Clearly it is helpful to explore the relationships between behaviour and its underlying constructs.

Behaviour refers to the actions which people take. It may be clearly defined and is observable either informally or by the use of carefully structured observation instruments in accordance with established protocols. The conditions under which particular behaviours occur vary, for example, by the presence of others, by the rewards or penalties associated with the behaviour, or by emotional variations in the individual.

Fair play and sportsmanship are terms that originated in the English language and have been widely adopted in others. However, it not always clear what they mean to sports participants nor what their relationship is to psychological constructs and the behaviours which they are thought to represent. Theoretical discussions of beliefs, attitudes and, most particularly, values, and their relationships to behaviour may illuminate the meaning of the terms. Broadly, beliefs refer to cognitions or perceptions about objects or events (what it is), attitudes to the affective response to that perception (how good or bad it is), and values to an assessment of the importance of the belief (how important it is). Let us now examine those ideas a little more closely.

Beliefs are cognitive structures which provide a framework from which people view the world. An individual's belief system may be said to determine his or her perceptions of reality and truth, judgements of value, and identification of appropriate goals and behaviour (Rokeach, 1968). The latter two outcomes have an evaluative dimension and may be construed as representing attitudes and values. The conceptual distinction between attitudes and values is of prime importance in the design of research because they demand different measurement techniques. While there are a range of techniques available for the measurement of attitudes the reliable measurement of values has been, and remains, a matter of debate (e.g. Braithwaite, 1982).

The concept of attitude was once described as the most important concept in social psychology (Allport, 1935) and has continued to be widely used in socio psychological research. It is commonly defined as a predisposition to respond in a positive or negative way to some specific stimulus, or attitude object and has a number of components: cognitive, affective, and behavioural (see Fishbein and Ajzen, 1975). Because attitudes are specific to particular objects or events it is possible to express equally positive or negative attitudes towards a number of stimuli. For example in sport it would be quite possible to express equally positive attitudes towards competitive success (winning) and to performing well (demonstrating skill).

Reference to values occurs frequently in the literature of fair play, though often without clear recognition of the nature of the concept (e.g. Hastad *et al.*, 1986). The construct spans the disciplines of anthropology, sociology and psychology and has aroused considerable interest in these fields since the 1950s (Spates, 1983). The cross-disciplinary nature of that interest reflects the importance of cultural influences on individual cognitions.

Finally, Schwartz suggests a series of conflicts between sets of value types. One such conflict is between Universalism/Benevolence and Power/Achievement (Schwartz, 1992: 35). In sport, that conflict could be expressed in terms of the competing demands of fair play and sportsmanship and of competitive success (winning).

Research into fair play in youth sports

Attitudes

Much of the research into aspects of fair play in sports has taken the form of attitudinal studies, possibly because of the relative ease of collecting data. The following conclusions are representative of those made from attitudinal research:

- a strong commitment to winning above playing well and playing fairly is associated with increases in age (Webb, 1969);
- instrumental and aggressive behaviour is more acceptable with increasing age (Lee and Williams, 1989);

- perceptions of acceptable aggression decrease with levels of moral reasoning (Bredemeier *et al.*, 1987);
- winning is more important for competitive participants than for recreational participants (Knoppers *et al.*, 1986);
- professional attitudes are stronger among boys than girls (McElroy and Kirkendall, 1980).

Values

Despite the influence of Rokeach little work using his approach has been conducted in sport. Simmons and Dickinson (1986) developed an instrument to measure values in athletic populations. While they drew upon Rokeach's work to provide a rationale there is no indication that the values they include in the instrument are drawn from any theoretical basis or from the populations of interest. The instrument comprised 14 items which yielded five factors: (a) achievement, (b) exercise in a pleasant setting, (c) sociability, (d) good health, and (e) self-fulfilment. Lee (1977), using the RVS, found that college athletes valued competence values rather more than moral values and, not surprisingly, were concerned predominantly with competitive success. However, no research using this instrument with children has been identified though other studies have indicated that the values of children in sport may differ from those of adults. There is evidence that many children place a greater emphasis on fun, developing skills, affiliation, fitness, and fair play, in preference to winning (Dubois, 1986; Roberts, 1993).

Rationale

Because values have been proposed as underlying the organisation of behaviour then the identification of values among young athletes is of prime importance in understanding better the processes by which they make decisions about their behaviour in sporting situations. Following the advice of Glaser and Strauss (cited in Spates, 1983) and Braithwaite and Laws (1985), we cannot assume that the values which young people express in sport necessarily fit adult preconceptions.

Hence it is important to adopt an inductive approach to establish salient values from the prospective population prior to examining the structure of value systems among junior athletes. The purpose of this project was to establish spontaneously expressed values which affect children's behaviour in competitive sport.

Kohlberg's strategy of interviewing in which a moral dilemma provides the basis for a discussion designed to elicit levels of moral reasoning (Colby and Kohlberg, 1987) is also considered suitable for eliciting values. Samples were drawn from sports which fulfil the following criteria: (a) mass participation, (b) have high public profile, (c) provide situations in which values may be clearly in opposition. In the United Kingdom football and tennis were considered suitable.

Method

Data were collected by semi-structured interview protocol which was developed through discussion with a working party drawn from a Council of Europe Committee of Experts in which the senior author took the chair.

Subjects

Subjects were (a) male football players ($n = 60$) in the East Midlands region of England, and (b) tennis players from schools and competitors at a junior tournament in the East Midlands ($n = 33$). All players were between 12 and 16 years of age, and participants in competitive sport as defined by representing teams in school or club leagues. The level of performance included school, club, district, regional and international. The total number of subjects available was 305, from which 93 were randomly selected.

Instrument

Each interview constituted a semi-structured discussion of two hypothetical situations which might occur in the subject's sport and produce a moral dilemma. Subjects were asked about possible and desirable actions in the situation, each of which was designed to elicit one of three different types of behaviour: (a) instrumental, (b) aggressive, and (c) altruistic. The interview was conducted in accordance with an agreed format. Six football and seven tennis situations were developed and randomly assigned to subjects. This procedure ensured that all of them were used in the study and hence elicited the maximum range of values available.

Procedures

Interview format

Interviews were conducted in quiet rooms from which, as far as possible, intruders were excluded. All interviews were recorded using micro-cassette recorders and later transcribed to facilitate content analysis. Subjects were asked to read a hypothetical situation allocated at random from the pool of items available for their sport. The interviewer checked subjects' comprehension of the situation described before commencing the discussion. Subjects were asked to imagine themselves in the situation and led through a series of stages designed to elicit their thoughts about (a) what they could do in the situation, (b) what most people might do, and (c) what they themselves would do. This provided a basis for a conversation about what was important to subjects about participating in their chosen sport.

Coding procedures

A small pilot study was conducted among players (*n* = 7) in a youth (under 13) football team, at one of the participating schools. The pilot studies were designed to (a) test the utility of dilemmas, and (b) establish preliminary coding. As a result of the utility criterion two football dilemmas were discarded from an original list of eight.

All interviews were transcribed in preparation for content analysis. For the coding process, values were operationally defined as guiding principles of behaviour or motivational goals which underlie the expression of a view about the desirability or otherwise of a particular form of behaviour arising during the discussion of a stimulus event. Using independent coding and subsequent discussion the researchers initially identified twelve value categories from the pilot study. As new categories were added inter-rater reliability was checked by independent coding of random samples of four transcripts on three occasions. Reliability was expressed as the percentage of total values identified which were classified similarly by both researchers. At each stage any discrepancies were discussed and classification of responses was clarified. Successive inter-rater reliability values obtained were 80, 78, and 86 per cent (mean = 81.3 per cent). A record was kept of the occurrence of the values in each interview and of the first appearance of each value in the set.

Results

Six transcripts were discarded. Analysis of the remaining transcripts resulted in the identification of 18 value categories. No new categories were added after the analysis of the nineteenth transcript. Frequencies of the occurrence of each value were recorded but are not central to this discussion. Categories and descriptors are given in Table 2.1.

The descriptors given in Table 2.1 represent a distillation of statements arising in the interviews and are further clarified by reporting examples of statements from which they were drawn. Figures in parentheses are subject code numbers.

- *Achievement:* Clearly in a sporting context achievement values are commonly expressed. Subjects occasionally distinguished between personal achievement and the achievement of the team in which they played, thus there was recognition of collective as well as personal achievement. In some cases the value was expressed as reaching a specific target, for example 'Scoring goals is a really good feeling, you know, achieving that goal is a good feeling' (111), or setting a performance standard, as in this tennis player who said 'The most important thing to me is being good and getting appreciation out of the game' (1008). In others it might be expressed in terms of performing to the limits of one's ability irrespective of the outcome, for example 'If you have lost and you have done your best you feel okay' (701).

Table 2.1 Spontaneously expressed values identified from football and tennis players aged 12–16 years

Value	Descriptor
1. Achievement	Being personally or collectively successful in play
2. Caring	Showing concern for other people
3. Companionship	Being with friends with a similar interest in the game
4. Conformity	Conforming to the expectations of other in the team
5. Conscientious	Doing one's best at all times, and not letting others down
6. Contract maintenance	Supporting the essence of agreeing to play the game, to play in the spirit of the game
7. Enjoyment	Experiencing feelings of satisfaction and pleasure
8. Fairness	Not allowing an unfair advantage in the contest/judgement
9. Good game	Enjoying the contest regardless of outcome; this usually embodies a balance between contestants
10. Health and fitness	Becoming healthy as a result of the activity and, in becoming fit, enhancing performance
11. Obedience	Avoiding punishment, being dropped, sent off or suspended
12. Public image	Gaining approval of others
13. Sportsmanship	Being of good disposition, accepting bad luck with the good, demonstrating positive behaviours toward opponents, and accepting defeats
14. Self-actualisation	Experiencing the activity for its own sake and accompanying transcendent feelings
15. Showing skill	Being able to perform the skill of the game well
16. Team cohesion	Doing something for someone else and for the sake of the team performance
17. Tolerance	Being able to get along with others despite interpersonal differences
18. Winning	Demonstrating superiority in the contest

- *Caring:* The value caring reflects a concern for others. It became evident in football when discussing possible actions in the case where an opponent might be injured when there is a chance to score. This evoked comments about stopping the play so that assistance could be given, for example 'I would kick it out – you don't know, he could have swallowed his tongue or anything, it could be really serious' (405). In some cases this sentiment was related to self and reflects the assumption of the Golden Rule. For example, subject 704 commented that he would 'probably kick it off the field' for the safety of the player. If I was down I would want the trainer on quickly'. More explicitly altruistic sentiments are exemplified by such remarks as '[it is] best not to hurt someone deliberately' (404) and 'people always push off little players, I mean it's only a game really. They should not do that' (906). A concern for the psychological well-being of others is evident in this remark from a tennis player 'It makes me really mad when people start chucking their racquets, cause it puts the other player off' (1009).

- **Companionship:** The importance of the companionship of others is evident in statements referring to opportunities to make new friends, such as 'It is in a way, because you meet people' (501), 'You make new friends and that, yes I quite like that' (311), and 'You meet lots of friends and you can arrange friendly matches' (1006). A second aspect of this value is that sport provides a common interest and setting for having fun, for example 'I enjoy the game, playing with mates' (212), and 'It's fun playing with other lads, having a laugh' (310) .

- **Conformity:** This refers to a willingness to live up to the behavioural expectations of the group, whether expressed by the team or the coach. This value is more evident among football players than tennis players and is exemplified by statements such as 'if you have a team plan you should follow it for the team's sake' (503) in relation to team strategies, and 'I think they would keep their mouths shut – because they have the advantage and I think the team mates would not be too pleased' (801) when discussing altruistic behaviour in the event of an injury.

- **Conscientious:** This value was frequently expressed as the need to meet one's commitments and not let others down and is exemplified by comments such as 'If you are given a job, the team is relying on you to do it and if you don't, you let them down' (211). It was evident among a significant proportion of the sample, particularly among football players.

- **Contract maintenance:** Playing within the 'spirit of the game' is important to many children. To break the rules is to destroy the game itself and break the social contract implicit in the contest. It is shown by statements such as 'they like to play fair, there is no point in winning if you can't do it properly' (703).

- **Enjoyment:** Most subjects considered that enjoying the game was very important to them. Enjoyment means different things to different people and not many were able to articulate the source of enjoyment clearly. In some cases it can come from achievement, for example 'Enjoyment – from scoring goals' (203). In other cases responses were less explicit and implied that the fun comes from the game experience rather than the outcome. Thus 'We just go out there to enjoy it.'

- **Fairness:** The principle of fairness is exemplified by comments about the balance of advantage between players. One boy summed it up simply by saying 'If you play football you have to let people have a fair game (301), while another gave a specific example: 'If you are in a 14-year-old group and there is a 16-year-old in the team, I don't think that is very fair, he is going to be a stronger lad and has had 3 years more experience' (308).

- **Good game:** Many subjects commented upon the importance of having a 'good game' in which the outcome is less important than the experience. This tennis player provides a good example: 'I don't mind as long as I have had a good game, even if I lose I don't mind' (1101). But this was not restricted to the tennis sample: 'Yes, it's a game, not just to win, but for fun, for the enjoyment of it...enjoying playing the game against someone else, doesn't matter if you lose as long as you have a game against another team playing with your friends' (201).

- *Health and fitness:* This value was evident as an awareness of the value of playing in order to get fit, for example '[It] keeps me fit' (1017), '[It] gets you fit' (1102), 'I feel as though I'm keeping fit' (1103). Among the tennis players fitness was perceived as an outcome of playing; however, football players tended to see it as a requirement of performance rather than an outcome.

- *Obedience:* The notion of obedience to authority is exemplified by comments such as 'saves getting booked or sent off' (203) and 'if you do get up and have a go you can get sent off, if you ignore it you are alright' (201). The importance of significant others in developing values is shown in this comment: 'they would get on with it even more because if they reacted like that they would be pulled off...my dad taught me not to react and now I don't think about it – you could get booked, sent off' (501). This value was more prevalent among football players than tennis players though it was expressed in both groups.

- *Public image:* The need to present a desirable public image is an important part of adolescent values and was also evident here. Players recognise that the image projected is important in impression formation and seek to gain the approval of others. Examples are 'It's untidy to have your shirt hanging out – bad image' (406) and 'You want to look smart so you gain respect, a good image shows you care, probably can play fairly, and well too' (603).

- *Sportsmanship:* The notion of sportsmanship was strongly evident in the interviews. It embodies prosocial behaviour which goes beyond the bounds of conformity to rules and may be altruistic. For example in response to a discussion of right action in the case of an injured player this player said 'they know what it is like to be ignored and they would want the ball kicked out...it is more important to think of the player really than to go on and score...sportsmanship, I think that is more important than being sent off' (501). A further element is that of good manners as in this tennis player 'Just show that you've got no hard feelings if you've lost' (1108).

- *Self-actualisation:* Some players referred clearly to the good feelings associated with playing a game. It is evident in such comments as 'Sometimes you get a good feeling, I can't explain any better than that' (103), 'I just like playing the game, it's really good' (105), 'I play because I love it' (402), and 'If you've done your best it gives a great feeling, there's nothing like it really' (1101). Further articulation of the good feelings is not easily made.

- *Showing skill:* This value was surprisingly less evident than expected. Typical comments gave evidence of both an internal satisfaction, as in 'If you are skilful you feel happy, confident, can show off, not big-headedly, but show your skill' (801), and of a need to impress, as in 'It's good to have a good technique... and look good on court instead of just sloppy play' (1005).

- *Team cohesion:* This is a team sport value though it did appear among tennis players with reference to doubles as in 'I get on well with my doubles partner, you have to work as a team' (1006). It reflects a recognition of the satisfaction to be gained from taking part in a group activity. 'If you win you are happy with yourself because you are helping the team win' (503). There is also an element of doing something for the sake of others as in 'You do it for the others' (302) and 'You have to lift the team when you are playing' (502).
- *Tolerance:* This value is used to refer to the importance of a degree of tolerance in the interpersonal relations engendered in playing sport, particularly in a team game. It is exemplified by the statement 'You may well want one idea, but your partner may want another idea' (1103). The context of the statement implies that such differences of opinion are to be tolerated and should not threaten the relationship.
- *Winning:* Taking part in sport implies being willing to see winning as a part of the activity. This is evident in that the vast majority of subjects expressed the value of winning. For some it provides the motivation as for this football player 'it's important to be part of the team, but winning is the pleasure' (503). In other cases it quite clearly influences decisions in the game, for example '[I] would commit a foul to make sure we won' (502). There is some evidence that this may become more important with age for some players, for example 'I go out to win now... I used to go out to enjoy myself and play my best; now I go out, play my best and win, determination, concentration, competitiveness!' (1006).

Discussion

This investigation of spontaneously elicited values has provided a fruitful avenue to the clarification of the development of sportsmanship among young athletes and enhanced our understanding of the benefits children obtain from sport. The loss of a small number of interviews for technical reasons is not critical to the data since it was demonstrated that all useful value categories were evident within the analysis of 19 interviews. Hence we have confidence that the values identified are representative of those which underlie decision-making in young athletes.

At first glance the data appear to demonstrate that there are values which are specific to sport, (e.g. good game, sportsmanship). However, even if this is the case, closer examination suggests that the values obtained here can be grouped at a higher-order level which represent more general categories. Thus these two values may simply be manifestations of more general principles which are particularly salient to sport.

A great many subjects considered Sportsmanship to be important, and when pressed to make a choice, many considered it to be more important than competitive success. Indeed a significant majority expressed the importance of playing within the spirit of the laws (contract maintenance) and to ensure that each contestant had no unfair advantage over the other (fairness). Further evidence for the levels of altruism existing within this sample can be found in a clear concern for the welfare of others, both physically and psychologically, shown by the value caring, and possibly tolerance; though since the latter appeared only infrequently it may not form an separate element in a collective value structure.

Perhaps the most consistent value of participating in sport is the personal pleasure to be gained from it. While most young people may experience some difficulty in articulating what it is that they enjoy about sport they certainly feel it very strongly. The value enjoyment is supported by others expressing a variety of pleasures to be gained from participating (e.g. companionship, good game, and self-actualisation). Recent research indicates that children have different achievement goals which relate to sports participation (see Roberts 1993) in the light of which it is reasonable to suggest that the attainment of these goals is a prime constituent of enjoyment. For example, children who gain satisfaction for showing skill may be expected to have an enjoyable experience when they play well, irrespective of the competitive outcome; others, who receive adult approval for participating, may enjoy the praise of their parents after a game even if the level of skill displayed is low.

If it can be demonstrated consistently that the values identified in this study represent the principles by which young athletes organise their experience of sport and judge their satisfaction from it then it, will be important to investigate the ways in which they develop their values. Hence we recommend that future research in this area should investigate (a) whether the values identified here are more widely applicable in youth sports, (b) the value systems of populations of young athletes in different sports, and (c) the relationships between athletes value systems and the value systems, both expressed and perceived, of significant others and sports institutions with which they are associated.

References

Allport, G.W. (1935) Attitudes. In Murchison, C. (ed.) *Handbook of Social Psychology.* Worcester, MA: Cambridge University Press, pp. 798–844.

Braithwaite, V.A. (1982) The structure of social values: Validation of Rokeach's twovalue model. *British Journal of Social Psychology*, 21, 203–11.

Braithwaite, V.A. and Laws, H.G. (1985) Structure of human values: Testing the adequacy of the Rokeach Value Survey. *Journal of Personality and Social Psychology*, 49, 250–63.

Bredemeier, B.J.L. (1994) Children's moral reasoning and their assertive, aggressive, and submissive tendencies in sport and daily life. *Journal of Sport and Exercise Psychology*, 16, 1–14.

Bredemeier, B.J.L. and Shields, D.L.L. (1993) Moral psychology in the context of sport. In Singer, R.N., Murphey, M. and Tennant, L.K. (eds) *Handbook of Research on Sport Psychology.* New York: Macmillan, pp. 587–99.

Bredemeier, B.J.L., Weiss, M.R., Shields, D.L.L. and Cooper, B.A.B. (1987) The relationship between children's legitimacy judgements and their moral reasoning, aggression tendencies, and sport involvement. *Sociology of Sport Journal*, 4, 48–60.

Colby, A. and Kohlberg, L. (1987) *The Measurement of Moral Judgement.* New York: Cambridge University Press.

Dubois, P.E. (1986) The effect of participation in sport on the value orientations of young athletes. *Sociology of Sport Journal*, 3, 29–42.

Fishbein, M. and Ajzen, I. (1975) *Belief, Attitude, Intention, and Behavior: An Introduction to Theory and Research.* Reading, MA: Addison-Wesley.

Hastad, D., Segrave, J.O., Pangrazi, R. and Peterson, G. (1986) Causal factors of deviant behavior among youth sport participants. In Vander Velden, L. and Humphreys, J.H. (eds) *Psychology and Sociology of Sport: Current Selected Research*, 1, 149–66. New York: AMS Press.

Knoppers, S. A., Schuiteman, J. and Love, B. (1986) Winning is not the only thing. *Sociology of Sport Journal*, 3, 43–56.

Lee, M.J. (1977) *Expressed Values of Football Players, Intramural Football Players, and Nonfootball Players.* Eugene, OR: Microform Publications.

Lee, M.J. and Williams, V. (1989) Over the top. *Sport and Leisure*, March–April, 27–28.

McElroy, M. and Kirkendall, D. (1980) Significant others and professionalised sport attitudes. *Research Quarterly for Exercise and Sport*, 51, 645–53.

Roberts, G.C. (1993) Motivation in sport: Understanding and enhancing the motivation and achievement of children in sport. In Singer, R.N., Murphey, M. and L.K.Tennant, L.K. (eds) *Handbook of Research on Sport Psychology.* New York: Macmillan, pp. 405–20.

Rokeach, M. (1968) *Beliefs, Attitudes, and Values.* San Francisco, CA: Jossey-Bass.

Rokeach, M. (1973) *The Nature of Human Values.* New York: The Free Press.

Schwartz, S. (1992) Universals in the content and structure of values: Theoretical advances and empirical tests in 20 countries. In Zanna, M.P. (ed.) *Advances in Experimental Social Psychology*, 25, 1–65. New York: Academic Press.

Simmons, D.D. and Dickinson, R.V. (1986) Measurement of values expression in sports and athletics. *Perceptual and Motor Skills*, 62, 651–58.

Spates, J. (1983) The sociology of values. *Annual Review of Sociology*, 9, 27–49.

Webb, H. (1969) Professionalization of attitudes towards play among adolescents. In Kenyon, G.S. (ed.) *Aspects of Contemporary Sport Sociology.* Chicago, IL: Athletic Institute, pp. 161–28.

Chapter 2 link: Relevance and update

This chapter, slightly modified from a paper originally published in 1995, introduces key constructs (beliefs, attitudes, and values) and their relationship with fair play. We have shortened the introduction and discussion to focus on the identification and description of 18 salient youth sport values.

The chapter has good ecological validity in drawing the values directly from young competitors through discussions of moral dilemmas in sport, thus it identifies some sport specific values that are absent from general surveys of human values (e.g. sportsmanship, good game). The frequency with which the values were expressed in this study was published later (Lee, 1997) and is shown in Figure 2.1. These values are used in Chapter 3 to develop the Youth Sport Values Questionnaire (YSVQ). It should be noted that the

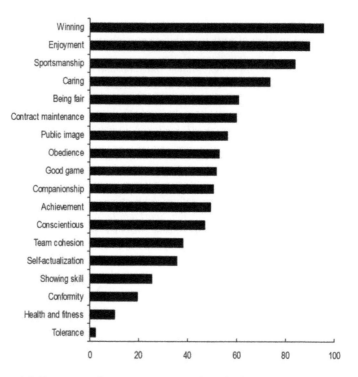

Figure 2.1 Frequency of spontaneous expression of values
Source: adapted from Lee (1997)

relative importance of these values in the *value systems* of young competitors differs substantially from the mere frequency of their expression shown here. This is illustrated in the Chapter 3 link.

The authors argue that this range of values is comprehensive and their view is supported by a Canadian study which administered the YSVQ to 1102 participants and asked them to write in other values, but found only duplicates (MacLean and Hamm, 2008). Hence the 18 values provide a comprehensive set of values to explore *value systems* in youth sport.

References

Lee, M.J. (1997) Values foundations of ethical decisions in children's sport. In A. Tomlinson and S. Fleming (eds) *Ethics, Sport and Leisure: crises and critiques.* Aachen: Meyer and Meyer (first published in 1995 by Chelsea School Research Centre, University of Brighton, as CSRC Topic Report 5), pp. 55–77.

MacLean, J. and Hamm, S. (2008) Values and sport participation: Comparing participant groups, age, and gender. *Journal of Sport Behavior*, 31(4), 352–67.

3   Which sport values are most important to young people?

The measurement of values in youth sport: Development of the Youth Sport Values Questionnaire

Martin J. Lee, Jean Whitehead and Nick Balchin

Values have been the subject of considerable research in mainstream psychology since the 1950s but have received limited attention in sport psychology until recently. This is due partly to a lack of understanding of the concept itself and partly to the lack of a suitable measurement instrument for them. Schwartz (1994: 21) has defined values as 'desirable trans-situational goals, varying in importance, that serve as guiding principles in the life of a person or a social entity'. He then commented that this definition implies that: (a) they serve the interests of individuals or groups, (b) they motivate action by giving it both direction and intensity, (c) they function as standards by which behaviour is evaluated, and (d) individuals learn values from the dominant values of the social groups to which they belong and through their own individual experiences. Furthermore, the qualification that values are trans-situational indicates that they guide behaviour in all life situations, and the view that they vary in importance implies that they may be ranked in order of importance. A final point in this context is that the process of examining values and value systems can be value free to the extent that the values chosen are derived from the population of interest, are not pre-selected by a researcher, and are conceived as, in Kluckhohn's (1951) terms, 'conceptions of the desirable'.

In everyday life, values may be expressed in such things as a desire for world peace, personal salvation, or honesty. In sport, they may include not only criteria of success, such as winning or playing well, but also fair play, sportsmanship, friendship, or tolerance, which are concerned with the quality of interaction during the activity.

Values have been an important topic for study in social sciences because they address the goals to which people and societies aspire and standards that they set for themselves. Discussions of values frequently occur in political, economic, religious, and educational debates, and the issues raised have been addressed by research in these and other fields (Braithwaite and Scott, 1991).

Measurement of values

Apart from his clarification of the concept of values, Rokeach (1973) also high-lighted differences in the way attitudes and values are measured. The concept of values addresses the desirability of a single belief and incorporates the important consideration of the relative importance of different beliefs in determining behaviour. This idea is expressed in the recognition of values as goals that vary in importance and can be organised in order of priority, as a hierarchy which is referred to as the value system (Rokeach, 1973; Schwartz, 1994). On the other hand, attitudes are typically measured by questions about the desirability of several beliefs about some single object or situation, with no implication of the priority of their relative importance. Therefore, it is possible to express equally strong attitudes towards different attitude objects. So, for example, a player may express strong support for winning and, simultaneously, for playing fairly.

Rokeach's particular methodological contribution was the Rokeach Value Survey (RVS) (Rokeach, 1967). This presents two lists of (a) 18 instrumental values (modes of conduct), and (b) 18 terminal values (end-states of existence), which respondents are required to arrange in order of importance to them as guiding principles in their lives. However, it produces data that are not readily amenable to sophisticated analyses.

The instrument has been criticised on the grounds of the adequacy of item sampling and the single item nature of the measures. The lists used by Rokeach are based on values derived from interviews with American adults and from a selection of personality descriptors assembled by Anderson (1968). Other research has indicated that the values included are a good representation of the available universe of values (see Braithwaite and Scott, 1991) but that the single item measures are subject to variation in interpretation and response. Braithwaite and Scott (1991) report that item consistency varies with the item, but comment that the utility of the instrument may depend upon the particular use to which it is put in a given situation.

Subsequently, Schwartz (1992; Schwartz and Bilsky, 1987, 1990) has produced an instrument based upon the RVS but which measures multi-item value domains. Schwartz and Bilsky (1987) argued that human beings must deal with three demands in life: the satisfaction of biological needs, the demands of co-ordinated social action, and the need for group functioning and survival. On this basis they proposed that the content of people's value systems may be described in terms of two fundamental motivational dimensions: (a) 'self-transcendence' to 'self-enhancement' (e.g. altruism and tolerance versus power and authority) and (b) 'openness to change' to 'conservation' (e.g. excitement and novelty versus self-restraint and obedience). The two dimensions provide a framework within which higher-order value domains can be organised such that adjacent domains are complementary and conflicting domains are in opposition. The model has since been modified and describes ten groups of values that are considered to govern the selection of behaviour and expression of attitudes, and is supported by extensive data (see Schwartz, 1992, 1994). While acknowledging the influence of Rokeach's conception of values, Schwartz refined their measurement by tapping the value types predicted by his theoretical model (Schwartz and Bilsky, 1987, 1990). After much experimentation he decided on a rating scale format that is similar to an attitude scale but in which the ratings can be transformed to rankings (Schwartz and Bilsky, 1990; Schwartz, 1992). This allows researchers to describe value systems among populations. However, describing the value system of a single individual is more problematic because the measure permits equal ratings, which one can expect to be differentiated by ranks when averaged across the sample but cannot be so easily distinguished for individuals.

Values in sport

Since values are considered universal in the sense that they are principles that govern all aspects of our lives, then they should also govern sport participation. For example, some athletes may value competitive success above all while others may value the development of skill or friendship. However, the concept and role of values has not been widely investigated in sport psychology and the number of studies using values as a fundamental concept in the study of fair play is limited (Lee and Cook, 1989; Shields and Bredemeier, 1995). Despite frequent references to values in the literature there has been little sustained attempt either to (a) adopt the 'concept of the desirable', (b) devise a suitable measure based on that principle, or (c) distinguish clearly values from attitudes. Nevertheless, in recent years, sports psychologists have shown a growing interest in values and begun to address these shortcomings. This has resulted in the presentation of data on values in youth sport, notably in Europe (e.g. Cruz *et al.*, 1999, 1995; Lee, 1997; Lee *et al.*, 1998; Mielke and Bahlke, 1995; Steenbergen *et al.*, 1998).

The use of the word 'value' in the sense of objects serving a purpose, for example sport being valuable, has attracted considerable attention in sport and health psychology (e.g. Eccles and Harold, 1991; Horn *et al.*, 1999; Powell, 1996). However, this focus may have diverted attention from the understanding of the concept of 'a value' as a guiding principle in life, the position that characterises the bulk of work on 'values' in contemporary psychology.

Eccles and her co-workers have been concerned particularly with achievement motivation and provide a model in which four types of subjective task value are identified: Utility value, attainment value, incentive value, and perceived cost (Eccles and Harold, 1991; Wigfield and Eccles, 1992). However, Wigfield and Eccles (1992) acknowledged the broader connotation of the value concept advanced by Rokeach and drew attention to the problems of drawing close correspondence between values and behaviour based upon them. They comment that greater correspondence is found in the attitude–behaviour relationship when attitudes are more specifically defined and that the same might be expected in the case of values. However, it is precisely because the adoption of the 'values as criteria' position allows a range of application beyond that of achievement behaviour that makes them useful as organising constructs.

Measurement of values in sport

Initial reviews of the literature (Lee and Cook, 1989; Lee *et al.*, 1990) indicated that the few studies that had addressed the concept of values in a sport setting used rather rudimentary instruments. Furthermore, sport psychologists have not always been clear about the distinction between attitudes and values at either the conceptual or operational levels. For example, Webb (1969) created the Professionalisation of Attitudes Scale, widely referred to as the Webb Scale, to measure professional attitudes in sport. It is, however, essentially a value scale because it arranges responses in order of importance. It requires athletes to rank 'playing well', 'winning', and 'playing fairly' in sport to produce a scale of 'professionalisation'. Thus, the ranking requires respondents to report preferences for three different value dimensions. However, although commendably simple and hence suitable for use with target samples of young competitors (versions for children aged 8–11 and adolescents 12–18 were developed) the scope of the values included is neither comprehensive nor derived from the population of interest. Hence, many important constructs may have been overlooked.

Some time later, Simmons and Dickinson (1986) drew upon a rationale derived from Rokeach in constructing a 14-item scale to measure athletes' values. When administered to young adults, the 14 items in the instrument reduced to five meaningful factors but there was no indication that the values used were drawn either from any theoretical basis or from the population of interest.

In order to overcome the criticism that measures were not salient to the target population, Lee and Cockman (1995) followed Braithwaite and Law's (1985) advice and used an inductive procedure to identify those values that adolescent athletes express spontaneously. They adapted Kohlberg's method (see Colby and Kohlberg, 1987) by discussing sport specific moral dilemmas in semi-structured interviews with 87 young male soccer, and male and female tennis, players in order to prompt the expression of salient values. Eighteen values were identified and no new categories were added after the analysis of 19 of the 87 transcripts. The authors concluded that a comprehensive set of values salient to moral decision making in sport had been identified.

However, to date there has been no instrument to measure the structure, or relative priorities, of value systems among youth sport participants that has been derived from values expressed by that population. The need for a measure of values in youth sport developed from the desire both to fill that gap and also to provide an alternative approach to the study of moral attitudes and behaviour in sport. In so doing it would draw more directly upon a social psychological tradition than the predominant cognitive-developmental model (e.g. see Shields and Bredemeier, 1995). Such an instrument would permit the description of the value systems of young athletes. But it would also facilitate the exploration of relationships between (a) values of athletes in different social contexts (b) athletes' values and those of significant others such as parents, coaches, teachers, peer group members, and (c) values and other variables such as socio-moral attitudes, participation and achievement motives, and sport attrition. The purpose of this series of studies, therefore, was to construct such an instrument.

Method

The research strategy was derived from Rokeach (1973), Braithwaite and Law (1985), and Schwartz (Schwartz and Bilsky, 1990; Schwartz, 1992). Rokeach provided the basic principle of measuring the relative importance of values as standards to guide behaviour by describing a hierarchical system of beliefs. Braithwaite and Law (1985) highlighted the importance of deriving salient values from the population of interest. Schwartz (Schwartz and Bilsky, 1990; Schwartz, 1992) provided the format of a rating scale as opposed to a ranking, which could be completed by young people and had the advantage of being more amenable to statistical analyses. The research programme took the form outlined in Figure 3.1.

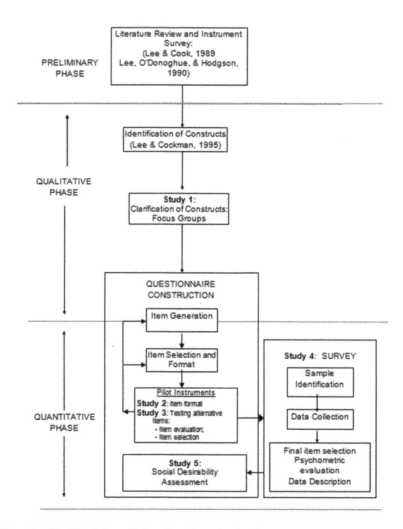

Figure 3.1 The Youth Sport Values Questionnaire development programme

The Youth Sport Values Questionnaire (YSVQ) was constructed by conducting a series of four studies to develop a reliable and valid instrument based upon the values identified by Lee and Cockman (1995). Study 4 also allowed the identification of value systems for a population of adolescent athletes in England. Following the formulation of the YSVQ, a fifth study was conducted to assess its vulnerability to social desirability response sets.

Study 1

Study 1 was designed (a) to establish the ecological validity for youth sport participants of the 18 values identified by Lee and Cockman (1995) and (b) to develop meaningful value statements, proxies, to represent each of them. Although each value identified had been given a label and a descriptor these were adult expressions of psychological constructs. In order to assess the values of young athletes it was necessary both to establish that the constructs had meaning for that population and that each value could be represented by a clearly understandable item in a questionnaire. These aims were achieved by the use of focus groups to facilitate the discussion and clarification of values, and the resolution of disagreements.

Participants and procedure

Participants were 50 sports club members (24 males, 26 females), aged 11 to 17 years drawn from five secondary schools in Southern England. Following informed consent procedures, interviews were conducted in eleven groups, each with between three and six members. The meaningfulness of sport values was examined by constructing a simple game for participants to complete prior to a group discussion. In the game two lists were presented in columns on a single sheet of paper. The first column was the list of value labels taken from the values identified by Lee and Cockman (1995). The second was a list of condensed, and therefore simplified, descriptors derived from the same source. These lists were broken into three loosely defined sets of similar values that represented interpretations of success, group identity, and self-expression. For numerical convenience, *health and fitness* was included in the group identity set. The lists were arranged within those groups such that no value was located opposite its descriptor. The task was to link each value to its descriptor by drawing a line between the items that the participants considered to match. Breaking the list into groups made the task easier, less time-consuming, and encouraged discrimination between similar values. Participants who finished the task early were asked to write a synonym for each value. When all had completed the task the responses were discussed and the disparate responses provided the basis for clarification of the concepts. Alternative words or phrases for the values were discussed until a degree of agreement and clarity was reached. All discussions were recorded and subsequently transcribed.

The transcripts revealed that the participants largely understood the value concepts, although the adult phrasing was not immediately accessible. Most easily understood was *health and fitness* (88 per cent correct links), while most difficult was *contract maintenance* (5 per cent correct links). The latter concept expresses the implicit contract that players of a game make with each other to play according to an agreed set of constraints, whether governed by the rules or not. Without such an agreement the game cannot proceed. While the term itself was not readily understood by participants it was, however, implied in subsequent discussions and, hence, represented a construct that was meaningful to them.

Following the analysis of transcripts further exemplars were developed, resulting in a pool of about six items to represent each value. However, following Rokeach (1973) we wanted to identify a manageable set of single values in order to describe a value system. Therefore, a panel of three experienced researchers selected the best single item as a proxy for each value on the basis of conceptual clarity and simplicity. The proxies were written as first-person statements. For example, the statement 'I don't spoil the game or competition' represented *contract maintenance*. The 18 initial proxies are given in Table 3.1.

Table 3.1 Selected value items from focus group interviews

Value	Value descriptor
1. Being fair	I am fair and don't cheat
2. Companionship	I am there with my friends
3. Compassion	I am concerned about the people around me in my sport
4. Conformity	I try to fit in with the group
5. Conscientious	I am reliable and give 100% when playing or competing
6. Contract maintenance	I don't spoil the game or competition
7. Enjoyment	I enjoy myself and have fun
8. Good game	I have a close game, race or event
9. Health and fitness	I get fit and healthy through sport
10. Obedience	I do what I am told
11. Personal achievement	I put in the best performance I can
12. Public image	I look good
13. Self-actualisation	I get a buzz or feel really good when playing
14. Showing skill	I do the skills or techniques well
15. Sportsmanship	I am well mannered, sporting and I am not a bad loser
16. Team cohesion	I lift the team when things are difficult
17. Tolerance	I try and get on with the other people in my sport, even if I don't like them
18. Winning	I win or beat other people

Study 2

The purpose of Study 2, which was the first of two pilot tests of the prototype questionnaire, was to establish a suitable format to present the content of the values in an understandable way for the target age group and to obtain a range of responses. In this research, we adapted two facets of the Schwartz Value Survey for use with young participants. First, we modified the instruction to rate each value on a measure of importance 'As a guiding principle in my life …' to the simpler 'When I do sport it is important to me that …'. Both Rokeach and Schwartz specify 'importance' as the criterion of evaluation. Second, the demand to consider the context of participating in sport was used to specify the situation clearly. Hence, this format reflects the criteria by which participants select their behaviour and value their participation in the activity. Finally, we used seven rather than nine response categories in order to reduce the demands of fine discrimination.

Study 3

The purpose of the second pilot study was to test alternative items for each value and use statistical criteria to select the best items that had been identified by the focus groups. In equivocal cases, conceptual criteria were given priority and the item-total correlations were used for guidance. Alternative items for three values were retained for further testing in Study 4.

Study 4

The purpose of Study 4 was to use the YSVQ to provide data on the prevailing value system in a population of competitive adolescent athletes aged 12 to 15 years inclusive. To meet this objective we conducted a survey to identify the relative importance of sports values in young competitors in six specified sports. There were three team sports: Soccer, rugby, and netball, and three individual sports: Tennis, badminton, and track and field athletics.

Instrument

The questionnaire used in the survey contained 23 items: 18 value statements, one alternative for each of the values *contract maintenance*, *good game* and *obedience*, and two items which made conflicting statements and could be used to screen for inconsistent responses. The two screening items, included as a consistency check, were: '… I can wear what I like.' and '… I wear the right kit for it.'

Participants and procedure

Participants were 1391 young competitors (647 males, 728 females, 16 gender not stated) aged 12–18 years (mean = 13.35 years, standard deviation, SD = 1.51). They were drawn from five major urban areas, London, Leeds, Manchester, Liverpool and the West Midlands and from non-urban schools in the southeast of

England. The target sample was aged 12–16 years ($n = 500$, mean $= 13.68$ years, SD $= .97$) and comprised 47 per cent males and 53 per cent females; 19 per cent from Metropolitan (urban) districts and 81 per cent from non-urban schools; and 75 per cent from team sports and 25 per cent from individual sports. Overall, 70 per cent represented their school or club, 26 per cent played at district level or county level, and 4 per cent at regional level or higher. No subjects were dropped for inconsistencies in the screening items.

Value systems

Table 3.2 shows the order of mean value rankings that formed the value system for the target sample. *Enjoyment* has the highest priority followed by *personal achievement*. *Winning* was given the least importance. A similar ranking was constructed from a further, more inclusive, sample of 614 (282 males, 318 females, 14 not stated) drawn from a wider range of age, sports, and level of performance. Correlations between the value systems of the two samples were very high ($r = .99$; $r_s = .98$, both $p < .01$). Differences in ranks were minor and mean differences between all these values were very small (mean $= .04$, SD $= .16$). We consider, therefore, that the data shown in Table 3.2 may be taken to represent the value system typical of adolescent athletes in England.

Table 3.2 Mean value rankings among adolescent athletes in England

Rank	Value label	Item	Mean	SD
1.	Enjoyment	I enjoy myself and have fun	4.22	1.02
2.	Personal achievement	I improve my performance	4.04	1.02
3.	Sportsmanship	I show good sportsmanship	3.90	1.07
4.	Contract maintenance	I always play properly	3.89	1.11
5.	Being fair	I try to be fair	3.73	1.18
6.	Compassion	I help people when they need it	3.68	1.12
7.	Tolerance	I accept other people's weaknesses	3.67	1.09
8.	Show skills	I do the skills or techniques well	3.59	1.15
9.	Obedience	I do what I am told	3.58	1.24
10.	Team cohesion	I make sure we all stick together	3.50	1.22
11.	Conscientious	I don't let people down	3.47	1.11
12.	Excitement	it is an exciting contest	3.22	1.38
13.	Health & Fitness	I do sport to get fit	3.20	1.46
14.	Self-actualization	I get a buzz or feel really good while playing	3.04	1.45
15.	Public image	I show a good image to others	2.94	1.38
16.	Companionship	I do things with my mates	2.00	1.65
17.	Conformity	I go along with everybody else	1.86	1.64
18.	Winning	I can show that I am better than others	1.27	1.75

We also examined the ratings and rankings of values across groupings within the criterion sample according to (a) gender, (b) sport type (team or individual), (c) age group, and (d) level of performance. These are presented in Table 3.3. Both ratings and rankings are very similar across these sub-groups. For gender, r = .95 for ratings and r_s = .93 for rankings (both $p < .01$). Similar results are reported for correlations between players of team and individual sports (r = .99; r_s = .96, both $p < .01$). Across age groups ($.92 < r < .97, .76 < r_s < .96$, all $p < .01$) and levels of performance ($.92 < r < .97, .81 < r_s < .93$, all $p < .01$) agreement was also very high. In these cases the highest correlations were found between adjacent groups. Analyses of differences between scores for different groups revealed that males gave higher mean ratings than females (t_{441} = 3.19, p = .002). There were no differences in mean ratings between team and individual sports (t_{441} = 1.04, p = .30). Trend analysis was conducted to identify trends in the data where the independent variable may be considered to be on a scale of equal appearing intervals. Thus, there was a significant decreasing linear trend across age group ($F_{1,441}$ = 4.73, p = .03), and a significant increasing linear trend across levels of performance ($F_{1,442}$ = 12.98, $p < .000$). In the age group data seven values reflected the decreasing trend but, in contrast, the importance of *winning* increased with age.

Discussion

The purpose of this series of studies was to construct an instrument to permit the description of the value systems of young athletes. In contrast to some earlier instruments (e.g. Webb, 1969; Simmons and Dickinson, 1986) the YSVQ has been constructed by developing meaningful items directly from the population of interest in a procedure that combined both qualitative and quantitative techniques. Lee and Cockman (1995) used interviews to identify salient value constructs. In this research items based on those constructs were developed by focus group discussions and then piloted to establish the structure and content of the instrument. The pilot testing produced a clear format that both presented brief items in the form of simply worded sentences and elicited a good range of response; it also identified the best indicator for each value. As shown by the second survey sample, which was more diverse in nature, the format of the instrument has enabled it to be easily accessed by young athletes in an age range 11–18 with similar results. Thus we believe that the language is appropriate, the stimulus item format is meaningful, and the response format manageable.

Utility

The purpose of the YSVQ is to identify the value priorities of young athletes. Because the response format is a rating scale, it can yield group scores for each value that may then be ranked in order of importance. The ranking describes the predominant value system within that group, which may then be compared to the value systems of other groups.

Table 3.3 Means, standard deviations and ranks of sports values among sports participants aged 12–15 years (inclusive) in England

Value label	Gender		Sport type		Age group				Level of performance		
	M	F	T	I	U13	U14	U15	U16	Sch.	Dist.	Reg.
Enjoyment	4.25 (1) (.96)	4.19 (1) (1.08)	4.19 (1) (1.05)	4.30 (1) (.96)	4.36 (1) (.91)	4.16 (1) (1.15)	4.09 (1) (.99)	4.28 (1) (.86)	4.16 (1) (1.01)	4.35 (1) (1.04)	4.42 (1) (1.07)
Achievement	4.19 (2) (.90)	3.90 (2) (1.07)	4.03 (2) (1.00)	4.06 (3) (1.07)	4.15 (4) (.97)	3.98 (2) (1.08)	3.91 (2) (1.03)	4.26 (2) (.85)	3.94 (2) (1.03)	4.25 (2) (.95)	4.37 (2=) (1.07)
Sportsmanship	3.94 (3) (1.05)	3.87 (3=) (1.08)	3.82 (4) (1.10)	4.12 (2) (.95)	4.22 (3) (.91)	3.84 (4) (1.13)	3.58 (3) (1.11)	3.93 (3) (.93)	3.82 (4) (1.10)	4.04 (3) (1.00)	4.37 (2=) (.76)
Contract maintenance	3.91 (4) (1.12)	3.87 (3=) (1.11)	3.86 (3) (1.14)	3.97 (4) (1.03)	4.25 (2) (.91)	3.90 (3) (1.12)	3.52 (4) (1.21)	3.61 (8) (1.08)	3.87 (3) (1.12)	3.95 (4) (1.10)	3.89 (6) (1.05)
Being fair	3.66 (5) (1.23)	3.78 (6) (1.13)	3.64 (6=) (1.20)	3.95 (5) (1.09)	3.98 (6) (1.15)	3.73 (5) (1.14)	3.43 (7) (1.21)	3.65 (6=) (1.16)	3.70 (5) (1.18)	3.75 (8) (1.18)	4.05 (5) (.97)
Compassion	3.64 (6) (1.06)	3.72 (7) (1.17)	3.65 (5) (1.15)	3.75 (7=) (1.05)	3.93 (7) (1.11)	3.68 (6=) (1.08)	3.38 (9=) (1.10)	3.65 (6=) (1.22)	3.65 (6) (1.12)	3.76 (6=) (1.12)	3.61 (11) (1.20)
Tolerance	3.52 (8) (1.20)	3.79 (5) (1.16)	3.64 (6=) (1.20)	3.75 (7=) (1.13)	3.90 (8) (1.11)	3.68 (6=) (1.17)	3.46 (5) (1.24)	3.43 (9) (1.24)	3.63 (7) (1.21)	3.76 (6=) (1.14)	3.84 (7=) (1.12)
Showing skill	3.63 (7) (1.12)	3.55 (10) (1.17)	3.53 (8=) (1.13)	3.74 (9) (1.18)	3.68 (11) (1.15)	3.55 (8) (1.16)	3.44 (6) (1.12)	3.82 (4) (1.15)	3.46 (10) (1.14)	3.86 (5) (1.13)	4.16 (4) (.90)
Obedience	3.48 (11) (1.29)	3.67 (8) (1.19)	3.51 (10) (1.29)	3.78 (6) (1.06)	3.99 (5) (1.19)	3.54 (9) (1.19)	3.27 (11) (1.17)	3.22 (15) (1.40)	3.61 (8) (1.24)	3.52 (12) (1.24)	3.53 (12) (1.22)
Team cohesion	3.40 (13) (1.19)	3.60 (9) (1.24)	3.53 (8=) (1.21)	3.43 (11) (1.25)	3.86 (9) (1.12)	3.32 (10) (1.26)	3.38 (9=) (1.27)	3.39 (10) (1.06)	3.49 (9) (1.26)	3.55 (11) (1.11)	3.47 (13) (1.31)
Conscientious	3.49 (10) (1.10)	3.45 (11) (1.13)	3.48 (11) (1.11)	3.45 (10) (1.13)	3.69 (10) (1.16)	3.28 (11) (1.07)	3.40 (8) (1.11)	3.74 (5) (1.00)	3.39 (11) (1.13)	3.67 (9) (1.04)	3.74 (9) (.99)

Table 3.3 continued

Value label	Gender		Sport type		Age group				Level of performance		
	M	F	T	I	U13	U14	U15	U16	Sch.	Dist.	Reg.
Excitement	3.51 (9) (1.25)	2.96 (13) (1.44)	3.20 (12) (1.38)	3.27 (13) (1.37)	3.27 (12) (1.39)	3.24 (13) (1.36)	3.07 (14) (1.35)	3.35 (12) (1.48)	3.08 (12=) (1.40)	3.57 (10) (1.25)	3.42 (14) (1.50)
Health/fitness	3.42 (12) (1.41)	3.01 (12) (1.49)	3.15 (13) (1.48)	3.34 (12) (1.41)	3.10 (13) (1.49)	3.25 (12) (1.56)	3.24 (12) (1.30)	3.26 (14) (1.39)	3.08 (12=) (1.47)	3.45 (13) (1.44)	3.84 (7=) (1.26)
Self-actualisation	3.26 (14) (1.45)	2.85 (14) (1.44)	3.04 (14) (1.47)	3.04 (14) (1.42)	2.95 (15) (1.51)	2.99 (14) (1.43)	3.10 (13) (1.40)	3.37 (11) (1.50)	2.88 (14) (1.45)	3.43 (14) (1.40)	3.37 (15) (1.34)
Public image	3.19 (15) (1.25)	2.73 (15) (1.46)	2.92 (15) (1.41)	3.00 (15) (1.32)	3.01 (14) (1.41)	2.82 (15) (1.36)	2.92 (15) (1.45)	3.28 (13) (1.19)	2.80 (15) (1.37)	3.21 (15) (1.38)	3.68 (10) (1.11)
Companionship	2.41 (16) (1.54)	1.62 (17) (1.58)	2.08 (16) (1.62)	1.78 (16) (1.58)	2.02 (17) (1.76)	2.02 (16) (1.53)	1.80 (16) (1.53)	2.33 (16) (1.65)	1.95 (16) (1.58)	2.13 (16) (1.71)	2.00 (17) (1.56)
Conformity	2.07 (17) (1.59)	1.66 (16) (1.66)	1.91 (17) (1.67)	1.73 (17) (1.56)	2.07 (16) (1.80)	1.74 (17) (1.51)	1.72 (17) (1.58)	2.09 (17) (1.72)	1.88 (17) (1.62)	1.81 (17) (1.70)	1.95 (18) (1.72)
Winning	1.98 (18) (1.83)	.64 (18) (1.41)	1.30 (18) (1.78)	1.18 (18) (1.66)	.99 (18) (1.67)	1.33 (18) (1.68)	1.28 (18) (1.82)	1.87 (18) (2.00)	1.07 (18) (1.63)	1.70 (18) (1.94)	2.06 (16) (2.01)
Mean	3.39	3.16	3.25	3.31	3.41	3.23	3.11	3.36	3.19	3.43	3.54
N	233	265	362	136	147	188	117	46	351	128	19

Notes: The mean for each value is given in the first row, followed by its ranking in brackets; standard deviations are bracketed in row two. M = male; F = female; T = Team; I = individual; U13 = 12–13 years; U14 = 13–14 years; U15 =14–15 years; U16 = 15–16 years; Sch. = school/club; Dist. = district; Reg. = regional or above. Two participants did not state their gender

The data show a good distribution of scores on all values. Since values are considered to be conceptions of the desirable some degree of social desirability and negative skewness on the scale used herein might be expected. However, there was no evidence of a social desirability response bias, the items yielded a wide range of responses, and skewness was modest. This suggests that the instrument should yield meaningful relationships with other stable psychological constructs.

In its present form, the YSVQ measures 18 discrete values that were identified as different from each other and represent those values that are commonly expressed by youth sport competitors. Hence, it is not appropriate to calculate a measure of internal consistency, but the instrument remains subject to the limitations of single item measures discussed by Braithwaite and Scott (1991). However, measures of re-test reliability after four weeks have been obtained in a subsequent study and are considered acceptable at this stage of development. The limited number of items encourages a good response rate from the target age group. While concerns about the demands of ranking a large number of items do not hold where a rating scale is used it may still be advantageous to use a relatively small number of items with adolescents.

Value systems of young athletes

The value system identified in the survey showed that the most important thing for young athletes is to enjoy their sport. This appears to be consistent with data on young people's reasons for doing sport that show the pre-eminence of fun among other motives, in samples from the USA, Canada, and Australia (e.g. Gould *et al.*, 1985; Kolt *et al.*, 1999). Second, it is instructive to note the structural relationship between *personal achievement* and *winning*, which are widely separated in the hierarchy. *Winning* is located at the bottom while *personal achievement* is located second. Similar relationships have been reported in the participation motivation literature (e.g. Klint &Weiss, 1987; Kolt *et al.*, 1999). However, it should be noted that studies of participation motives differ in focus and content from studies of values. The study of participation motives commonly addresses the utility value of the items while the value concept addresses the criteria for the selection and evaluation of behaviour, during the activity, on a broader front. Thus studies of participation motives do not include such issues as compassion, tolerance, or fair play.

The high correlations of value rankings across the different criterion groups presented above suggest that the structure of value systems identified is consistent among those groups while differences in mean ratings indicate the differential importance of sporting values to them. Hence, girls are seen to attach less importance to sporting values than boys, sporting values appears to become less important with increasing age but more important at higher levels of performance. These trends may be explained by a lower level of commitment to sport by girls, a decline in commitment during adolescence as other interests become more prominent, and a necessary increase in commitment as participants aspire to higher levels of achievement.

Limitations

Following the advice of Braithwaite and Law (1985) to derive values from the population of interest, we adopted a qualitative approach to identifying salient constructs. This was followed by a strategy of constructing questionnaire items that represented those constructs. In such a strategy statistical criteria become important in making decisions and it is possible that some subtleties of meaning will become lost in the translation. For example, the value *good game* became expressed as *excitement* when the original idea contained a more complex and wider range of concepts. The inclusion of more items to address each construct would help alleviate this problem.

While we assumed that the content of the YSVQ is comprehensive because the values expressed in Lee and Cockman's (1995) interviews were found in only a small sample of the available data there is another possibility. The original interviews were carried out using moral dilemmas as stimuli. This was specifically to access the cognitions that underpinned the participants thinking about moral issues. It is possible that other stimulus events would reveal an additional range of constructs.

It would be desirable to establish the construct and predictive validity of the YSVQ. For example, the prediction of ethical attitudes from social or moral values would illustrate the value expressive function of attitudes proposed by Katz (1960). While this form of the YSVQ may permit such investigation it may be more effectively conducted with multi-item scales to evaluate super-ordinate value domains. With that in mind we have begun to extend the YSVQ to examine appropriate value groupings.

Future directions

This instrument breaks new ground and provides the potential for examining such issues as the tension between competitive success and moral behaviour as predicted by Schwartz's (1992) model. The identification of value systems might lead to comparisons between the value priorities held by young people in life and in sport, in different sports, and in different sport contexts or countries. Exploration of relationships between athletes' values and those, expressed or perceived, of significant others will promote the understanding of value transference in sport and hence the role of parents, teachers, coaches, and sports institutions in that process. Finally, the instrument permits the examination of relationships between value systems and other variables, such as achievement motivation, that are of interest to psychologists in youth sport.

We are currently developing the instrument further, using multi-item scales that are representative of higher-order groupings, in order to extend further the social psychological explanations of sportspersonship. The identification of groups of values will facilitate the understanding of the influence of value structures and the mechanisms that predict attitudes and behaviour in sport. Perhaps, ultimately, this line of research will promote an alternative perspective for the examination of sport in modern society.

References

Anderson, N.H. (1968) Likeableness ratings of 555 personality-trait words. *Journal of Personality and Social Psychology*, 9, 272–9.

Braithwaite, V. A. and Law, H. G. (1985) Structure of human values: Testing the adequacy of the Rokeach Value Survey. *Journal of Personality and Social Psychology*, 49, 250–63.

Braithwaite, V.A. and Scott, W.A. (1991) Values. In J.P. Robinson, P.R. Shaver and L.S. Wrightsman (eds) *Measures of Personality and Social Psychological Attitudes*, 1, 661–753. London: Academic Press.

Colby, A. and Kohlberg, L.(1987) *The Measurement of Moral Judgements*. New York: Cambridge University Press.

Cruz, J., Boixados, M., Valiente, L. and Capdevila, L. (1995) Prevalent values in young Spanish soccer players. *International Review for the Sociology of Sport*, 30, 353–73.

Cruz, J., Boixados, M, Capdevila, M., Mimbrero, J., Torregrosa, M. and Valiente, L. (1999) Evaluacion del fairplay en el deporte professional y de iniciacion [Assessment of fair play in professional and beginners sport]. In *Participacion deportiva: Perspectiva ambiental y organizacional*. Serie Icd de Investigacion en Ciencias del Deporte, no. 24. Madrid: Ministerio de Educacion y Cultura.

Eccles, J.S. and Harold, R.D. (1991) Gender differences in sport involvement: Applying the Eccles' expectancy-value model. *Journal of Applied Sport Psychology*, 3, 75–135.

Gould, D., Feltz, D. and Weiss, M. (1985) Motives for participating in competitive youth swimming. *International Journal of Sport Psychology*, 16, 126–40.

Horn, T.S., Kimiecik, J., Maltbie, J., Wong, W. and Rojas, K.K. (1999) Parents' beliefs and values regarding their children's participation in youth sport programs. *Journal of Sport and Exercise Psychology*, 21, s58.

Katz, D. (1960) The functional study of attitudes. *Public Opinion Quarterly*, 24, 163–204.

Klint, K.A. and Weiss, M.R. (1987) Perceived competence and motives for participating in youth sports: A test of Harter's competence motivation theory. *Journal of Sport Psychology*, 9, 55–65.

Kluckhohn, C. (1951) Value and value-orientations in the theory of action: An exploration in definition and classification. In T. Parsons and E. Shils (eds) *Towards a General Theory of Action*. Cambridge, MA: Harvard University Press, pp. 388–433.

Kolt, G.S., Kirby, R.J., Bar-Eli, M., Blumenstein, B., Chadha, N.K., Lui, J. and Kerk, G. (1999) A cross-cultural investigation of reasons for participation in gymnastics. *International Journal of Sport Psychology*, 30, 381–98.

Lee M.J. (1997) Moral well-being: The role of physical education and sport. In N. Armstrong, B. Kirby and J. Welsman (eds) *Children and Exercise*, XIX, 542–62. London: E. & F.N. Spon.

Lee, M. J. and Cockman, M. J. (1995) Values in children's sport: Spontaneously expressed values among young athletes. *International Review for the Sociology of Sport*, 30, 337–52.

Lee, M. J. and Cook, C. (1989) *Review of Literature on Fairplay with Special Reference to Children's Sport*. London: Sports Council Research Unit.

Lee, M. J., O'Donoghue, R. and Hodgson, D. (1990) *The Measurement of Values in Children's Sport*. Strasbourg: Council of Europe (CDDS).

Lee, M.J., Whitehead, J. and Balchin, N. (1998) Socio-moral values among young athletes. Poster session presented at the 24th International Congress of the International Association of Applied Psychology, San Francisco, California, August.

Mielke, R. and Bahlke, S. (1995) Structure and preferences of fundamental values of young athletes: Do they differ from non-athletes and young people with alternative leisure activities. *International Review for the Sociology of Sport*, 30(3–4), 419–37.

Powell, W. (1996) Task-value as a mediator for aerobic exercise adherence. Poster session presented at Annual Conference of the Association for Applied Sport Psychology, Williamsburg, Virginia, October.

Rokeach, M. (1967) *Value Survey*. Sunnyvale, CA: Halgren Tests.

Rokeach, M. (1973) *The Nature of Human Values*. New York: The Free Press.

Schwartz, S. H. (1992) Universals in the content and structure of values: Theoretical advances and empirical tests in 20 Countries. In M. P. Zanna (ed.) *Advances in Experimental Social Psychology*, 25, 1–65. London: Academic Press.

Schwartz, S. (1994) Are there universal aspects in the structure and contents of human values? *Journal of Social Issues*, 50, 19–45.

Schwartz, S.H. and Bilsky, W. (1987) Toward a psychological structure of human values. *Journal of Personality and Social Psychology*, 53, 503–62.

Schwartz, S.H. and Bilsky, W. (1990) Toward a theory of the universal content and structure of values: Extensions and cross-cultural replications. *Journal of Personality and Social Psychology*, 58, 878–91.

Shields, D.L.L. and Bredemeier, B.J.L. (1995) *Character development through physical activity*. Champaign, IL: Human Kinetics.

Simmons, D.D. and Dickinson, R.V. (1986) Measurement of values expression in sports and athletics. *Perceptual and Motor Skills*, 62, 650–8.

Steenbergen, J., Buisman, A.J., De Knop, P. and Lucassen, J.M.H. (1998) *Waarden en normen in de sport: Analyse en beleidsperspectief* [*Values and Norms in Sport: Analysis and Policy Perspectives*]. Houten: Bohn Stafleu Van Loghum.

Webb, H. (1969) Professionalisation of attitudes towards play among adolescents. In G. S. Kenyon (ed.) *Aspects of Contemporary Sport Sociology*. Chicago, IL: The Athletic Institute, pp. 161–78.

Wigfield, A. and Eccles, J.S. (1992) The development of achievement task values: A theoretical analysis. *Developmental Review*, 12, 265–310.

Chapter 3 link: Relevance and update

This chapter, abridged from an article published in 2000, overviews the history of the study and measurement of values and develops the Youth Sport Values Questionnaire (YSVQ) to assess the *value systems* of young competitors using the values identified in Chapter 2. Figure 3.2 integrates material from both chapters. It shows that enjoyment was most important to these young competitors, followed by achievement and a group of socio-moral values consistent with fair play and sportsmanship. Winning was given the lowest rank.

The *value system* contrasts the frequency with which the values were mentioned in Chapter 2. Although winning was most frequently referred to in the context of moral dilemmas it was least important when compared with other values. *Value systems* matter because it is not enough to know which values youngsters have. We must also know which values are most important because these will dominate in situations where values conflict.

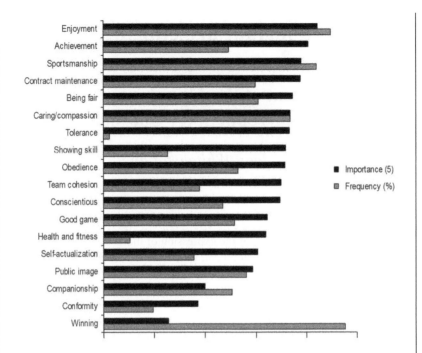

Figure 3.2 The importance of values in youth sport and their expressed frequency
Source: Whitehead (2011)

A different pattern is shown by the value of tolerance which was rarely expressed but placed in the top half of the value system. This illustrates an important distinction between values and participation motives, with which they are often confused. People are not motivated to participate in order to be tolerant, to be fair, or to play by the rules but when they do participate these instrumental values are important to them.

Reference

Whitehead, J. (2011) Understanding fair play in youth sport through children's values and attitudes: some insights of Martin Lee. *Physical Education Matters*, 6(1), 23–24, 26–27.

4 How important are ethical attitudes?

Development of the Attitudes to Moral Decisions in Youth Sport Questionnaire

Martin J. Lee, Jean Whitehead and Nikos Ntoumanis

The view that sport is a theatre for the expression of moral behaviour and indeed has an influence on moral development, has been widespread, yet research to investigate the credibility of the claims has been somewhat equivocal (Shields and Bredemeier, 1995). The bulk of early research into fair play, or violations of its principles, was conducted through a variety of attitudinal studies (e.g. Blair, 1985; Goodger and Jackson, 1985; Maloney and Petrie, 1972). The results of these studies in North America suggest that instrumental attitudes are more commonly associated with older athletes, competitive success, males rather than females, and higher levels of participation. However, Lee and Williams (1989) found no reliable relationships between the endorsement of fouls and experience, playing position, or level of performance, among young athletes in the United Kingdom. Subsequently several studies by Kavussanu (e.g. Kavussanu and Ntoumanis, 2003) have sought to clarify the roles of the many interacting variables which underpin inconsistent findings in this field.

The influence of sport participation on moral behaviour outside of the sporting context is also equivocal. Segrave and Hastad (1982, 1984; Segrave *et al.*, 1985) have reported a negative relationship between sport participation and delinquency. However, Telama and Liukkonen (1999) reported that boys involved in organised sport were more disposed to aggression than boys who did not do sport. In contrast to the work of Segrave and his co-workers, Begg *et al.* (1996) conducted a longitudinal study that showed that high involvement in individual sports – but not in team sports – was associated with increased delinquency.

Bredemeier and her co-workers have provided the major impetus to the study of moral development and behaviour in youth sport in an extensive research programme that drew heavily upon the structural-developmental models developed by Kohlberg (1976; Colby and Kohlberg, 1987) and Haan (1978). Nevertheless, after prolonged investigation and careful evaluation of the evidence, Shields and Bredemeier (1995) concluded that there is not sufficient evidence for establishing a causal link between physical activity and moral development.

More recently, the assessment of attitudes towards fair play among young athletes has been the subject of research by Vallerand and his co-workers (see, for example, Vallerand and Losier, 1994; Vallerand *et al.*, 1997), and by Boixadós and Cruz (1995) and Boixadós *et al.* (2004). Vallerand and Losier (1994) provided an alternative socio-psychological perspective. They observed that Haan, in particular, has had a great influence on the study of moral behaviour in sport, but that the theory relied exclusively on the developmental aspects of moral dialogue between protagonists. The catalogue of research by Bredemeier and her co-workers derived from this perspective addressed the issue of sportsmanship largely through a focus on aggressive behaviour. Consequently, Vallerand and Losier contended, attention was diverted from other issues relevant to sportsmanship research, and indeed, the 'content of sportsmanship behaviours has yet to be identified' (Vallerand and Losier, 1994: 230).

Vallerand (1994) argued (a) for a socio-psychological approach to the study of sportsmanship that recognises the social origins of ethical behaviour, (b) that it was necessary to define the content of sportsmanship as a pre-requisite for the investigation of sportsmanship behaviour, orientations, and development, and (c) that an understanding of the concept by athletes is reached through interaction with salient adults and peers. Thus, the nature of sportsmanship emerges by a consensus within a social context. Vallerand further argued that this process implies that the definition of sportsmanship is best obtained from the athletes themselves. Thus, the resulting Multi-dimensional Sportsmanship Orientation Scale (MSOS; Vallerand *et al.*, 1997) has proved to be a major step toward recognising the social-psychological roots of the concept and provided an operational definition that drew upon the lived experience of the athletes themselves.

The MSOS was developed through a number of stages by identifying potential items suggested by an open-ended questionnaire that asked adolescent athletes to provide their definition of sportsmanship and examples of sportsmanlike behaviour. Items were categorised to provide good coverage of the facets of the constructs involved prior to selection. An EFA revealed five factors that explained 50 per cent of the variance. The final form of five scales, each of five items, was piloted with a large sample of adolescent athletes and gave satisfactory psychometric properties. The scales represent (a) Commitment to participation, (b) Respect for social conventions, (c) Respect for rules and officials, (d) Respect for opponents, (e) A negative approach to participation. The last focuses on the importance of winning at all costs and is scored with reverse polarity. The MSOS, then, identifies primarily positive socio- moral attitudes involved in sports participation with only a single scale that addresses unsportsmanlike behaviour.

Boixadós and Cruz (1995) advanced a multidimensional definition of fair play incorporating (a) respect for rules, (b) good relationships with opponents, (c) equality of opportunity and conditions, (d) avoidance of 'victory at all costs', (e) honour in victory and defeat, and (f) commitment to do one's best. However, when data from a 35-item questionnaire administered to teenage soccer players were subjected to EFA, they revealed three attitude components: (a) rough play, (b) spirit of the game and enjoyment, and (c) commitment to winning, of which two could be construed as representing antisocial constructs. The final scale comprised 27 items and explained 30.8 per cent of the variance, supporting the authors' comment that the scale did not represent all aspects of the fair play concept. In a subsequent study, (Boixadós *et al.*, 2004) cheating was incorporated in the rough play scale and 16 items explained 46 per cent of the variance in the Fair Play Attitudes Scale (Escala d'Actituds de Fair play; EAF-C).

Concept of cheating

Neither of the preceding instruments directly addresses attitudes towards cheating, which appears to occupy the minds of parents, players, fans and coaches. Perhaps one of the problems is that the category 'cheating' may also be difficult to define both conceptually and operationally, in much the same way as Vallerand has argued about sportsmanship. Furthermore, there appear to be other conceptually similar categories of behaviour that occur in sport by which players violate the implicit nature of the contract to compete fairly and seek to gain a 'dishonourable' advantage. These may be described as 'professional fouls' and gamesmanship.

In examining the first class of dishonourable behaviour – cheating – Reddiford (1998) pointed out that the rules, definitions and ends of a game, or sport, provide the structure of the activity. Hence, those who wish to compete in such activities implicitly agree to abide by those rules in the pursuit of the stated ends. Since the rules define what is and what is not permitted, they must also define the skills that may be brought to bear in the pursuit of the stated ends. Thus, in order to compete successfully it follows that players, and coaches, should know the rules and what they allow as well as what they prohibit. To be more precise they should know what the officials (referees, umpires, etc.) in any particular contest will allow. Hence, Reddiford argued that cheating is characterised by three features. First, it involves seeking to make illegitimate gains, by violating the rules of the game. Second, it involves the concealment of true intentions, that is, deception is essential. Third, cheating is successful if the victim, and/or an independent party (e.g. the official) is convinced that all is well. However, the third feature appears to address the criterion by which success of cheating is judged rather than being an essential characteristic of the behavioural category. Nevertheless, it appears that cheating refers to infractions of the rules in order to gain some unfair advantage in which there is a degree of successful deception. However, merely to operate the art of deception is not enough to merit the charge of cheating because skilful players will always attempt to deceive their opponents, as part of their skill. Deception of that sort lies within the rules of the game and may characterise skilful performance. Thus, in cricket, a skilful bowler will seek to lure the batsman into a false stroke by disguising the type of delivery he is making.

A second category of dishonourable behaviour, often known as the 'professional foul', occurs when players deliberately break the rules knowing that, despite suffering a penalty, they will gain advantage. In this case, Reddiford's third feature of cheating is not met. For example, in soccer a defender may trip an opposition attacker, preferring to give away a free kick but giving the defence time to re-organise. Although there may be an expectation of detection the tactical outcome of the penalty renders the act advantageous.

Third, there is a category of actions that do not actually violate the rules of the sport but that do appear to violate the spirit of the contest, perhaps using the laws to gain some advantage that might be considered to be unfair or dishonourable. Thus, for example, the receiver in tennis may pause to retie a shoelace as his opponent is about to serve, thereby upsetting the server's rhythm, or the fielders in cricket may try to upset the batsman by derogatory comments, a practice commonly known as 'sledging'. Such actions appear to fall into the category initially called 'gamesmanship' by the British humourist Stephen Potter (1947). Potter described how sophisticated, and perhaps less technically skilful, players adopted strategies to upset their opponents and win without actually cheating. A wide range of behaviours may be described as gamesmanship but most would appear to focus on distracting or psychologically destabilising opponents. These actions are neither examples of violating the rules of the game nor do they involve deception, yet they may be considered to be a form of cheating in that there is a motivation to gain an unfair advantage by adopting behavioural strategies that are not covered by the rules of the game. Currently we are not aware of any instrument that seeks to identify such behaviour or attitudes towards it.

Stephens *et al.* (1997) have addressed the issue of cheating directly in a youth soccer population. They developed an instrument, the Judgements about Moral Behavior in Youth Sport Questionnaire (JAMBYSQ), which examines attitudes towards three types of non-moral behaviour: cheating, aggression and lying to officials. Stephens *et al.* (1997) utilised a social constructivist approach that acknowledges the influence of both developmental and social forces on moral thinking. By using a restricted number of scenarios (i.e., three) to represent the target attitudes JAMBYSQ explores the participants' deontic judgement, moral atmosphere within the team, action tendencies, and motivational precursors to action. This technique has the advantage of exploring different aspects of moral reasoning, judgement, and attitude while focusing on a single incident. It does not, however, permit researchers to distinguish among some of the dimensions of dishonourable behaviour outlined above.

Finally, in consideration of the arena in which cheating takes place, Shields and Bredemeier (1995) argued that moral exchanges in sport occur in a context of bracketed morality, in which responsibilities differ from everyday life and where game reasoning leads participants to adopt more egocentrism and a narrower emphasis on winning. A related argument from the perspective of achievement goal theorists (e.g. Nicholls, 1989) is that an ego orientation, which involves a preoccupation with demonstrating superiority, may be accompanied by a lack of concern for justice and fairness.

Purpose

The project reported here was therefore designed to serve two purposes. The first was to develop an instrument to measure attitudes towards moral decision making in sport among youth populations, with particular focus on the distinction between those actions that could be fairly described as cheating and other classes of actions that might also be described as immoral, instrumental, or antisocial, such as gamesmanship. Second, after developing the instrument we intended to describe the levels of these attitudes among a population of adolescent athletes in England. These purposes were addressed through a series of five studies that incorporated both qualitative and quantitative methods.

Study 1: Identification of items

The purpose of this study was to obtain suitable items for a pilot questionnaire. The selected method was that of the Focus Group, which is frequently used to explore and clarify issues amongst a target population. The advantages of this method are that participants can (a) disagree with each other, thereby identifying differences of opinion of which the researcher may be unaware, (b) expand on their comments through discussion between themselves, and (c) clarify their explanations (Frey and Fontana, 1993). It is a suitable method for interviewing young people because they can feel safer and more relaxed in the company of a strange interviewer when others are present.

Method

Interviews were conducted with 11 groups of sport participants (males $n = 24$, females $n = 26$) aged 11–17 years, drawn from five schools in the south of England. The numbers in each focus group varied from 3 to 6 participants (mode = 5). Participants were grouped for homogeneity on a suitable variable (age or sex) to encourage participation. All interviews were recorded, transcribed, and subjected to content analysis. Participants were assured of confidentiality of their responses. Three interviewers were used; two male and one female. Training was undertaken to ensure consistency of approach between interviewers.

Stimulus subjects for discussion were drawn from a survey of experienced contributors to youth sport, which included coaches, administrators, and teachers (Lee, 1998). These experts identified nine categories of unethical behaviour that were of concern. Of these, four addressed issues central to our exploration of unethical attitudes, such as cheating, gamesmanship, the absence of fair play, and the importance of winning at all costs. Participants were asked to draw on their own experience to discuss the importance of these issues in the context of their own participation in sport.

Results

When added to responses from the earlier experts survey (Lee, 1998), the content analysis resulted in a pool of 189 potential questionnaire items. Subsequent cate-gorisation of these items identified personal conduct, cheating, fair play, gamesmanship, and attitudes towards winning as the most frequently mentioned constructs. Other commonly mentioned topics, such as parental roles and aggres-sion, were considered to be beyond the scope of the current investigation. The item pool was further reduced to 56 items by a panel of experts, which included three members with experience in constructing attitude questionnaires, and one member with experience in children's reading and language skills. The criteria used to select potential items were (a) coverage of the whole range of opinion and (b) ease of understanding by young people.

Discussion

These qualitative processes produced a list of items from which to develop an instrument suitable as a measure of ethical attitudes among athletes between 11 and 17 years of age. The items had good ecological validity because the topics were proposed by experts in youth sports and the item content was provided by young competitors. Subsequent reduction by other experts provided 56 items with good coverage of the underlying constructs. The items provided a foundation on which to identify viable factors in the next study.

Study 2: Identification of potential factors

The purpose of this study was to make a preliminary identification of potentially viable factors by testing the pool of pilot items derived from Study 1. Fifty-six items were selected and placed in random order in a questionnaire with an introduction that stated:

> In the list below there are some things that people have said about cheating and fair play in sport. Please read each one and circle one of the numbers beside it to show how much you agree or disagree with it. Some of these are not very different so you will have to be careful.

A five-point response scale was given, anchored by *strongly agree* (1) and Strongly *disagree* (5).

In order to identify potentially viable factors in a new area of study, several EFA's were performed on complete questionnaires ($n = 384$). Table 4.1 gives factor loadings for this final EFA and for confirmatory factor analyses (CFA) reported in the subsequent studies.

Discussion

In Study 2 we used EFA to explore the data and identify potentially viable factors related to moral decision making. The content of the six largest factors was salient. Cheating represents a violation of the rules and is central to the study of unethical behaviour. Gamesmanship represents a violation of the spirit rather than the rules of the game. A focus on keeping winning in proportion counters pressure for the unethical behaviour involved in winning at all costs. It gives an indication of the extent to which respondents are able to contextualise their actions and may relate to Shields and Bredemeier's (1995) notion of bracketed morality. Respect for sport

Table 4.1 Descriptive statistics and factor loadings of the three major factors in Studies 2 to 5

Factor and item	Mean	SD	EFA	CFA-1	CFA-2	CFA-3	CFA-4
I. Acceptance of cheating							
It is OK to cheat if nobody knows	1.61	.91	.83		.82	.86	.89
I would cheat if I thought it would help me win	1.86	.93	.81	.72	.82	.82	.76
If other people are cheating, I think I can too	1.88	.95	.51	.67	.61	.66	.59
I cheat if I can get away with it	1.98	1.07	.73	.85	.64		
When I get the chance I fool the official	1.82	1.02	.49	.85	.61		
I always play by the rules[a]	4.11	.92	−.60	−.46			
I would cheat if I thought it would help the team win	2.00	1.00	.64				
II. Keeping winning in proportion							
Winning and losing are a part of life	4.36	.81	.71	.68	.77	.84	.77
It is OK to lose sometimes because in life you don't win everything	4.18	.42	.65	.67	.71	.62	.82
If you win properly it feels better than if you did it dishonestly	4.60	.83	.57	.47	.52	.56	.47
You have to think about the other people and not just winning	3.94	.90	.53	.65	.38		
I get annoyed by people trying to 'win at all costs'	3.77	1.02	.63	.45			
Winning is all that matters[a]	2.14	1.06	−.31	−.52			

Table 4.1 continued

Factor and item	Mean	SD	EFA	CFA-1	CFA-2	CFA-3	CFA-4
III. Acceptance of gamesmanship							
I sometimes try to wind up the opposition	3.09	1.27	.71	.71	.80	.79	.80
It is not against the rules to psyche people out so it's OK to do	3.21	1.14	.81		.65	.63	.73
Sometimes I waste time to unsettle the opposition	2.67	1.15			.68	.66	.69
If I don't want another person to do well then I put them off a bit	2.56	1.17	.53	.79	.58		
It is a good idea to upset your opponent	2.04	1.05			.74		
I would never psyche anybody out[a]	2.80	1.16	−.85	−.39			
It is understandable that players swear in the heat of the moment	3.65	1.99	.52	.35			

Notes: Loadings for all factors are presented in the same column but refer to the factor named alongside. Items in italics were added to the Acceptance of Gamesmanship factor in Study 4. EFA: Final exploratory factor analysis of the three factors selected in Study 2. CFA-1: Confirmatory factor analysis of the initial 3-factor model in Study 3. CFA-2: Confirmatory factor analysis of the unidimensional scales in Study 4. CFA-3: Confirmatory factor analysis of the 3-factor model developed in Study 4. CFA-4: Confirmatory factor analysis of the 3-factor model confirmed in Study 5.
[a] Reverse-scored item.

addresses the ethical context of the sporting contract and is consistent with work by other researchers. Shame is a key emotion evoked when one's sense of personal morality is violated. Acceptance of responsibility for personal behaviour is essential for the maintenance of ethical conduct. However, factors IV to VI were rejected because they accounted for little variance. Nevertheless, we report them here because their content merits future research.

Factors I to III, as finally selected, explained 50 per cent of item variance. This is comparable to the variance explained by Vallerand's MSOS (50 per cent), and the EFA-C (46 per cent) of Boixadós *et al.* (2004). Hence these factors were considered to be conceptually and psychometrically suitable for the next pilot study.

Study 3: Evaluation of the three-factorial structure

[This study is omitted. It confirmed the factorial structure of the instrument in a new sample.]

Study 4: Model revision and evaluation of gender invariance

The purposes of this study were to make exploratory modifications to the model in order to (a) improve the structure of the three-factor model, (b) test the gender invariance of the model, and (c) describe mean differences in ethical attitudes as a function of gender, age, competitive level, and type of sport. A large sample with a wide geographical distribution was selected to (a) provide comprehensive data on attitudes among a youth population, and (b) permit separate analyses with males and females. The latter analyses were desirable because if scales can be constructed that have a similar meaning for males and females, subsequent interpretation of any gender differences in mean scores is more valid than if the factorial structure differs for each gender group. Modifications to the model were made in a *restricted framework,* in accordance with the two-step approach advocated by Anderson and Gerbing (1988).

Method

Young sport participants ($n = 1126$; males $n = 566$, females $n = 546$, unclassified $n = 14$) were drawn from 25 schools in large urban areas (London, Leeds, Manchester, Liverpool and the West Midlands) and from non-metropolitan areas in southeast England. They were aged from 11 to 16 years (mean $= 13.48$, SD $= 1.18$) and were drawn from more than 15 team ($n = 669$) and individual ($n = 217$) sports in which they competed for their school or sports club ($n = 769$) or a higher level team (i.e. district or county, $n = 302$; or regional or above, $n = 55$). Teachers administered the questionnaires using a well-tested protocol to ensure confidentiality.

In accordance with the two-step approach advocated by Anderson and Gerbing (1988), separate CFA's were first performed on the scales for Acceptance of Cheating, Acceptance of Gamesmanship, and Keeping Winning in Proportion in order to obtain close-fitting scales which would serve as a foundation for the three-factor model. Anderson and Gerbing considered that the achievement of unidimensional measurement is necessary in order to assign meaning to a construct and is crucial in theory testing and development. We wanted to meet this standard in order that the scales could be used independently by researchers.

Results

The analyses of individual factors resulted in each case in the achievement of close-fitting scales by deleting certain items. Initially a three-factor 14-item model was formed from the close-fitting scales for Acceptance of Cheating (five items), Acceptance of Gamesmanship (five items), and Keeping Winning in Proportion (four items). Five items were cut to obtain a three-factor nine-item model that was invariant across gender.

The revised three-factor model was acceptable when all parameters were constrained, but an even better fit was obtained when the constraints on factor variances and co-variances were relaxed because inter-factor correlations were higher for females than for males. The instrument was called 'Attitudes to Moral Decisions in Youth Sport Questionnaire' (AMDYSQ). In this model the factor correlation between Acceptance of Cheating and Acceptance of Gamesmanship was $r = .55$ (female $r = .65$, male $r = .45$), the correlation between Acceptance of Cheating and Keeping Winning in Proportion was $r = -.50$ (female $r = -.52$, male $r = -.48$), and the correlation between Acceptance of Gamesmanship and Keeping Winning in Proportion was $r = -.12$ (female $r = -.21$, male $r = .07$). Fit indices for all samples in this final model are given in Table 4.2, whereas factor loadings are given in Table 4.1.

Descriptive survey

Participants endorsed Keeping Winning in Proportion (mean = 4.37, SD = .68) more strongly than Acceptance of Gamesmanship (mean = 2.81, SD = .94) and Acceptance of Cheating (mean = 1.69, SD = .72). Moreover, the individual scales showed differences as a function of gender, age, competitive level, and type of sport. These differences were explored using latent means structure analyses.

Gender

The results of the latent means structure analysis showed significant gender differences on all three scales. Females scored higher than males on Keeping

Table 4.2 Fit indices for the three-factor models tested in Studies 4 and 5

Model	Items	χ^2	d.f.	p	SRMR	RMSEA	CFI	NNFI
Study 4								
All	9	51.10	24	.00	.04	.04	.97	.96
Male	9	36.51	24	.05	.04	.03	.98	.97
Female	9	51.39	24	.00	.06	.05	.95	.93
Multisample	9	100.75	63	.00	.06/.05	.04	.95	.94
Study 5								
All	9	33.54	24	.09	.05	.03	.98	.98
Male	9	35.42	24	.06	.09	.05	.93	.89
Female	9	19.95	24	.70	.04	.00	.98	.97
Multisample	9	51.13	63	.86	.09/.05	.00	.96	.96

Notes: This multisample model was constrained for invariance of factor loadings and error variances sequentially (see text for details). Here separate SRMR indices are given for male (first) and female groups.

Winning in Proportion ($B = .10$; $p < .05$; effect size $d = .10$) but males scored higher for Acceptance of Cheating ($B = .21$; $p < .01$; $d = .31$) and Acceptance of Gamesmanship ($B = .58$; $p < .01$; $d = .95$).

Age

Latent mean structure analysis comparing younger (i.e. aged 11–13 years) and older (i.e. aged 14–16) athletes showed that the latter reported higher Acceptance of Cheating ($B = .26$; $p < .01$; $d = .38$) and Acceptance of Gamesmanship ($B = .29$; $p < .01$; $d = .44$). However, there were no significant differences in Keeping Winning in Proportion ($B = -.04$; $p > .05$; $d = .09$).

Competitive level

Differences between competitive levels (school or club team vs. district team or above) were found in Acceptance of Gamesmanship ($B = .22$; $p < .01$; $d = .34$), but not in Acceptance of Cheating ($B = .02$; $p > .05$; $d = .04$) or in Keeping Winning in Proportion ($B = -.03$; $p > .05$; $d = .05$).

Sport type

Differences between participants in team and individual sports were shown by team sport competitors scoring higher than individual sport athletes on Acceptance of Cheating ($B = .17$; $p < .05$; $d = .25$) and Acceptance of Gamesmanship ($B = .27$; $p < .01$; $d = .42$), but not on Keeping Winning in Proportion ($B = -.07$; $p > .05$; $d = .16$).

Discussion

This study employed exploratory modifications to the instrument within a restricted confirmatory framework. In so doing so, we developed three individual scales and subsequently a three-factor model that appears conceptually sound, psychometrically valid, and invariant across gender. However, this model has to be cross-validated in Study 5. Using this model, we found that levels of acceptance of cheating and gamesmanship were greater among males, older athletes, and athletes from team sports. Acceptance of gamesmanship was also higher among athletes at higher competitive levels. Keeping winning in proportion was higher in females, thus females exhibited a more moral position on each scale.

Study 5: Confirmation of the revised factorial structure, concurrent validity, and social desirability effects

The purposes of this study were (a) to confirm the structure of the gender-invariant model in a new sample, (b) to test concurrent validity with a related questionnaire, and (c) to test social desirability effects. [We report only concurrent validity as this is a foundation for the development of AMDYSQ-2 in Appendix 2.]

Results

Concurrent validity

A seven-factor CFA was performed on the AMDYSQ and MSOS scales, using a robust ML method. This model had a good fit (χ^2 = 555.39, d.f. = 356, p < .001, RMSEA = .044, SRMR = .063, CFI = .94, NNFI = .93). The inter-factor correlations (see Table 4.3) show that, as predicted, the scale for Keeping Winning in Proportion had significant positive correlations with all the prosocial MSOS scales. In contrast, Acceptance of Cheating and Acceptance of Gamesmanship correlated significantly and negatively with these scales. The highest correlation for the AMDYSQ scale for Keeping Winning in Proportion was with the MSOS scale for Respect for Opponents. This is a logical relationship, because players who want to win at all costs would be unlikely to have respect for opponents. Similarly, the highest correlations between the AMDYSQ scales for Acceptance of Cheating and Gamesmanship and the MSOS scales were for the Respect for Rules and Officials scale. Since cheating is defined in terms of contravention of rules, and officials' interpretations of those rules, and gamesmanship is defined as a form of manipulation of the competitive contract, these results are to be expected and offer support for the concurrent validity of the AMDYSQ.

The low to moderate size of the correlations between the factors of the two instruments demonstrates that the AMDYSQ scales tap different facets of morality than those evaluated by the MSOS. Hence, the new instrument does not duplicate an existing measure, but provides new information for researchers.

Table 4.3 Correlations among attitudes and social desirability

Scale	1	2	3	4	5	6	7	8
1. Cheating	–	.74**	–.42**	–.30**	–.37**	–.35**	–.42**	–.36**
2. Gamesmanship		–	–.32**	–.11*	–.22**	–.30**	–.42**	–.41**
3. Winning in proportion			–	.48**	.53**	.66**	.57**	.10
4. Commitment				–	.60**	.50**	.74**	.39**
5. Conventions					–	.82**	.76**	.21**
6. Opponents						–	.76**	.34**
7. Rules and officials							–	.39**
8. Social desirability								–

Notes: AMDYSQ scales: Acceptance of Cheating, Acceptance of Gamesmanship, Keep Winning in Proportion. MSOS scales: Commitment to Sport, Respect for Conventions, Respect for Opponents, Respect for Rules and Officials. PRQ scale: Social Desirability. Correlations among attitudes are taken from a confirmatory factor analysis. Correlations with social desirability are Pearson product–moment correlations.*p < .05, **p < .01, n = 307 listwise.

Inter-correlations among the three AMDYSQ scales (*r*'s ranged from –.42 to .74) were somewhat lower than those among the MSOS scales (*r*'s ranged from .50 to .82), indicating discriminant validity.

Discussion

This study provided strong psychometric support for the robustness and validity of the AMDYSQ. First, using an independent sample, the data cross-validated the fit of a gender invariant model. Second, concurrent validity was demonstrated by positive correlations between the prosocial MSOS scales and Keeping Winning in Proportion, and by negative correlations between the same MSOS scales and Acceptance of Cheating and Acceptance of Gamesmanship. Third, the social desirability effects were negligible for Keeping Winning in Proportion, and low to moderate for the two antisocial scales of the AMDYSQ. The pattern of gender latent means on each of the three scales was consistent with what was observed in the previous study.

General discussion

The process described above has resulted in a new measure of attitudes towards moral decision making in youth sport – AMDYSQ – that is social psychological in its approach and differs in both content and structure from existing instruments. It accesses different facets of sportspersonship than those measured by the MSOS (Vallerand *et al.*, 1997) in that it specifically addresses two essentially antisocial attitudes – the acceptance of cheating and of gamesmanship – while also including a prosocial scale – keeping winning in proportion. It also addresses different dimensions of moral attitudes from the JAMBYSQ (Stephens *et al.*, 1997), while both have cheating in common. AMDYSQ has not been designed to address deontic judgements or moral atmosphere, but its format could be adapted to widen its application. For example the stem 'In my team . . .' could precede such a statement as 'people think it is OK to cheat if nobody knows'.

While attitudes towards cheating have received direct treatment in the sport psychology literature (e.g. Stephens *et al.*, 1997), we believe that this is the first time that a measure of gamesmanship has been reported. The distinction between these two concepts is important because, while cheating can be defined by reference to the explicit rule structure of a particular sport, gamesmanship constitutes a violation of the spirit of the contest that is not specifically addressed by the rules but harms the contractual integrity implicit in sport competitions. Furthermore, because its manifestations depend so much on the creativity of the protagonists, it is such a diverse construct as to be extremely difficult to describe comprehensively.

Scale content

The items that represent the constructs underlying the scales have undergone comprehensive statistical analyses in order to meet rigorous criteria. More importantly, they also represent important conceptual elements of those constructs. In the Acceptance of Cheating scale, the item 'I would cheat if I thought it would help me win' represents Reddiford's (1998) first feature of cheating, that of making illegitimate gains. The second item, 'It is OK to cheat if nobody knows', combines Reddiford's second and third features, notably successful concealment of intention. The third item, 'If other people are cheating I think I can too', goes beyond Reddiford's categories by highlighting the importance of normative influence on attitude formation; such type of influence is central to research on moral atmosphere. Thus although the scale has only three items, it represents different components of attitudes towards cheating.

In contrast, although gamesmanship embraces a wide variety of instrumental behaviours that may be limited only by the imagination of the contestants, we felt that it was advantageous at this stage to focus on a single identifiable aspect; hence, the scale comprises items that are interpersonal in nature and concerned with disturbing or distracting the opponent. The diversity of behaviours that are jointly represented by cheating and gamesmanship has made it difficult to devise an instrument to cover all eventualities but in which the two constructs are not considered synonymous. Whilst the correlations between them are positive, the magnitude is such as to suggest that there is still a significant amount of variance that is specific to each. Hence, we can conclude that the scales measure distinct but related constructs.

From the point of view of assessing moral attitudes it may be that gamesmanship is a particularly useful indicator on empirical as well as conceptual grounds. The data suggest that Acceptance of Gamesmanship may discriminate among participants more effectively than Acceptance of Cheating because (a) it is less skewed, and (b) it showed greater differences in gender, age, competitive level, and sport type. It has also related differently to other variables. For example, in comparison with the cheating scale, the gamesmanship scale showed a higher correlation with ego orientation and status values, and a lower correlation with moral values (Lee and Whitehead, 1999). In the present study it had lower correlations with the MSOS scales for commitment and conventions.

Although the discussion has emphasised the uniqueness of gamesmanship and cheating, the scale for 'keeping winning in proportion' is also important because it provides a prosocial rather than antisocial dimension and, hence, provides a degree of balance. Further, the data indicate that this prosocial scale is not susceptible to social desirability effects.

Finally, examination of data collected during the construction of these scales suggests that it would be fruitful to develop further a scale for shame that assesses the emotional response to the actor's dishonourable behaviour. In this context, it would be instructive to distinguish between those responses that result from self-knowledge of transgressions (e.g. guilt), and the public knowledge thereof, (e.g. shame; Reber, 1985).

Gender invariance

An important feature in the construction of the AMDYSQ was the selection of items to provide scales that would be invariant across gender. Factor structure in questionnaires frequently differs for males and females; therefore mean differences may reflect a difference in the interpretation of the items (i.e. different factor structure) as well as a systematic difference in the degree of support for the construct. Although gender differences are always present and can fluctuate due to sampling variations, we hoped to reduce their effect by eliminating the items with the greatest gender differences in factor loadings. An alternative would have been to retain non-invariant items and construct gender-specific scales, but this strategy would have been less parsimonious and would prevent cross-gender comparisons.

Gender invariance was achieved at the cost of reduction of the number of items per scale but the resulting brevity of the scales has both advantages and disadvantages. On the positive side, the short scales produced findings that were equivalent to those obtained with longer individual scales in earlier work (Lee, 1998) and, hence, are more parsimonious. Furthermore, shorter scales minimise potential problems that might arise with inattention among younger populations. On the negative side, the desire to meet stringent criteria of uni-dimensionality, such as can be achieved by item elimination using CFA, seems to militate against the identification of some aspects of the multifaceted concepts of cheating and gamesmanship. Both of these constructs embrace a variety of characteristics and behaviours that are not easily captured in a short psychometric scale. As Georgi (2002: 4) has pointed out, a test is a symbolic instrument that is 'a substitute for a situation that is fuller, richer, more complex, more lived, and more ambiguous than that addressed by the test itself'. However, the short scales given herein have extremely good coherence and internal reliability, but necessarily as a compromise, they measure the richness of complex concepts in a more limited fashion.

Survey results: mean scores and subgroup mean differences

The data from a survey of a large sample of British adolescent athletes (i.e. Study 4) indicated that these participants do not support cheating, are largely neutral towards gamesmanship and like to keep winning in proportion. Essentially, they like to participate in an activity in which people play by the rules, do not take advantage of others and recognise that other things in life are more important. Hence, we consider that the athletes in our samples may be described as adopting an ethical approach to their sports participation. We recognise, however, that our conclusion may not generalise to older athletes as they attempt to progress from junior to senior levels of sport.

Limitations and applications

While the AMDYSQ is potentially valuable for the investigation of immoral, or instrumental, attitudes in youth sport, in particular of attitudes towards gamesmanship, there remains scope for further elaboration of the latter construct by the development of a greater variety of items pertaining to a similar variety of sports situations. However, while that should result in greater external validity of the construct, the probability is that it would be more difficult to establish high levels of internal validity within the scale.

Although the reliability of the cheating and gamesmanship scales is good there is a need to improve that of Keep Winning in Proportion and to establish the stability of all three scales over time. But, in so doing, future investigators would be well advised to take account of the genesis of the instrument with adolescent populations, which are prone to rapidly changing attitudes, and conduct such studies with a variety of age groups and over varying time spans.

In Study 5 we initiated the evaluation of construct validity by examining concurrent validity with a criterion test of sportspersonship (Vallerand *et al.*, 1997). We also explored the validity of the responses of our participants by determining that they were no strong social desirability effects. Further studies are needed to test different facets of validity, and in particular to test whether relationships with other conceptually relevant variables conform to theoretical predictions. To date, our ongoing work indicates that these attitudes are correctly predicted by logical antecedents. Future research should also examine correlations between the ethical attitudes and their logical consequences.

The AMDYSQ may serve as a useful addition to existing instruments. Since its emphasis is on negative attitudes, it might usefully be employed in conjunction with the MSOS which is comprised predominantly of positive scales. It would be fruitful to explore further whether different aspects of achievement orientations and motivational climate can predict support for cheating in sport. We have argued that the more general construct of values underpins the specific motivational orientations that are brought to bear in sports settings (Lee and Whitehead, 2001) and we have examined more complex relationships between values, achievement orientations and moral attitudes. Initial findings indicate that achievement orientations mediate the influence of values upon both prosocial and antisocial attitudes in sport [see Chapter 5 of this book]. Hence, it is logical to propose that future investigations include personal values, and the perceived values and motivational climate of significant others and institutions as independent factors that influence moral attitudes.

In conclusion, the AMDYSQ appears to be a sound instrument with a strong factor structure and gender invariance, and is suitable for use in investigations of previously unexplored dimensions of moral decision making among youth sport populations. It has also provided some preliminary data on the level of ethical attitudes among young athletes.

References

Anderson, J.C. and Gerbing, D.W. (1988) Structural equation modelling in practice: A review and recommended two-step approach. *Psychological Bulletin*, 103, 411–23.

Begg, D.J., Langley, J.D., Moffitt, T. and Marshall, S.W. (1996) Sport and delinquency: An examination of the deterrence hypothesis in a longitudinal study. *British Journal of Sport Medicine*, 30, 335–41.

Blair, S. (1985) Professionalization of attitudes towards play in children and adults. *Research Quarterly for Exercise and Sport*, 56, 82–3.

Boixadós, M. and Cruz, J. (1995) Construction of a fairplay attitude scale in soccer. In R. Vanfraechen-Raway and Y. Venden Auveele (eds) *Proceedings of the IXth European Congress of Sport Psychology: Part 1*. Borgerhout: Vlaamse Vereniging voor Sport Psychologie, pp. 4–11.

Boixadós, M., Cruz, J., Torregrosa, M. and Valiente, L. (2004) Relationships among motivational climate, satisfaction, perceived ability, and fair play attitudes in youth soccer players. *Journal of Applied Sport Psychology*, 16, 301–17.

Colby, A. and Kohlberg, L. (1987) *The Measurement of Moral Judgement. Vol.1: Theoretical Foundations and Research Validation*. Cambridge University Press. Cambridge.

Frey, J.H. and Fontana, A. (1993) The group interview in social research. In Morgan, D.L. (ed.) *Successful Focus Groups: Advancing the State of the Art*. London: Sage, pp. 20–34.

Georgi, A. (2002) The question of validity in qualitative research. *Journal of Phenomenological Psychology*, 33, 1–18.

Goodger, M. and Jackson, J. (1985) Fair play: Coaches attitudes towards the laws of soccer. *Journal of Sport Behavior*, 8, 34–41.

Haan, N. (1978) Two moralities in action contexts: Relationship to thought, ego regulation and development. *Journal of Personality and Social Psychology*, 36, 286–305.

Kohlberg, L. (1976) Moral stages and moralization: The cognitive–developmental approach. In Lickona, T. (ed.) *Moral Development and Behavior: Theory, Research and Social Issues*. New York: Holt, Rinehart and Winston, pp. 31–53.

Lee, M.J. (1998) *Young People, Sport, and Ethics: An Examination of Values and Attitudes to Fair Play among Youth Sport Competitors*. London: English Sports Council.

Lee, M.J. and Whitehead, J. (1999) *Report of Award R000222219: The Effect of Values, Achievement Goals, and Perceived Ability on Moral Attitudes in Youth Sport*. Swindon: Economic and Social Research Council.

Lee, M.J. and Whitehead, J. (2001) Belief systems as antecedents of moral attitudes in youth sport: a rationale. In Papaioannou, A., Goudas, M. and Theodorakis, Y. (eds) *In the Dawn of the New Millennium, Vol. 2: Proceedings of the 10th World Congress of Sport Psychology*. Thessaloniki: Christodoulidi Publications, pp. 187–8.

Lee, M.J. and Williams, V. (1989) Attitudes towards professional fouls in youth soccer. *Sport and Leisure*, 1, 27–8.

Maloney, T.L. and Petrie, B. (1972) Professionalization of attitude toward play among Canadian school pupils as a function of sex, grade and athletic participation. *Journal of Leisure Research*, 4, 184–95.

Nicholls, J.G. (1989) *The Competitive Ethos and Democratic Education*. Harvard, MA: Harvard University Press.

Potter, S. (1947) *The Theory and Practice of Gamesmanship, or the Art of Winning without Actually Cheating*. London: Penguin.

Reber, A.S. (1985) *The Penguin Dictionary of Psychology*. Harmondsworth: Penguin.

Reddiford, G. (1998) Cheating and self-deception in sport. In McNamee, M.J. and Parry, S.J. (eds) *Ethics and Sport*. London: E. and F.N. Spon, pp. 225–39.

Segrave, J.O. and Hastad, D.N. (1982) Delinquent behavior and interscholastic athletic participation. *Journal of Sport Behavior*, 5, 96–111.

Segrave, J.O. and Hastad, D.N. (1984) Interscholastic athletic participation and delinquent behavior: An empirical assessment of relevant variables. *Sociology of Sport*, 1, 117–37.

Segrave, J.O., Moreau, C. and Hastad, D.N. (1985) An investigation into the relationship between ice hockey participation and delinquency. *Sociology of Sport*, 2, 281–98.

Shields, D.L.L. and Bredemeier, B.J.L. (1995) *Character Development and Physical Activity*. Champaign, IL: Human Kinetics.

Stephens, D.E., Bredemeier, B.J.L. and Shields, D.L.L. (1997) Construction of a measure designed to assess player's descriptions and prescriptions for moral behavior in youth sport soccer. *International Journal of Sport Psychology*, 28, 370–90.

Telama, R. and Liukkonen, J. (1999) The relationship between goal orientation, prosocial behavior, and physical activity among schoolchildren. Paper presented at Youth Sports in the 21st Century, Institute for the Study of Youth Sports, Michigan State University, East Lansing, Michigan, May.

Vallerand, R. (1994) A social psychological analysis of sportsmanship. 1: Theoretical perspectives. Unpublished manuscript, Universite du Quebec, Montreal.

Vallerand, R.J. and Losier, G.F. (1994) Self-determined motivation and sportsmanship orientations: An assessment of their temporal relationship. *Journal of Sport and Exercise Psychology*, 16, 229–45.

Vallerand, R.J., Brière, N.M., Blanchard, C. and Provencher, P. (1997) Development and validation of the Multidimensional Sportspersonship Orientation Scale. *Journal of Sport and Exercise Psychology*, 19, 197–206.

Chapter 4 link: Relevance and update

One purpose of this chapter, which is abridged from a 2007 article, was to develop the Attitudes to Moral Decision-making in Sport Questionnaire (AMDYSQ) to explore attitudes which underlie moral decision making and facilitate a test of the relationship between values and attitudes in Chapter 5.

AMDYSQ measures attitudes to 'acceptance of cheating', 'acceptance of gamesmanship', and 'keeping winning in proportion' with short scales that are invariant across gender to ensure that any differences found reflect the same construct. Results showed the greatest endorsement for keeping winning in proportion followed by gamesmanship then cheating. Females had the more ethical attitudes.

An original feature of AMDYSQ is the measurement of gamesmanship, which violates the spirit of the game but does not break the rules. This British concept, introduced by Potter's (1947) book about gamesmanship as the art of winning without actually cheating, has been misunderstood internationally and is sometimes mistakenly equated with sportspersonship. The shaded columns in Table 4.4 show low negative correlations between gamesmanship assessed in this chapter and the sportsmanship value identified in Chapter 3.

Although AMDYSQ was constructed to measure moral decision making without a focus on aggression it has nevertheless been used as an indicator of acceptance of aggression in a series of studies of moral disengagement (Appendix 2.)

Table 4.4 Correlations among sportsmanship variables and two gamesmanship scales (*n* = 549)

1	2	3	4	5	6	7
1. I show good sportsmanship	.52**	.44**	.42**	.39**	−.18**	−.25**
2. I try to be fair		.40**	.34**	.37**	−.16**	−.24**
3. I play properly			.44**	.38**	−.08	−.12**
4. I help people when they need it				.31**	−.09*	−.10*
5. I do what I am told					−.13**	−.20**
6. Gamesmanship 3 items						.89**
7. Gamesmanship 5 items						

**p > .01; *p > .05

Relationships with reactive and instrumental aggression which related negatively and positively, respectively, to sportsmanship might be explored (Chantal *et al.* 2005).

Chapter 5 tests the value-expressive function of attitudes, using the cheating and gamesmanship scales. In that study the scales were improved but not published, hence Appendix 2 describes the relationship of AMDYSQ with other variables, and the construction of AMDYSQ-2. The item 'I think fairness is more important than winning' was introduced into the scale for Keeping Winning in Proportion to improve its suitability for youth sport.

Reference

Chantal, Y., Robin, P., Vernat, J-P. and Bernache-Assollant, I. (2005) Motivation, sportspersonship, and athletic aggression. *Psychology of Sport and Exercise*, 6, 233–49.

5 How do values influence attitudes and achievement goals?

Relationships between values, achievement orientations and attitudes in youth sport

Martin J. Lee, Jean Whitehead, Nikos Ntoumanis and Antonis Hatzigeorgiadis

It has been widely proposed that 'sport develops character' in the sense that moral attitudes developed in sport transfer to other contexts. However, Shields and Bredemeier (2007) conclude that there is little to support this view and, in fact, participants adopt a different moral framework when competing than otherwise. However, it may be that the focus on the mere content of the activities as the source of personal qualities is misguided and the process by which these activities are encouraged is the determining factor in the developmental process. It is our intention, therefore, to examine the fundamental psychological motivations that result in young athletes exhibiting socially desirable or undesirable attitudes in sport.

Human values have been regarded as dominant influences in society, guiding people's actions and governing their perceptions of reality (e.g. Allport, 1961; Rokeach, 1973), but have received little attention in sport psychology. In contrast, achievement motivation has become a dominant model for the study of motivation in this field (e.g. Duda, 1992). While the role of achievement motives in determining behaviour in sport is readily recognisable that of values is less obvious. However, if values determine how people justify decisions in life then they will influence attitudes and behaviour in sport.

This research, therefore, was developed to examine the relationships between values, achievement orientations and attitudes in youth sport. Specifically we examined the role of achievement orientation in mediating the value expressive function of attitudes.

The nature of values

Values are defined as beliefs that certain goals or behaviours are more or less preferable to their alternatives (e.g. Rokeach, 1973). They serve the interests of individuals or groups, motivate action by giving it direction and intensity, provide standards by which behaviour is evaluated, and are learned by individuals from the dominant values of their social groups and through their own experiences

(Schwartz, 1994). Because the same values have been identified in different societies they are considered universal (Schwartz, 1992).

Values and attitudes

An attitude has been defined as 'a learned predisposition to respond in a consistently favorable or unfavorable manner with respect to a given object' (Fishbein and Ajzen, 1975: 5). Thus attitudes differ from values because they are bipolar, specific to an attitude object, and they have no hierarchy of importance. One of the functions of attitudes is that of expressing the more general principles embodied in values in relation to specific target objects or issues (Katz, 1960; Rokeach, 1973). Because they are object specific they are more numerous than values. Furthermore, many attitudes can arise from a single value, and one attitude can reflect more than one value.

The relative importance given to values demands that they are ranked either by individuals or as a representation of the value system of a social group (see Bardi and Schwartz, 2003). Attitudes have no such relative quality and two or more may be equally endorsed. Further, values are expressions of the desirable while attitudes express both positive and negative sentiments. Thus attitudinal and behavioural decisions result from the relative importance attached to the underlying values. In this research we use social attitudes as operational proxies for moral attitudes. Specifically we refer to prosocial attitudes which are cooperative and supportive of the social situation, and antisocial attitudes which are disruptive and antagonistic to it.

Values in sport

Since values are considered to be general principles that guide behaviour across situations then they should underpin decision-making in sport and those values that pertain to achievement and morality are particularly significant. However, early studies in this area did little to distinguish values from attitudes, to use values as conceptions of the desirable, or to develop values instruments (Lee *et al.*, 2000). More recent research has addressed some of these issues (e.g. Cruz *et al.*, 1995; Kavalir, 2004). Lee and Cockman (1995) identified 18 values spontaneously expressed by young athletes in discussions of moral dilemmas in their sport. Subsequently, Lee *et al.* (2000) used these to construct the Youth Sport Values Questionnaire (YSVQ) which identified value systems of adolescent athletes.

The YSVQ also identified moral, competence and status values in an acceptable factorial model (unreported) as particularly relevant for further study. These value types have high ecological validity because they were drawn from young athletes and they relate closely to the universalism, self-direction, and power domains identified by Schwartz (1992). They are appropriate for this study because they provide parsimonious coverage of the nature and structure of salient values in youth sport. They also reflect three dimensions explored by Webb

(1969): playing fairly, playing well, and winning. Moral and status values represent a value conflict in accordance with Schwartz' structural model, while competence and status values are expected to underpin different achievement orientations. Lee (1996) explored the value expressive function of attitudes in sport and found that moral values predicted prosocial attitudes positively and antisocial attitudes negatively.

This research will further examine the value-expressive function of attitudes by identifying the influence of moral, competence and status values on antisocial and prosocial attitudes.

Achievement goal theory

This social–cognitive approach holds that the demonstration of ability is central to achievement and that success is interpreted subjectively according to the concept of ability adopted for each activity. Different psychological consequences arise from using an effort-based concept of ability and the concept of ability as a capacity which limits the effect of effort. When an effort-based interpretation of ability is used, people are in a state of *task-involvement*. They focus on mastering a task and judge success by self-referenced criteria such as understanding and completing it, or overcoming a challenge. When the adequacy of ability in relation to others is paramount, people are in a state of *ego-involvement*. They focus on demonstrating ability and judge success by normative criteria such as establishing superiority over others or gaining success more easily. While these goal *states* are transitory, socialisation and experience lead people to develop *dispositional orientations* towards one or other perspective. These more stable orientations underpin the activation of the goal states (Nicholls, 1989).

A mediating role for achievement orientations

Achievement orientations are seen as organising constructs that lead to characteristically different psychological and behavioural outcomes (Duda and Whitehead, 1998). Indeed, composite goal-belief factors generalise across school and sport contexts and are components of personal theories about how the achievement context works (Duda and Nicholls, 1992). Such views include antecedent beliefs about the purpose of sport and consequent social attitudes, and they also include moral content. Nicholls (1989) argued that a preoccupation with winning may be accompanied by a lack of concern for justice, fairness, and the welfare of others in competition.

In a review of correlates of achievement orientations Biddle *et al.* (2003) concluded that task orientation is related to higher moral functioning, prosocial attitudes, and sportspersonship and a belief that the purpose of sport is to develop mastery. Hence task orientation should mediate the effect of competence values on prosocial attitudes. In contrast, ego orientation is related to endorsement of aggression, poor sportspersonship, and beliefs that ability and deception cause success, and that the purpose of sport is to gain social status. Hence, ego orientation should mediate the effect of status values on antisocial attitudes. However, because moral values have no achievement element, we do not expect achievement orientations to mediate the effect of moral values on social attitudes.

Rationale

The value-expressive role of attitudes and achievement goal theory suggest that both values and achievement orientations predict moral attitudes in youth sport. These theories can be integrated to the extent that the prioritising function of values implies that they should not only prompt the adoption of appropriate attitudes but also encourage the adoption of achievement orientations that are consistent with underlying values. Furthermore, since values are trans-situational principles which guide behaviour and achievement orientations address behaviour only in the achievement domain values can be considered as antecedents of achievement orientations, and moral attitudes as consequences of both. Thus achievement orientations should mediate the effect of relevant sport values on moral attitudes.

The purpose of the research was twofold. First it was necessary to refine the YSVQ (Lee *et al.*, 2000) to facilitate the measurement of appropriate values types (Study 1). Then, in Study 2, we tested the following hypotheses. First, values will have a direct effect on social attitudes: (a) moral values will positively predict prosocial attitudes; (b) moral values will negatively predict antisocial attitudes; (c) competence values will positively predict prosocial attitudes; and (d) status values will positively predict antisocial attitudes. Second, integrating predictions of achievement goal theory, we hypothesise that achievement orientations will mediate some of these effects: (a) task orientation will mediate the effect of competence values on prosocial attitudes; and (b) ego orientation will mediate the effect of status values on antisocial attitudes.

Study 1: Modification of the values questionnaire (YSVQ-2)

The purpose of this study was to modify the YSVQ (Lee *et al.*, 2000) to assess moral, competence, and status values. That instrument was constructed to assess the value systems of young athletes, that is, the hierarchical ranking of the importance of their values (Rokeach, 1973). The 18 YSVQ values were drawn directly from adolescent athletes and they represent a comprehensive set of values salient to moral decision-making in youth sport. This follows the advice of Braithwaite and Laws (1985) who recommend the development of items from the population of interest. Each value is represented by a proxy item in the form of a personal statement. For example, the value of public image is represented by the item 'I look good'. However, the YSVQ consists only of single-item measures, hence in the present study it was extended to create multi-item assessment of three higher order value types.

The questionnaire is headed 'What is important to me in sport' and respondents are asked to 'Please circle one of the numbers beside each item to show how important it is to you in your main sport'. Responses are on a seven-point scale with the following response labels, each starting with the phrase 'This idea is ...':

- ... extremely important to me (5)
- ... very important to me (4)
- ... important to me (3)
- ... quite important to me (2)
- ... slightly important to me (1)
- ... not important to me (0) and
- ... the opposite of what I believe (−1)

This asymmetric scale was developed by Schwartz (1992) for cross-cultural research. Although values are conceptions of the desirable, and normally draw approval, there was a need for disagreement to be expressed when a particular value conflicted with the culture.

Method

The instrument was revised in two phases. The purpose of the first phase was to identify the most suitable items in the existing data to represent the moral, competence, and status scales. The purposes of the second phase were (a) to construct and pilot a revised instrument, and (b) to make exploratory modifications to produce a YSVQ-2 questionnaire that would be cross-validated in Study 2 (see Anderson and Gerbing, 1988).

[10 paragraphs of detail have been removed. Please consult the original article for this information.]

Discussion of Study 1

These procedures provide good initial evidence that we have constructed a sound instrument to assess moral, competence, and status values in youth sport. The 13-item model provides more extended coverage than the seven-item model identified by Lee *et al.* (2000). The instrument now includes five moral values (obedience, fairness, sportspersonship, helpfulness and contract maintenance), three competence values (achievement, showing skill, and self-direction), and three status values (winning, public image and leadership). This broadening is particularly important for the competence and status value types that were under-represented in the YSVQ. The CFA's demonstrate that the uni-dimensional scales for moral, competence, and status values can be used independently. These scales had little or no contamination by social desirability and shared no more than 2.5 per cent variance with the social desirability index. Finally, a three-factor model formed from these scales had a good fit to the data, and is suitable for cross-validation in Study 2. Whereas the YSVQ assessed value *systems* the YSVQ-2 also assesses value *structure* and it is in this context that it was used in Study 2.

Table 5.1 Descriptive statistics and factor loadings for the 13-item YSVQ-2 model

Means and items	Mean	SD	Skewness	Kurtosis	F1	F2	F3	R^2
Moral values (F1)								
I do what I am told	3.49	1.33	−.81	.32	.61	0	0	.38
I show good sportsmanship	3.76	1.21	−.90	−.36	.76	0	0	.58
I help people when they need it	3.67	1.26	−.85	.50	.56	0	0	.32
I always play properly	3.61	1.26	−.88	.37	.73	0	0	.53
I try to be fair	3.64	1.25	−.90	.67	.60	0	0	.36
Competence values (F2)								
I become a better player	3.79	1.19	−1.09	1.21	0	.70	0	.49
I use my skills well	3.73	1.17	−.96	1.05	0	.71	0	.50
I set my own targets	3.31	1.47	−.73	−.13	0	.50	0	.25
I improve my performance	3.80	1.16	−.86	.34	0	.71	0	.50
Status values (F3)								
I show that I am better than others	1.09	1.73	.68	−.60	0	0	.70	.49
I am the leader in the group	.97	1.58	.74	−.21	0	0	.67	.45
I win or beat others	1.81	1.81	.22	−1.02	0	0	.85	.72
I look good	1.72	1.80	.24	−.99	0	0	.70	.49
Factor correlations					F1	F2	F3	
				F1		.85	.18	
				F2			.49	
				F3				

Study 2: Testing the conceptual relationships

The central purpose of the second study was to test the conceptual relationships between values, achievement orientations and sporting attitudes. A secondary purpose, although undertaken first, was to cross-validate the factor solution of the YSVQ-2 obtained in Study 1 with a new sample. Subsequently, measurement models were tested for all constructs, then a direct model and a mediation model were examined to test the structural relationships hypothesised in the introduction.

Method

Participants and procedures

Participants (n = 892; males n = 503, females n = 389) aged 12 to 15 (mean age = 13.89, SD = 1.05) were recruited in southern England. They were drawn from 22 community sport clubs that represented the 12 most popular sports in the United Kingdom (Mason, 1995), and from four state secondary schools. They competed for their school or club (n = 617) or at a higher level (n = 271, missing n = 4), and in team sports (n = 531) or individual sports (n = 299, missing n = 62). Under controlled and ethically approved conditions participants completed the three questionnaires described below in a counter-balanced order. The data were collected between one and two months after the start of the summer and winter sport seasons.

Instruments

The Youth Sport Values Questionnaire-2 (YSVQ-2)

The three-factor 13-item model that provided a good fit in Study 1 was administered.

The attitudes measure

A 23-item attitude instrument was constructed using two antisocial scales from the Sport Attitudes Questionnaire (SAQ; Lee *et al.*, 2001) and two prosocial scales from the MSOS (Vallerand *et al.*, 1997). The SAQ is a longer version of the Attitudes to Moral Decision-making in Youth Sport Questionnaire (AMDYSQ; Lee *et al.*, 2007). We used its two antisocial scales to measure acceptance of cheating (e.g. 'I would cheat if I thought it would help me win') and acceptance of gamesmanship (e.g. 'I sometimes try to wind up the opposition').

The MSOS includes four scales that focus on a prosocial approach to sportspersonship and all were considered conceptually suitable to complement the two antisocial scales. In a pilot test the two psychometrically strongest prosocial scales were selected and a CFA on the four antisocial and prosocial scales showed an acceptable fit. The selected MSOS scales measured commitment to sport participation (e.g. 'I go to every practice') and respect for social conventions (e.g. 'I shake hands with the opposition – win or lose'). The composite questionnaire contained five items for each of these MSOS scales, with six cheating and seven gamesmanship items for the SAQ scales. All responses were made on a 5-point scale anchored by 'strongly disagree' (1) and 'strongly agree' (5).

Perceptions of Success Questionnaire

The adolescent version of the Perceptions of Success Questionnaire (POSQ) (Roberts *et al.*, 1998) was selected to measure achievement orientations. In pilot tests, we added two items at the end of the scale ('I do things more easily than others' and 'I learn something new to me') to represent facets of the ego and task orientation constructs that were not in this questionnaire. A preference to succeed without effort improves the identification of ego orientation as a concept of ability, complementing its focus on obtaining superiority over others, while a learning item complements the focus of task orientation on effort. Hence the POSQ administered in this study comprised seven items for each orientation. Responses were on the five-point scale described above.

Data analyses

Cross-validation of the YSVQ-2 was undertaken using participants with complete scores on this instrument ($n = 755$; males $n = 427$, females $n = 328$). Subsequent measurement and structural models were tested using participants with complete scores on all variables ($n = 549$; males $n = 317$; females $n = 232$).

For the hypothesis testing, we selected three indicators (Olmstead and Bentler, 1992) to represent each construct because we had too many items to maintain an acceptable ratio of sample size to estimated parameters. Indicators were selected by three experienced judges to (a) parsimoniously represent the conceptual breadth of a construct, (b) reduce over-emphasis on one facet of a construct, and (c) avoid items with similar wording that could inflate paths between constructs. All items that were previously added to the values instrument and achievement orientation scales were included because they met these criteria. The indicators are given in the Table 5.2.

Measurement models

The fit of the indicators selected for each instrument was tested by CFA as described in Study 1. The Robust ML method was used because the normalised estimate of Mardia's coefficient indicated multivariate non-normality. We also examined invariance across gender using the procedure of Byrne *et al.* (1989).

Structural models

A direct model and a mediated model were used to test the hypotheses given in the introduction. These models were also tested for invariance of path coefficients across gender, as described above.

Results

Cross-validation of the YSVQ-2

The hypothesised three-factor structure was supported by good fit indices for the total, female, multi-gender non-constrained and constrained models. In the male sample the CFI and NNFI indices were weaker than RMSEA and SRMR indices (Table 5.3). Overall, the good fits confirm that we have constructed a

Table 5.2 Indicators of the measurement models

Item	Loading
Values	
Moral	
I try to be fair	.64
I show good sportsmanship	.77
I help other people when they need it	.57
Competence	
I set my own targets	.62
I use my skills well	.71
I become a better player	.73
Status	
I am a leader in the group	.67
I show that I am better than others	.77
I look good	.52
Attitudes	
Commitment	
I go to every practice	.49
I always try my hardest	.73
I don't give up after mistakes	.51
Conventions	
I shake hands with the opposition – win or lose	.76
I congratulate the opposition for a good play or performance	.69
I congratulate the opposition after I've lost	.77
Cheating	
I would cheat if I thought it would help me win	.73
I cheat if I can get away with it	.84
Sometimes I have to cheat	.81
Gamesmanship	
It's a good idea to upset your opponents	.79
I sometimes try to wind up the opposition	.76
If I don't want another person to do well I put them off a bit	.65
Achievement orientations	
Task orientation	
I learn something new to me	.60
I perform to the best of my ability	.54
I overcome difficulties	.76
Ego orientation	
I do things more easily than others	.75
I do something that others cannot do	.70
I show other people that I am the best	.71

Notes: For values items the stem is 'When I do sport it is important to me that…'.
For attitude items the instruction is 'Show how you play in your main sport'.
For achievement orientation items the stem is 'In my sport I feel successful when…'.

Table 5.3 Fit indicators for the measurement and structural models in Study 2

	χ^2	d.f.	CFI	NNFI	RMSEA	90% CI for RMSEA	SRMR
Cross validation of YSVQ-2							
Total	170.64	62	.95	.94	.05	.04–.06	.05
Males	168.04	62	.91	.89	.06	.05–.08	.06
Females	122.11	62	.96	.95	.05	.04–.07	.05
Multi-gender non-constrained	256.57	124	.94	.94	.04	.03–.04	.06
Multi-gender constrained	279.99	137	.94	.94	.04	.03–.04	.08
Measurement models for indicators							
Values (9 items)	53.21	24	.97	.96	.05	.03–.06	.05
Attitudes (12 items)	75.16	48	.98	.98	.03	.02–.05	.04
Achievement orientations (6)	11.36	8	1.00	.99	.03	0–.06	.03
Structural models							
Direct	310.76	179	.96	.95	.04	.03–.04	.06
Mediated	515.59	310	.95	.94	.04	.03–.04	.06

Notes: The Satorra-Bentler χ^2 and the fit indices from the Robust ML solution are reported, except for SRMR indices which are from the ML solution. χ^2 $p = .23$ for achievement orientations, and $p < .01$ for other models. Fit indices for the male, female and multi-gender models are available from the second author on request. Measurement models were constrained for factor loadings and covariances. Structural models were constrained for structural paths.

psychometrically sound instrument. It is also invariant across gender, as shown by the absence of change in the CFI and RMSEA indices between the constrained and unconstrained models. The correlation between the Moral and Competence factors was $r = .76$ (smaller than in Study 1), between Competence and Status factors $r = .43$, and between Status and Moral factors $r = .18$.

Measurement models

Fit indices were acceptable for all three measurement models (Table 5.3). In the values model, correlations were $r = .72$ between moral and competence values, $r = .43$ between competence and status values, and $r = .11$ between status and moral values. In the attitudes model, the correlation between the two antisocial factors was $r = .71$, and between the two prosocial factors $r = .46$. Correlations between prosocial and antisocial factors ranged from $r = -.07$ to $r = -.35$. For achievement orientations the correlation between task and ego orientation was $r = .28$. Factor loadings for all instruments were moderately high (.49 to .84), and gender invariance of factor loadings and factor correlations was supported.

Structural models

The structural models and path coefficients for the total sample are shown for the direct and mediated models in Figures 5.1 and 5.2, respectively. Based on the YSVQ-2 measurement model, the Competence factor was allowed to correlate with the Moral and Status factors. The four attitude factors were hypothesised to load on two second-order factors representing Prosocial (Commitment to Sport and Respect for Social Conventions) and Antisocial (Acceptance of Cheating and Acceptance of Gamesmanship) factors. Fit indices for the models discussed below are given in Table 5.3 and are considered acceptable.

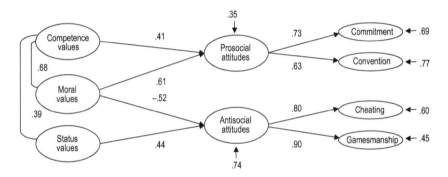

All paths significant at *p* < .05

Figure 5.1 The direct model: Standardized path coefficients for the total sample

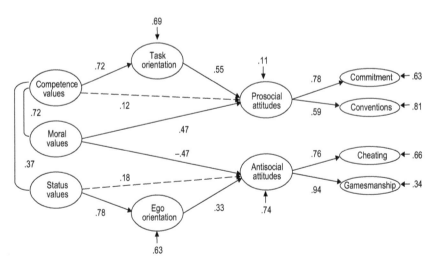

Paths indicated by solid lines are significant at *p* < .05

Figure 5.2 The mediated model: Standardized path coefficients for the total sample

THE DIRECT MODEL

As hypothesised, moral values positively predicted prosocial attitudes and nega-tively predicted antisocial attitudes. Similarly, competence and status values positively predicted prosocial and antisocial attitudes, respectively. All path coef-ficients were moderate to high and significant, with paths from moral values being higher than those from competence and status values. Loadings of the atti-tude scales on the second-order factors were high. Overall, the model explained 88 per cent of variance in the prosocial attitudes and 45 per cent of variance in the antisocial attitudes. Common variance was lower between the two prosocial scales than the two antisocial scales.

THE MEDIATED MODEL

Baron and Kenny (1986) argue that the mediating role of a variable is determined by the reduction in the original direct path between two variables when a third variable is introduced. If the original path becomes zero, full mediation can be claimed, whereas if it drops partial mediation can be claimed. Hence we inserted paths from competence values to task orientation, and from task orientation to prosocial attitudes. Similarly, we inserted paths from status values to ego orienta-tion, and from ego orientation to antisocial attitudes. Our objectives were (a) to ascertain whether the model had an acceptable fit, and (b) to examine any reduc-tion in the direct path coefficients.

The new paths from competence values to task orientation and from status values to ego orientation were high (β = .72 and β = .78 respectively, $p < .05$). The new path from task orientation to prosocial attitudes was moderately high (β = .55, $p < .05$), and the new path from ego orientation to antisocial attitudes was smaller but significant (β = .33, $p < .05$).

Task orientation partially mediated the effect of competence values on proso-cial attitudes, as shown in a reduction of the direct path coefficient from β = .41 ($p < .05$) in the direct model to β = .12, not significant) in the mediated model. The variance explained by this direct path fell from 17 per cent to .01 per cent. Ego orientation partially mediated the effect of status values on antisocial atti-tudes. The direct path coefficient fell from .44 ($p < .05$) to .18 (not significant), and the explained variance fell from 19 per cent to .03 per cent. Overall, 99 per cent of variance in prosocial attitudes and 45 per cent of variance in antisocial attitudes was predicted. In all, the mediation model confirms our predictions that sport values underpin achievement orientations, and that achievement orienta-tions mediate the relationships between certain values and attitudes.

INVARIANCE ACROSS GENDER.

In both the direct and mediated models satisfactory fit indices were obtained for the male and female models, and also for invariance of factor pattern across gender in the non-constrained and constrained models.

Discussion of Study 2

Our research purposes were, first, to examine the direct effect of moral, competence, and status values on prosocial and antisocial attitudes and, second, to examine the mediating role of achievement orientations. We found that prosocial attitudes were predicted positively by both competence and moral values, whereas antisocial attitudes were predicted positively by status and negatively by moral values. Task orientation partially mediated the effect of competence values on prosocial attitudes and ego orientation partially mediated the effect of status values on antisocial attitudes. The relationships were gender invariant.

These findings are important for several reasons. First, the direct effects demonstrate the value-expressive function of attitudes (Katz, 1960) in youth sport. The prosocial attitudes of commitment to sport and respect for its social conventions express moral and competence values. Similarly the antisocial attitudes of cheating and gamesmanship express status values and inversely express moral values. This illustrates that an attitude can reflect more than one value (see Rokeach, 1973) and, moreover, that moral attitudes are derived from both moral and non-moral values. However, moral values predicted both prosocial and antisocial attitudes.

Second, competence and status values strongly predicted task and ego orientation, respectively. Thus, values underpin achievement orientations which, by their nature, illustrate personal theories or world views about achievement contexts. Our findings are consistent with Rohan's (2000) proposal of a process whereby personal value systems lead through world views to attitudes and behavioural decisions. This outcome widens our understanding of possible antecedents of achievement orientations. Nicholls (1989) argued that these orientations arise from cognitive development, socialisation and experience; these are also the roots of value systems (Rokeach, 1973). These data suggest that the role of value systems lies in underpinning achievement orientations and that an institutional value system may function to promote a dominant motivational climate.

Third, and perhaps most importantly, achievement orientations were partial mediators of the effect of competence and status values on attitudes. The mediation was not complete, because the direct paths did not drop to zero. This suggests a cognitive mechanism for the influence of these values on attitudes. For example, high competence values lead participants to display commitment and respect the social conventions of sport because they first adopt an achievement orientation in which success is judged by effort and improvement.

Shields and Bredemeier (2007) argue that achievement orientations include latent moral theories because in addition to a cognitive interpretation of success, they include a motivational intention. They propose that the motives to make oneself better or to look good are adopted for ethical reasons. It follows that values should be antecedents of achievement orientations as our results show. However, we found the mediation of ego orientation to be based on items focused more on cognitive interpretation than motivational intention.

Ego orientation predicted antisocial attitudes less effectively than task orientation predicted prosocial attitudes. It may be that athletes who want to show superiority only condone cheating and gamesmanship when they doubt their ability to succeed honestly. In our case, however, a supplementary (unreported) test showed no moderation by perceived ability. Alternatively, Elliot (1997) argues that maladaptive outcomes of ego orientation accompany avoidance, rather than approach, motivation. Thus ego-oriented athletes who want to avoid looking bad are more likely to seek an unfair advantage than those who expect to look good. POSQ items, however, measure only ego-approach motivation. The directional effects of approach and avoidance motivation on prosocial and antisocial attitudes should be examined.

General discussion

These studies have refined the YSVQ (Lee *et al.*, 2000) demonstrated the value-expressive role of attitudes and examined the role of achievement orientations in mediating the influence of values on prosocial and antisocial attitudes in youth sport competitors. Refining the YSVQ produced three scales measuring different value domains which underpinned prosocial and antisocial attitudes. We then introduced a measure of achievement orientation and found that it had a mediating effect on the influence process. These findings lend support to the view that attitudes towards moral decisions in sport are founded in the value system of the actor and in the prevailing interpretation of success by the actor.

Furthermore we consider that we have identified a psychological mechanism by which moral growth or character development can be achieved through participation in youth sport. If sport is to act as an agent of moral growth, coaches, teachers, and parents should promote moral and competence values rather than status values. This can be achieved by positive modelling on the part of significant others and encouraging both the understanding of moral dilemmas in sport and the importance of making self-referenced evaluations of success. Since competence values are mediated by achievement orientations, encouragement will be facilitated by the creation of task involving conditions and minimising ego involving conditions.

Limitations and future directions

This research has the limitations of a cross-sectional study. Longitudinal research is required to examine the change in these variables over time. The study was also restricted to competitors in early or mid-adolescence who displayed generally favourable ethical attitudes. It should be extended to older competitors and higher levels of competition.

Our direct and mediation models were robust across all samples and it was not necessary to add or delete any paths. Further testing should examine the generalisation of effects, and the mediation model should be adapted to include both approach and avoidance forms of task and ego orientation. We have found a good model fit in a study which used the TEOSQ (Task Ego Orientation in Sport Questionnaire; Duda and Nicholls, 1992) instead of POSQ to measure achievement orientation (Whitehead *et al.*, 2003). Generalisation could also be examined by extending the range of ethical attitudes to include other scales from MSOS and AMDYSQ.

The YSVQ-2 could be extended to examine other issues, such as the conflict between moral and status values. While future research could assess other sport related values, using multi-item scales would be demanding on the attention span of young athletes. We recommend that values are selected to extend our sampling of compatible and conflicting domains because this could provide insight into mechanisms underpinning value conflict and a basis for intervention.

In the interests of instrument development the YSVQ-2 or its derivatives would also benefit from a study of the effect of anchoring the scales with adolescent populations. Bardi (personal communication) suggests that anchoring would improve the degree of differentiation between value domains. This should be done in accordance with the protocol described by Schwartz (1992) in which respondents read all values statements and identify the most and least important to them. The questionnaire would then be completed by items being rated relative to these extremes.

Some values research might parallel work in achievement orientations, as in exploring how competitors' value systems relate to those of significant others. However, our study opens the way for further combined research, since achievement orientations contribute to world views of the achievement context (Duda and Nicholls, 1992), and values can extend this perspective because they cover a more comprehensive motivational field and have a prioritising function (Schwartz, 1992).

This research was limited to cognitive variables. Bardi and Schwartz (2003) showed that values and behaviour yield a common structure across 10 value types. They suggested that value related behaviour is not limited to conscious decision-making processes but can also arise from habitual or spontaneous behaviour. Incidents of fair play or cheating in sport are likely to arise from spontaneous decisions on the field of play, for example deliberately obstructing an opponent in an illegal manner, or from calculated decisions both on and off the field, such as in attempts to deceive a referee or to take drugs to gain a long term advantage. Hence it is important to establish in what conditions values and sport behaviour are related. Kandel (2006) has shown that spontaneous responses may be initiated 200 ms. before a conscious decision can be made, hence the term cheating might be inappropriate for actions not under conscious control.

We suggest that while the observation of real-life sports events may not yield sufficient data in the time available suitably modified computer games could yield a good source of behavioural tendencies of both a spontaneous and considered nature in a time efficient manner.

Conclusion

The view that sport provides a fertile environment for the development of desirable personal and social qualities is commonly expressed by more optimistic educators despite the lack of supporting evidence. However, our data indicate that whether such outcomes are positive (i.e. promote prosocial attitudes) or negative (i.e. promote antisocial attitudes) depends on the value systems that are encouraged and transmitted in the teaching/coaching process. Since sports activities constantly provide situations where competitors are faced with moral dilemmas significant others can use them to encourage competitors to understand and confront the moral dimensions of the decisions they take. Such strategies provide opportunities to both express and encourage value transmission in accordance with the prevailing value system held by significant others.

Because values, mediated by achievement orientations, contribute to the development of prosocial and antisocial attitudes in youth sport both contribute to the paradox that faces sport coaches and teachers, that is, how to develop competition between opponents while also promoting fairness. Significant others should, we consider, endeavour to encourage young people to strive for personal excellence and competitive success while, at the same time, encouraging fairness and respect for both the rules and those opponents.

In summary, the unique contributions of this research were the development of a new instrument to measure sport values, the demonstration that these values underpin both ethical attitudes and achievement orientations in youth sport, and that achievement orientations mediate the effect of some values on ethical attitudes. This work provides a basis for future research into values, attitudes, and behaviour in youth sport and physical education.

References

Allport, G.W. (1961) *Pattern and Growth in Personality*. New York: Holt, Rinehart and Winston.

Anderson, J. C. and Gerbing, D.W. (1988) Structural equation modeling in practice: A review and recommended two-step approach. *Psychological Bulletin*, 103, 411–23.

Bardi, A. and Schwartz, S.H. (2003) Values and behavior: Strength and structure of relations. *Personality and Social Psychology Bulletin*, 29, 1207–20.

Baron, R.M. and Kenney, D.A. (1986) The moderator–mediator variable distinction in social psychological research: Conceptual, strategic, and statistical considerations. *Journal of Personality and Social Psychology*, 51, 1173–82.

Bentler, P.M. (2003) *EQS 6 Structural Equations Program Manual*. Encino, CA: Multivariate Software.

Biddle, S.J.H., Wang, C.K.J., Kavussanu, M. and Spray, C.M. (2003) Correlates of achievement goal orientations in physical activity: A systematic view of research. *European Journal of Sport Science*, 3, 1–20.

Bollen, K.A. (1989) *Structural Equations with Latent Variables*. New York: John Wiley.

Braithwaite, V.S. and Laws, H.G. (1985) Structure of human values: Testing the adequacy of the Rokeach Value Survey. *Journal of Personality and Social Psychology*, 49, 250–63.

Byrne, B. M., Shavelson, R. J. and Muthén, B. (1989) Testing for the equivalence of factor covariance and mean structures: The issue of partial measurement invariance. *Psychological Bulletin*, 105, 456–66.

Cruz, J., Boixadós, M., Valiente, L. and Capdevila, L. (1995) Prevalent values in young Spanish soccer players. *International Review for the Sociology of Sport*, 30, 353–73.

Duda, J.L. (1992) Motivation in sport settings: A goal perspectives approach. In G.C. Roberts (ed.) *Motivation in Sport and Exercise*. Champaign, IL: Human Kinetics, pp. 57–91.

Duda, J.L. and Nicholls, J.G. (1992) Dimensions of motivation in schoolwork and sport. *Journal of Educational Psychology*, 84, 290–9.

Duda, J.L. and Whitehead, J. (1998) Measurement of goal perspectives in the physical domain. In Duda, J.L. (ed.) *Advances in Sport and Exercise Psychology Measurement*. Morgantown, WV: FIT Press, pp. 21–48.

Elliot, A.J. (1997) Integrating the "classic" and "contemporary" approaches to achievement motivation: A hierarchical model of approach and avoidance achievement motivation. In M. Maehr and P. Pintrich (eds) *Advances in Motivation and Achievement*, 10, 143–79. Greenwich, CT: JAI Press.

Fishbein, M. and Ajzen, I. (1975) *Belief, Attitude, Intention and Behavior: An Introduction to Theory and Research*. Reading, MA: Addison-Wesley.

Hu, L. and Bentler, P. M. (1999) Cutoff criteria for fit indices in covariance structure analysis: Conventional criteria versus new alternatives. *Structural Equation Modeling*, 6, 1–55.

Kandel, K.R. (2006) *In Search of Memory: The Emergence of a New Science of Mind*. New York: W.W. Norton.

Katz, D. (1960) The functional study of attitudes. *Public Opinion Quarterly*, 24, 163–204.

Kavalir, P. (2004) Sport in the value system of Czech adolescents: Continuity and change. *International Journal of the History of Sport*, 21, 742–61.

Kluckhohn, C. (1951) Value and value-orientations in the theory of action: An exploration in definition and classification. In Parsons, T. and Shils, E. (eds) *Towards a General Theory of Action*. Cambridge, MA: Harvard University Press, pp. 388–433.

Lee, M.J. (1996) *Young People, Sport and Ethics: An Examination of Fairplay in Sport*. London: Sports Council.

Lee, M.J. and Cockman, M. J. (1995) Values in children's sport: Spontaneously expressed values among young athletes. *International Review for the Sociology of Sport*, 30, 337–52.

Lee, M. J., Whitehead, J. and Balchin, N. (2000) The measurement of values in sport: Development of the Youth Sport Values Questionnaire. *Journal of Sport and Exercise Psychology*, 22, 307–26.

Lee, M.J., Whitehead, J., Ntoumanis, N. and Hatzigeorgiadis, A. (2001) Development of the Sport Attitude Questionnaire. In Papaioannou, A., Goudas, M. and Theodorakis, Y. (eds) *In the Dawn of the New Millennium, Vol 2: Proceedings of the 10th World Congress of Sport Psychology*. Thessaloniki: Christodouli Publications, pp. 191–2.

Lee, M.J., Whitehead, J. and Ntoumanis, N. (2007) Development of the Attitudes to Moral Decision-making in Youth Sport Questionnaire (AMDYSQ). *Psychology of Sport and Exercise*, 8, 369–92.

Mason, V. (1995) *Young People and Sport in England, 1994: A National Survey*. London: Sports Council.

Melech, G. (2001) Value-development in adolescence. Unpublished doctoral dissertation, The Hebrew University of Jerusalem, Israel.

Nicholls, J.G. (1989) *The Competitive Ethos and Democratic Education*. Harvard, MA: Harvard University Press.

Olmstead, R.E. and Bentler, P.M. (1992) Structural equations modeling: A new friend? In Bryant, F.B., Edwards, J., Tindale, R.S., Posavac, E.J., Heath, L., Henderson, E. and

Suarez-Balcazar (eds) *Methodological Issues in Applied Social Psychology*. New York: Plenum, pp. 135–158.

Reynolds, W.M. (1982) Development of reliable and valid short forms of the Marlowe-Crowne Social Desirability Scale. *Journal of Clinical Psychology*, 38, 119–25.

Roberts, G.C., Treasure, D. and Balague, G. (1998) Achievement goals in sport: The development of the Perception of Success Questionnaire. *Journal of Sports Sciences*, 16, 337–47.

Rohan, M.J. (2000) A rose by any name? The value construct. *Personality and Social Psychology Review*, 4, 255–77.

Rokeach, M. (1973) *The Nature of Human Values*. New York: The Free Press.

Schwartz, S. H. (1992) Universals in the content and structure of values: Theoretical advances and empirical tests in 20 countries. In M.P. Zanna (ed.) *Advances in Experimental Social Psychology*, 25, 1–65. London: Academic Press.

Schwartz, S.H. (1994) Are there universal aspects in the structure and content of human values? *Journal of Social Issues*, 50, 19–45.

Shields, D.L.L. and Bredemeier, B.J.L. (2007) Advances in sport morality research. In Tenenbaum, G. and Eklund, R.C. (eds) *Handbook of Sport Psychology*, 3rd. edn. Indianapolis, IN: John Wiley, pp. 662–84.

Vallerand, R.J., Brière, N.M., Blanchard, C. and Provencher, P. (1997) Development and validation of the Multidimensional Sportspersonship Orientation Scale. *Journal of Sport and Exercise Psychology*, 19, 197–206.

Webb H. (1969) Professionalization of attitudes towards play among young adolescents. In Kenyon, G.S. (ed.) *Aspects of Contemporary Sociology*. Chicago, IL: The Athletic Institute, pp. 161–78.

Whitehead, J., Lee, M.J. and Hatzigeorgiadis, A. (2003) Goal orientations as mediators of the influence of values on ethical attitudes in youth sport: Generalization of the model. *Journal of Sports Sciences*, 21(4), 364–5.

Chapter 5 link: Relevance and update

This chapter, which is abridged from a 2008 article, first built on Chapters 2 and 3 by developing the YSVQ-2 to measure higher-order *moral, competence*, and *status* values with multi-items scales which have been cross-validated internationally (Appendix 1).

The new measures were then used to test the influence of values on antisocial attitudes (cheating and gamesmanship from Chapter 4) and prosocial attitudes (commitment and respect). Competence values predicted prosocial attitudes, status values predicted antisocial attitudes, and moral values predicted prosocial attitudes positively and antisocial attitudes negatively. Moreover, the effect of competence and status values on prosocial and antisocial attitudes, were mediated by task and orientation respectively. This suggests that values influence some attitudes by first activating different conceptions of success. It also implies that teachers and coaches should promote moral and competence values and task orientation to encourage prosocial attitudes and reduce any focus on status values and ego orientation to minimise antisocial values.

The model is robust. It was supported for each gender, for high and low levels of perceived ability. Elements of it have been replicated to some extent internationally with other variables. In Italy Lucidi *et al.* (2013) confirmed the model and extended it to include behavioural measures of cheating and gamesmanship. In Lithuania Šukys (2010) found moral values related positively to prosocial behaviour towards team mates and opponents, and negatively to antisocial behaviour to opponents, using Kavussanu and Boardley's (2009) scales. In Greece, working with physical education students, Vatali (2011) related the values to task-involving and ego-involving motivational climates.

Importantly the model explained more variance in the prediction of prosocial attitudes than of antisocial attitudes hence other mediators should be explored to understand the influence of moral and status values on cheating and gamesmanship. Chapter 13 implies that the differential effect of performance approach and avoidance goals could be explored, and also identifies relationships between moral disengagement and both values and attitudes.

References

Kavussanu, M. and Boardley, I.D. (2009) The Prosocial and Antisocial Behaviour in Sport Scale. *Journal of Sport and Exercise Psychology*, 31, 97–117.
Lucidi, F., Mallia, L., Zelli, A., Nicolais, G., and Baldacci, A. (2013) Cheating and gamesmanship in youth Italian players: from attitude to behaviour. Paper presented at the ISSP 13th World Congress of Sport Psychology, Beijing, China.
Šukys, S. (2010) Adaptation and validation of the Prosocial and Antisocial Behavior in Sport Scale and Youth Sport Scale for Lithuanians. *Education, Physical Training, Sport*, 78(3), 97–104.
Vatali, D. (2011) Relationship among values and motivational climate in physical education students. Paper presented at the 3rd International Conference of the Psychological Society of Northern Greece.

6 Are sport values similar in other nations?

Exploring cross-cultural value systems

Jean Whitehead and Carlos E. Gonçalves

A characteristic feature of personal values is that they are relatively few in number and the same values are found universally although their relative importance varies in different cultures (Rokeach, 1973; Schwartz, 1992). Their function depends on their ranking within the hierarchical *value system* of an individual or a social or cultural group, and also on the overall *value structure* or correlational relationships among the values. Thus far this book has introduced the assessment of *value systems* by the YSVQ (Lee *et al.*, 2000; Chapter 3) and made a preliminary examination of the *structure* of higher order values in relationships among the moral, competence and status values types assessed by the YSVQ-2 (Lee *et al.*, 2008; Chapter 5).

In this chapter we first compare the youth sport *value system* found in the UK with corresponding *value systems* found in other nations which have used the Youth Sport Values Questionnaire (YSVQ; Lee *et al.*, 2000) and derive a preliminary international youth sport *value system*, or hierarchy of values. We then compare this youth sport *value system* with a global hierarchy of human values found by Schwartz and Bardi (2001) using the Schwartz Values Survey (SVS; Schwartz, 1992) based on data from 56 nations. This facilitates the integration of the values in the global SVS hierarchy with SVS data from young Australian and Singaporean swimmers (Aplin and Saunders, 2009) to explore how national *value systems* may influence the development of sport potential. We conclude with data from the YSVQ-2 which extends the cross-national sport comparison and prepares for Chapter 8 (by Bardi and Schwartz), in which the Schwartz *value structure* that underlies the SVS is described, and the youth sport values are located within it.

The development of *value systems* is influenced by cultural factors such as the individualistic or collectivist nature of societies and their religious heritage. Thus cross-cultural research has traditionally studied similarities and differences between nations, and the source of these differences. The *emic* approach focuses on *differences* between cultures, while the *etic* approach focuses on *similarities*. In this chapter we will focus on identifying similarities across cultures. Our reasons are twofold. First, when Schwartz and Bardi (2001) looked for similarities across human values, they found a remarkable degree of agreement, leading to new insights. In particular their pan-cultural hierarchy was useful in providing a baseline from which to interpret national differences. Second, our data do not come from matched samples, in which extraneous variables have been controlled; hence any differences may not be reliable.

Our intention is therefore to present preliminary exploratory work, using the first data to become available in a new field for sport study, to guide more systematic future research. Although the *value systems* of young participants will be influenced by their national culture, we expect that a shared experience of competition in youth sport will underpin some consistencies in the sport *value systems* of participants in different countries. If this is so, it is important to discover which features are similar and understand the more universal role of these features, in order to adapt research and practice accordingly.

How similar are youth sport *value systems* across nations?

Lee and his co-workers identified a comprehensive range of 18 values that are salient in youth sport (Lee and Cockman, 1995; Chapter 2) and created the YSVQ to show the hierarchical priorities of these values in the UK (this book, Table 3.2). *Enjoyment* was the most important value, followed by *personal achievement*, and a group of socio-moral values. *Winning* was least important. Rokeach (1973) observed that values at the extremes of a *value system* are more clearly determined than intermediate values, where there is little difference between adjacent ranks. Thus we will explore the similarity of the highest and lowest ranked values across nations.

The 'target' sample, on which the YSVQ was constructed, comprised 500 participants who were selected from a larger sample of 1375 to meet criteria of age (12–15 years), gender, competitive level, and participation in one of 6 nationally popular team and individual sports, hence this was considered to be a representative sample for the UK. An under 16 sample was selected to minimise the distracting effect of major school examinations normally taken at 16 years, which is the minimum school leaving age in the UK. Additional analyses were made of the *value systems* of subgroups defined by gender, age, participation in individual or team sports, and level of competition. Correlations were high to very high, hence the data demonstrated a high degree of consistency of *value systems* across subgroups. In this section we will present similar correlations across national samples, and show graphically the *value system*, or hierarchical priorities of values in the UK and other nations.

Method

Data for the national samples were drawn from published and unpublished studies by researchers who have used the YSVQ (Lee *et al.*, 2000) or translations of it (Table 6.1). This is convenience sampling, but when there was a choice we have selected sub-samples of similar age to the UK sample to provide the best comparison. In the first analyses we include three UK samples to illustrate the range of variability within a nation. These UK samples answered the final version of the

Table 6.1 Source of the national samples for the YSVQ value systems

Nation	Sample size	Age	Participation level	Reference
UK1	M = 233; F = 265	12–15 years	High school or club	Lee *et al.* (2000)
UK2	M = 258; F = 233	12–15 years	High school or club	Lee *et al.* (2008, study 1)
UK3	M = 427; F = 328	12–15 years	High school or club	Lee *et al.* (2008, study 2)
Portugal	M = 220; F = 224	13–16 years	High school or club	Gonçalves and Coelho e Silva (2004)
Spain	M = 247; F = 190	12–16 years	Club leagues	Torregrosa and Lee (2000)
Germany	M = 29; F = 46	11–18 years	Sports clubs	Alfermann and Lee (1997)
Canada	M = 106; F = 99	14–18 years	High school	MacLean and Hamm (2008)

YSVQ (Appendix 4) using the items in Table 3.2 of this book. These are the *proxy items* that were finally selected to represent the initial value descriptors derived from focus group interviews and given in Table 3.1. The Canadian version of the YSVQ used the *value descriptors* in Table 3.1, whereas the Portuguese, Spanish, and German samples used translations of the final items that were back-translated and pilot tested in their own countries. These samples were of high school age and participated in inter-school or inter-club competition, in clubs that were not professionally focused. They form the basis for our analyses. However, it should be noted that the Spanish sample contained only team sport competitors.

Results and discussion

How well do national *value systems* correlate with each other? Table 6.2 presents both parametric correlations for the similarity between the raw scores (national means) for the 18 values and non-parametric correlations for the similarity between rank orders. The latter are usually lower, because ranking methods can be distorted by the varying intervals between adjacent ranks.

These data show, in bold type, that the UK samples correlate highly with each other ($.85 < r < .95$; $.94 < \rho < .95$) and, in the shaded sections, that the UK samples also correlate significantly although to a lesser extent with samples from mainland Europe ($.64 < r < .82$; $.52 < \rho < .78$). In contrast, the UK has only one significant correlation with Canada ($r = .49$).

The mainland European samples, which used local translations of the YSVQ, are shown in italics to correlate significantly with each other ($.67 < r < .88$; $.76 < \rho < .76$), but not with Canada. The highest correlations in mainland Europe are between Spain and Portugal ($r = .88$; $\rho = .76$), two nations with geographical closeness in southern Europe, and similar cultural and religious heritage.

Table 6.2 Correlations among value systems for six nations

	n	Age	UK1	UK2	UK3	Portugal	Spain	Germany	Canada
UK1	500	11–15	–	.94**	.85**	.64**	.76**	.76**	.49*
UK2	483	11–15	.95**	–	.92**	.73**	.83**	.80**	.44
UK3	755	11–15	.94**	.94**	–	.78**	.83**	.82**	.28
Portugal	423	13–16	.53*	.63**	.67**	–	.88**	.67**	.08
Spain	437	12–16	.67**	.67**	.73**	.76**	–	.68**	.27
Germany	75	11–18	.78**	.77**	.78**	.63**	.70**	–	.41
Canada	205	14–18	.31	.29	.27	.11	.21	.47	–

Notes: **p < .01; *p < .05; Parametric correlations (Pearson's *r*) above the diagonal; non-parametric correlations (Spearman's ρ) below the diagonal.

Germany's highest correlations are with the UK (*r* = .82; ρ = .78), in northern Europe.

These data indicate that despite the variety in the samples, and the difficulties that may occur in translation, youth sport *value systems* in Western Europe have much in common. Further generalization of the pattern of national relationships was found in a younger age group. A modified 13-item version of the YSVQ was completed by a large Italian primary school sample of 3197 (Borraccino, 2011). Parametric correlations on 7 identical items ranged from *r* = .71 to *r* = .89 within Europe and the correlation with Canada was .16. However, although the Canadian *value system* showed little overall relationship with the European nations, this sample had an older minimum age (14 years), reflective of the high school system in North America. Moreover, the Canadian values did show similarities with Europe at the extremes of the values hierarchy, as illustrated in Figure 6.2.

Do nations agree about the most and least important values?

The UK *value system* is shown graphically in Figure 6.1 alongside a composite rating of values in Portugal, Spain, Germany, and Canada. Across all nations *enjoyment* and *personal achievement* were most important, and *winning* was least important.

Several values, particularly in the lower half of the hierarchy have greater importance in other nations than in the UK. However, the raw data are misleading because samples differed in the mean importance that they gave to sport values. On a scale of –1 to 5, the mean rating varies from 2.87 (quite important) in the small German sample to 4.02 (very important) in the Portuguese sample (Table 6.3). Thus a value rated 3.5 in Portugal is less important than most other values, whereas a rating of 3.5 in Germany means that the value is more important than most other values. Nevertheless, all nations rated many individual values as 'very important'. The negative skewness in all samples shows that values were typically rated at the higher end of the scale and are thus regarded as

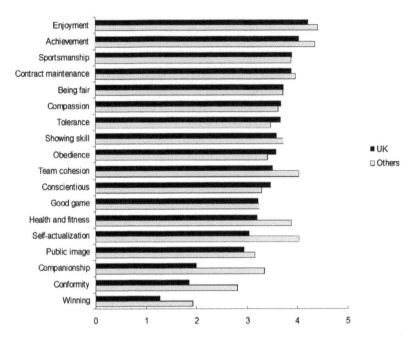

Figure 6.1 Ratings of the 18 YSVQ values by the UK and 4 other national high school
      samples (overall mean)

important guiding principles. The three UK samples had similar means hence
subsequent analyses will use only UK1.

   Using the data in Table 6.3 we have converted the raw data from each sample
into standardised scores (z-scores with a mean of zero and a standard deviation of
1.0) and we present these data in Figure 6.2. Thus values which are rated above
the mean for a nation are plotted to the right, and those rated below the mean to
the left. A normal distribution of scores would fall between –3 and +3.

Table 6.3 Descriptive statistics for value ratings in six nations

	Items	Mean	SD	Minimum	Maximum	Skewness	Kurtosis
Portugal	18	4.02	.59	2.07	4.50	−2.50	7.14
Canada	18	3.83	.72	2.23	4.96	−.11	.11
Spain	18	3.55	.69	1.42	4.39	−1.72	4.83
UK3	18	3.34	.78	1.52	4.46	−1.33	1.37
UK1	18	3.27	.80	1.27	4.22	−1.38	1.31
UK2	18	3.21	.75	1.09	4.26	−1.63	3.14
Germany	18	2.87	1.01	1.03	4.39	−.50	−1.12
Italy	7	3.33	.39	2.37	3.74	−.15	3.15

Note: Shaded values are beyond the normal range. High kurtosis shows a narrow range of scores

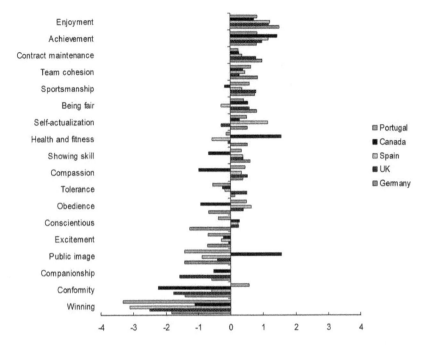

Figure 6.2 Standardized *z*-scores for ratings of 18 YSVQ values in 5 nations

In Figure 6.2 the 18 values are listed on the left in descending order of the mean value rating across all 5 nations. In comparison with Figure 6.1, which ranks values according to the original UK data, values of *team cohesion, self-actualisation,* and *health and fitness* are higher up the hierarchy, while *tolerance* and *compassion* move down. Within each value the national bars are plotted in descending order of the mean importance of sport values in the national samples.

These data confirm the initial impression given in Figure 6.1. They show international similarities in value priorities in the universal ranking of *enjoyment* and *achievement* at the top of the hierarchy and *winning* at the bottom. Moreover, *enjoyment* and *achievement* have positive *z*-scores from every individual nation and there is little variability among the nations. Similarly, *winning* has the lowest international mean and negative *z*-scores from every nation. In a normal distribution 95 per cent of the population falls within 2 standard deviations of the mean, hence the magnitude of these low ratings is unusual. Other values with universal positive scores are *contract maintenance* (keeping a contract) and *team cohesion.* Lee *et al.* (Chapter 3) observed initially that *achievement* was followed by a group of five socio-moral values. It would be unusual if this ranking was replicated across all nations, but the socio-moral values of *contract maintenance, sportsmanship,* and *being fair* retain a high position. This suggests that a positive moral attitude is accepted in the young competitors.

The figure also shows distinctive national differences in the intermediate ranks. For example, Canada's high ratings for *health and fitness* and for *public image*, and low ratings for *showing skill* and *compassion*, are in opposition to the ratings of other nations, and indicate why the Canadian sample had low overall correlations with the European data. However, it is inappropriate to offer post hoc explanations of observed national differences because the samples were not carefully matched. Specifically, the Canadian researchers have told us that their data came from an elite private high school with a high public image. Similarly, a contributory factor in the higher ranking of *team cohesion* may be the absence of competitors in individual sports in the Spanish sample. In some cases, a translated item might have a subtly different interpretation from the original. More data should be obtained from systematic research and selection of samples on the basis of theoretical predictions before conclusions are drawn.

How does the youth sport *value system* relate to a pan-cultural hierarchy of human values?

In the wider context of adult values, not restricted to sport, Schwartz and Bardi (2001) observed that most cross-cultural studies of values have focused on national differences based on such variables as genetic heritage, personal experience, and social location. In contrast, they sought national similarities and found remarkable consistency in the value priorities of representative samples, teachers, and students across 56 nations. The representative samples included a diversity of age, gender, occupation, education level, cultural region, economic and political systems, history, socio-economic development, and other variables. These researchers employed the SVS (Schwartz, 1992) which uses 56 items to assess the importance of 10 motivationally-based value types 'as a guiding principle in my life'. These value types are described by Bardi and Schwartz in Chapter 8 of this book.

The pan-cultural hierarchy obtained from these samples is presented in Figure 6.3. It shows values of *benevolence* (preserving the welfare of those with whom one is in frequent content) to be most important, slightly ahead of *self-direction* (independent thought and action) and *universalism* (protecting the welfare of all). *Power* values (social status and dominance over others) are least important. Schwartz and Bardi (2001) interpret this hierarchy as a logical outcome of three requirements for human existence and social functioning. That is, members must value their in-group, cooperate for effective functioning, and also receive some gratification as individuals.

We offer three observations on the relationship of the values at the extremes of the youth sport hierarchy to this adult *value system*. First, the sport value of *winning* is represented by Schwartz's category of *power* values, not his category of achievement values. Power values are seen here to be unambiguously the least important values in adult life. Thus the low ranking of winning, identified initially by Lee *et al.* (2000) in the UK, and then found in this chapter to be similar in other nations, is entirely consistent with the global hierarchy of human values. Second, the value of *enjoyment* which is at the top of the youth sport *value system*, represents

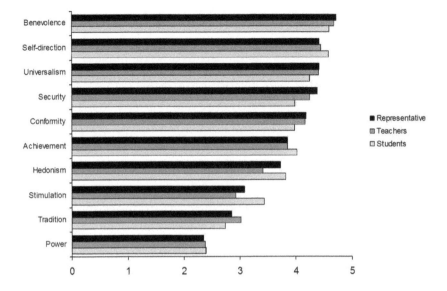

Figure 6.3 A global value system shown by the pan-cultural hierarchy of human values of Schwartz and Bardi (2001)

Schwartz' category of hedonism which is located in the lower half of his adult hierarchy. In this case the placing of the youth sport values is inconsistent with the global hierarchy. We suggest that this might occur because the priorities in youth sport are less likely to reflect needs of human survival which underlie the SVS hierarchy than the characteristic of a voluntary activity, freely chosen by young athletes because it is attractive to them. Finally, the high placing of *personal achievement* in the youth sport hierarchy, which represents self-referenced achievement, corresponds with the high place of *self-direction* in the adult hierarchy.

Here we must point out that this chapter focuses only on an exploration of hierarchical *value systems*. There are also structural relationships among Schwartz's values which cannot be determined from a hierarchy of priorities. These are centrally important in the study of values, and the resulting relationships among conflicting and compatible values underpin informed interventions. These are explained by Bardi and Schwartz in Chapter 8 where the probable location of the YSVQ and YSVQ-2 values within the global Schwartz model is also described.

Do national *value systems* influence the realisation of sport potential?

Is there a sub-culture for elite sport?

We have so far reported youth sport data for 'national' samples, but many sport groups are not representative of their national population and form their own subcultures within different sports and at different levels of experience. In a comprehensive study of the values of young Singaporean and Australian swimmers (13–16 years) with different levels of commitment to swimming, Aplin and Saunders (2009) administered the Schwartz SVS which measures the 10 value categories illustrated in Figure 6.3. In Table 6.4 we have correlated their youth sport data with the global adult data of Schwartz and Bardi (2001) to illustrate that *value systems* of the progressively more elite swimmers diverged systematically from the pan-cultural human *value system*, as shown in the progressively lower correlations highlighted. However, a comparison of the global *value system* with matched groups of Singaporean and Australian swimmers at the top of the last two columns shows that strong cultural differences in *value systems* remained, since the Singaporeans had significant relationships with the pan-cultural hierarchy but the Australians did not.

National differences

In further exploration of these national differences Table 6.5 shows the ranking and rating of the Schwartz basic values by Australian and Singaporean swimmers. The differences between the two nations, when the importance of values for each individual was held constant, were significant, and 44 per cent of the variance in scores was explained by nationality. Singaporeans regarded *universalism, benevolence* and *tradition* as more important than did Australians, while Australians gave greater priority to *achievement, hedonism, stimulation* and *self-direction*. These values cluster around contrasting poles of the Schwartz model as will be described in Chapter 8 which focuses on *value structure*.

Table 6.4 Correlations among SVS values in the general population and in competitive swimmers

	General				Swimmers			
	Represent-ative	Teachers	Students	Sub-specialist	Specialist	Elite	Singa-pore	Aust-ralia
General (Schwartz and Bardi, 2001)								
Representative		.99**	.96**	.91**	.78**	.46	.87*	.41
Teachers	.99**		.93**	.94**	.74**	.37	.87**	.30
Students	.96**	.95**		.88**	.85**	.60	.88**	.57
Swimmers (Aplin and Saunders, 2009)								
Subspecialist	.80**	.83**	.80**		.83*	.49	.95**	.40
Specialist	.62	.61	.72*	.85**		.85**	.93**	.79*
Elite	.20	.16	.32	.41	.72*		.64*	.99**
Singapore	.74*	.73*	.83*	.90**	.94**	.56		.55
Australia	.15	.10	.47	.29	.61	.98**	.43	

Notes: **$p < .01$; *$p < .05$; Parametric correlations (Pearson's r) above the diagonal; nonparametric correlations (Spearman's ρ) below the diagonal

Table 6.5 Ranking, rating and differences in value types in Australian and Singaporean swimmers

Rank	Singapore Value type	Mean	SD	Australia Value type	Mean	SD	National differences	F	Sig.	η^2
1	Achievement	4.71	1.09	Hedonism	5.07	1.13	Power	1.48	.23	.02
2	Benevolence	4.69	.84	Achievement	4.95	.87	Achievement	8.42	.01	.09
3	Conformity	4.66	.99	Self-direction	4.59	.75	Hedonism	26.54	.00	.35
4	Self-direction	4.37	1.09	Stimulation	4.48	1.42	Stimulation	1.25	.00	.11
5	Universalism	4.22	.91	Conformity	4.32	1.17	Self-direction	7.22	.01	.08
6	Security	4.21	1.01	Security	4.16	1.03	Universalism	18.47	.00	.19
7	Hedonism	3.93	1.76	Benevolence	4.11	.78	Benevolence	10.51	.00	.12
8	Stimulation	3.76	1.61	Universalism	3.44	.89	Conformity	.67	.42	.01
9	Tradition	3.52	1.11	Power	3.29	1.26	Tradition	7.62	.01	.09
10	Power	3.24	1.38	Tradition	2.75	1.25	Security	1.35	.25	.02

Notes: On the left of the table values are separately ranked for each nation. On the right the values are listed in their order in the Schwartz model. Values in which Australians scored higher have lighter shading, and values in which Singaporeans scored higher have darker shading.

Source: Aplin and Saunders (2009)

The *value systems* of these swimmers share some characteristics of adult *value systems* in their own country but Aplin and Saunders (2009) argue that they are distinctive enough to represent a swimming sub-culture.

Implications

Aplin and Saunders argue that the traditional Singaporean values, which focus on developing economic security and racial harmony, make if difficult for swimmers to develop the level of commitment shown by Australians, who give more importance to *self-direction*, *stimulation*, and *hedonism*. We expected that, although individual youth sport *value systems* would be influenced by national culture, a shared experience in competitive sport would underpin some consistencies. The SVS data for these swimmers demonstrate that competitors did show strong cultural differences in their *value systems*, with Singaporeans being closer to the global system, but there were also consistent differences in values associated with systematic increases in sport commitment (Aplin and Saunders, 2009). Further relationships between values and swimming performance are discussed in Chapter 13 about future directions.

A concluding note on YSVQ-2 data from a wider geographical area

This chapter has focused on *value systems* assessed in youth sport by the YSVQ, and in adult life by the SVS. We conclude with complementary cross-cultural data from the YSVQ-2 (Lee *et al.* 2008; Chapter 5). This simplifies the hierarchical relationships by using only three higher order youth sport values, and also facilitates discussion of the structural relationships among these three key values in Chapter 8. Moreover the data are drawn from four continents and thus extend the potential generalisation of the pattern of results.

Conceptual framework for the YSVQ-2

Whereas the YSVQ assesses 18 values by single items, the YSVQ-2 assesses youth sport values by multi-item scales, as is the case in the SVS (Chapter 8). *Moral*, *competence*, and *status* values were selected as the first higher order sport values to be assessed in this way.

The scales represent key reference points in the structure of human values proposed by Rokeach (1973) and extended by Schwartz (1992). First, the *moral* and *competence* values represent Rokeach's interpersonal and intrapersonal values, since our moral items are socio-moral and our competence values are self-referenced. Second, the interpersonal *moral* and *status* values illustrate the opposing self-transcendent and self-enhancing poles of Schwartz. Third, given that sport represents a classical achievement situation (McClelland *et al.*, 1953), our *competence* and *status* values represent intrapersonal and interpersonal interpretations of achievement. Although we derived them from the major dimensions of leading value researchers, they have some correspondence with the task and ego goal orientations which have provided a central paradigm for research in youth sport for some decades. Fourth, these values represent the three parsimonious categories of Webb (1969) in one of the earliest value studies in sport: playing fairly, playing well, and winning.

The cross-cultural and concurrent validity of the YSVQ-2 are given in Appendix 1. We have deferred the presentation of that data in order that the structural location of the sport values measured by the YSVQ and YSVQ-2 can first be related to SVS values by Bardi and Schwartz in Chapter 8.

Supplementary findings with the YSVQ-2

The following YSVQ-2 data supplement the YSVQ data from Western Europe and North America with complementary data from Eastern Europe, Asia, Africa, and South America (Table 6.6).

The YSVQ-2 does not include the value of *enjoyment*, but the standardised data in Figure 6.4 reflect the other priorities shown in the YSVQ data although with different terminology. The higher-order *competence* value type, which is self-referenced in nature and includes values of *personal achievement* and *self-direction*, is consistently ranked highest. The *status* value type, which is comparative in nature and includes values of *winning* and *public image*, has the lowest rank. *Moral* values, including *fairness* and *keeping a contract*, hold an intermediate position. The Lithuanian sample is not drawn from youth sport but comprises elite university competitors many of them at international level. We include it to show that, although these elite competitors have a lower regard for

Table 6.6 National samples with YSVQ-2 data

Nation	Sample size	Age	Participation level	Reference
UK	M = 427; F = 328	12–15 years	Inter-school, club or higher	Lee *et al.* (2008)
Portugal	M = 206; F = 217	13–16 years	High school	Gonçalves, C. *et al.* (2005)
Greece	M = 111; F = 101	12–15 years	Inter-school, club or higher	Gymnopoulou and Vatali (2009)
Lithuania	M = 138; F = 32	University	Elite team players	Šukys (2010)
Kenya	M = 181; F = 92	10–18 years	Youth sport leagues	Kanyiba Nyaga (2011)
Japan	M = 364; F = 109	15–17 years	High school	Fukami *et al.* (2012)
Hong Kong	M = 77; F = 23	11–18 years	Junior golf	Chan *et al.* (2013)
Brazil	M = 50; F = 92	12–18 years	School and club teams	Gonçalves, M. *et al.* (2012)

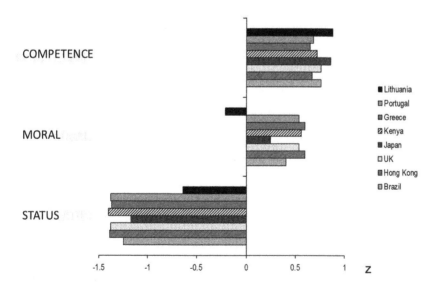

Figure 6.4 Rank order of YSVQ-2 standardized scores for competence, moral and status values in eight nations

moral values than the youth sport competitors, even at this elite level the *status* values, which include values of *winning* and *public image*, have the lowest priority.

In sum, these simple data demonstrate that the *competence* values which illustrate an intrapersonal perspective on achievement are given higher priority around the world than are the *status* values which illustrate the interpersonal perspective. It suggests that personal best performance is more highly valued than winning. In Webb's terms, playing well is somewhat more important than playing fairly which is far more important than winning.

Conclusions, limitations, and future directions

At the start of this exploratory chapter we expected that although the *value systems* of young competitors would be influenced by their national culture, a shared experience of youth sport would underpin some consistencies in value priorities. The data support both expectations.

Cultural influences on *value systems* were illustrated in the correlational data. European nations showed a high degree of similarity in their youth sport *value systems*, with the greatest similarities occurring between nations that are close in geographical location and religious heritage. However, Western Europe showed little overall similarity with Canada. Likewise, Aplin and Saunders's (2009) data showed cultural differences in the contrasting *value systems* of Singaporean and Australian swimmers.

Nevertheless, the hierarchical data show strong consistencies across western European and North American samples, in the values at the extremes of the YSVQ hierarchies. *Enjoyment* and *achievement* were most important, and *winning* was least important. Supplementary comparisons with the YSVQ-2 which does not include *enjoyment* showed that the low ranking of *status* values, including *winning*, and a high ranking of *competence* values including *personal achievement*, extended to samples from Eastern Europe, Asia, Africa, and South America. Moreover, when the youth sport hierarchies were compared with the pan-cultural hierarchy of adult values (Schwartz and Bardi, 2001) this low ranking of *winning* in sport was seen to be consistent with the low ranking of *power* values in daily life while the high ranking of *personal achievement* and *competence* in youth sport corresponded to the importance of *self-direction* values in adult life.

The low priority given to *winning* is a striking universal finding and appears characteristic of human *value systems*. This should inform the media and policy makers who sometimes argue that a low priority on *winning* is the outcome of deficient local teaching or coaching methods. However, we must also point out that *all* values were regarded – both by definition and by participants – as important guiding principles in youth sport, or in life, hence *winning* is an important value, and this low ranking is relative to other values. Nevertheless, our data suggest that sport participation is most likely to be prolonged when young competitors believe that they are improving and having fun. Competitors in many sports focus on obtaining a personal best performance which is more under their own control than is winning.

A limitation of the research is the use of convenience sampling and the inclusion of some unpublished data. Future research should verify our findings and select samples systematically to explore *value systems* related to different nations, sports, ages, and levels of competition. This book focuses on youth sport, and it is likely that values in adult professional sport will differ. Recent work by Fisher and Schwartz (2012) in more than 60 countries found more variation in *value systems* within nations, than between them, such that they questioned a major role for cultural influence. However, as cross-cultural research proceeds, our preliminary international values hierarchy for youth sport provides an initial baseline from which to interpret data from nations who rate the importance of sport values differently. This chapter has been confined to the study of *value systems*. Chapter 8 provides an integrated view of the complementary roles of *value systems* and *value structure*.

References

Alfermann, D. and Lee, M.J. (1997) Unpublished data, University of Leipzig, Germany.

Aplin, N. and Saunders, J. (2009) *Values and the Pursuit of Sports Excellence: Swimmers from Singapore and Australia.* Saarbrücken: VDM Verlag.

Bardi, A. and Schwartz, S.H. (2013) How does the value structure underlie value conflict? Chapter 8, this book.

Borraccino, A. (2011) I valori nello sport [Values in sport]. In R. Grimaldi, *Valori e modelli nello sport: Una ricerca nelle scuole del Piemonte con Stefania Belmondo.* Milan: Franco Angeli.

Chan, Y., Whitehead, J., Hatzigeorgiadis A. and Chow, B. (2013) Sport values and ethical attitudes in young Hong Kong golfers. Paper presented at the ISSP 13th World Congress of Sport Psychology, Beijing, China.

Fischer, R. and Schwartz, S. (2011) Whence differences in value priorities? Individual, cultural or artifactual sources. *Journal of Cross-Cultural Psychology*, 42(7), 1127–44.

Fukami, K., Kondo, A., Ishidate, K., Fukami, M. and Mizouochi, F. (2012) Social attitudes in sport of high school students: verification of measurements-composition. *The Ohmon Research Bulletin of Physical Education*, Nihon University, 45(1), 1–8.

Gonçalves, C.E and Coelho e Silva, M. (2004) Values in youth sport: a study across gender, type of sport, and context. In *Proceedings of the Vth Annual Congress of the Spanish Association of Physical Education.* Valencia: University of Valencia.

Gonçalves, C.E., Cardoso, L., Freitas, F., Lourenço, J. and Coelho e Silva, M. (2005) Valores no desporto de jovens: concepções, instrumentos e limitações [Values in youth sport: concepts, instruments and limits]. *Boletim da Sociedade Portuguesa de Educação Física*, 30–1, 93–110.

Gonçalves, M.P., Oliveira, L.C. and Moura, M.A.R. (2012) Validation of the Youth Sport Values Questionnaire-2 in Brazil. Unpublished preliminary data. Universidade Federal do Vale do São Francisco, Brazil.

Gymnopoulou, V. and Vatali, D. (2009) Relationships among goal orientations and values in adolescent students. In *Proceedings of 10th Thematic Congress of Northern Greece Physical Education Teachers Association.* Thessaloniki: Northern Greece Physical Education Teachers Association, p. 53.

Kanyiba Nyaga, L.R. (2011) Valued outcomes in youth sport programs in Kenya: Towards the government's Vision 2030. Doctoral dissertation, Springfield College, MA.

Lee, M.J. and Cockman, M. (1995) Values in children's sport: Spontaneously expressed values among young athletes. *International Review for Sociology of Sport*, 30(3/4), 337–50.

Lee, M.J., Whitehead, J. and Balchin, N. (2000) The measurement of values in youth sport: Development of the Youth Sport Values Questionnaire. *Journal of Sport and Exercise Psychology*, 22, 588–610.

Lee, M.J, Whitehead, J., Ntoumanis, N. and Hatzigeorgiadis, A. (2008) Relationships among values, achievement orientations, and attitudes in youth sport. *Journal of Sport and Exercise Psychology*, 30(5), 588–610.

MacLean, J. and Hamm, S. (2008) Values and sport participation: Comparing participant groups, age, and gender. *Journal of Sport Behavior*, 31(4), 352–67.

McClelland, D.C., Atkinson, J.W., Clark, R.A. and Lowell, E.L. (1953) *The Achievement Motive*. New York: Appleton-Century-Crofts.

Rokeach, M. (1973) *The Nature of Human Values*. New York: The Free Press.

Schwartz, S.H. (1992) Universals in the content and structure of values: theoretical advances and empirical tests in 20 countries. In M.P. Zanna, *Advances in Experimental Social Psychology*, 25, 1–65. New York: Academic Press.

Schwartz, S.H. and Bardi, A. (2001) Value hierarchies across cultures: Taking a similarities perspective. *Journal of Cross-Cultural Psychology*, 32, 268–90.

Šukys, S. (2010) Adaptation and validation of the Prosocial and Antisocial Behavior in Sport Scale and Youth Sport Values Questionnaire into Lithuanian. *Lithuanian Academy of Physical Education: Education, Physical Training, Sport* 3(78), 97–104.

Šukys, S. and Jansonienė, A.J. (2012) Relationship between athletes' values and moral disengagement in sport, and differences across gender, level and years of involvement. *Education, Physical Training, Sport*, 84(1), 55–61.

Torregrosa M. and Lee, M. (2000) El studio de los valores en psicologia del deporte [The study of values in sport psychology]. *Revista de Psicologia del Deporte*, 9(1–2), 71–83.

Webb, H. (1969) Professionalization of attitudes towards play among adolescents. In G.S. Kenyon (ed.) *Aspects of Contemporary Sport Sociology*. Chicago, IL: The Athletic Institute, pp. 161–78.

Whitehead, J., Telfer, H. and Lambert, J. (2013) What questions remain? Chapter 13, this book.

7 How do values relate to motivation?

Values and motivational processes in youth sport: An AGT and SDT perspective

Isabel Balaguer, Isabel Castillo, Eleanor Quested and Joan L. Duda

A major consideration among coaches, teachers, and others significant to the sporting experience is the role of sport as a vehicle to promote young performers' optimal social and psychological functioning. For many years, researchers as well as practitioners have mused on what personal and social factors facilitate versus forestall the promotion of adaptive behaviours, thoughts and emotions among young athletes. Two theoretical constructs that researchers have utilised in attempting to answer these questions are *motivation* and *values*. In the sport context, the study of the determinants and consequences of motivation has been a major research focus over the past four decades. However, in comparison, the topic of values has received scant attention in the sport literature. As a result, little is known regarding the interplay between values and motivation in this domain.

In mainstream cultural values discourse, it has been proposed that values do impact motivation (Rokeach, 1973; Schwartz, 1994). Rokeach (1973) considered values as having an inherent motivational component, and in the same vein, Schwartz (1994) described values as fundamentally motivational in their function. Other researchers also argue that a deeper understanding of how values relate to motivation is important because this would provide greater insight into human behaviour as well as uncover possibilities of how human functioning can be optimised (Parks and Guay, 2009).

In this chapter, we aim to extend current thinking on motivation in the sport domain. Specifically, we will go beyond considerations of motivation as purely a quantitative entity and describe how motivation can be differentiated in terms of *quality*, drawing from achievement goal theory (AGT; Ames, 1992; Dweck, 1999; Nicholls, 1989) and self-determination theory (SDT; Deci and Ryan, 1985, 2000). In the context of these theories, we will consider how personal values are linked to motivation-related individual differences in how competence is judged and success defined (i.e. differences in dispositional achievement goals) and motivation regulations (i.e. the degree of self-determination reflected in reasons for engagement) within sport. Both AGT and SDT consider that motivation is reflected in the goal-directed behaviour of individuals in particular settings and highlight the motivational significance of the meaning behind such striving. Not all these meanings (as captured in achievement goals and motivation regulations) are assumed to be created equal; theory, and related empirical evidence in different contexts including sport, inform us that only when these motivational processes are adaptive (i.e. reflect quality motivation) are we likely to witness engagement that results in optimal functioning and personal growth. That is, the strength of both AGT and SDT is that they clarify the motivation-related mechanisms that contribute to the promotion of positive as well as compromised involvement in activities such as sport (Deci and Ryan, 2000; Dweck, 1999; Nicholls, 1989). According to these theoretical frameworks, adaptive and personal growth conducive to sport engagement is more likely to occur when athletes adopt a strong task goal focus and have more intrinsic and autonomous reasons for their participation.

Personal values are understood to interrelate with goals and act as an overarching guide of action for individuals in different contexts of action. To examine which values are related to the motivational processes (i.e. achievement goals and motivation regulations) emphasised in both AGT and SDT is the principal objective of the present work.

In this chapter, we first introduce the achievement goal (Ames, 1992; Dweck, 1999; Nicholls, 1989) and the self-determination (Deci and Ryan, 1985; 2000) theories, in order to present their principal constructs and predictions. Then, we briefly describe the concept of personal values as guides of action. Next, we present an empirical study exploring the interplay between personal values, motivation regulations and goal orientations in the sport context.

Achievement goal theory

Achievement goal theory proposes that individuals' achievement-related goals are key determinants of motivation-related cognitions, affect, and behaviour (Ames, 1992; Dweck, 1999; Nicholls, 1989). According to Nicholls (1989), there are at least two major achievement goals operating, namely a task (or mastery) goal and an ego (or performance) goal, which stem from how competence is construed. When task-involved, one's perceived level of competence is self-referenced and dependent on the individual's own demonstration of learning, performance improvement and/or task mastery. The importance of working hard and working well with others is also linked to individuals' tendency to be task-involved. When ego-involved, one feels competent and thereby successful when comparatively superior ability is demonstrated. That is, perceptions of competence are other-referenced when ego goals prevail and it is important to show that one is better than others (or not worse). A central feature of AGT is the premise that task and ego goal perspectives are orthogonal. That is, one can be high in one and low in the other, or high in both or low in both (Duda, 2001).

With respect to achievement processes and associated behavioural patterns, AGT (Dweck, 1999; Nicholls, 1989) holds that it is not only the level of perceived competence that is pertinent to goal striving and resulting learning/performance, but also how such competence is judged. More specifically, it is proposed that a task goal focus will result in optimal learning and sustained performance as well as greater perseverance, regardless of whether the performer perceives his or her competence to be high or low (Dweck, 1999; Nicholls, 1989). This is because it has been assumed, and empirically supported in the sport context (Roberts, 2012), that task involvement will translate into more concentrated effort and intrinsic interest in the activity, and a greater utilisation of effective strategies to meet task demands.

An extensive literature has examined the correlates and effects of dispositional (i.e. achievement goal orientations) and situational (i.e. the motivational climate) task and ego achievement goal emphases in sport settings (for reviews, see Duda, 2001; Duda and Balaguer, 2007; Duda and Hall, 2001; Duda and Whitehead, 1998). Collectively, this research provides evidence regarding the motivational advantages of a strong task goal emphasis, from the standpoint of dispositional tendencies or the motivational climates deemed to be operating. That is, from the standpoint of AGT, a strong task orientation lays the bases for quality motivation and positive engagement in achievement settings such as sport.

Self-determination theory

SDT (Deci and Ryan, 1985; Ryan and Deci, 2000a) centres on the 'why' of behaviour and proposes that human motivation varies in the degree to which behaviour is freely initiated and regulated by a sense of choice and volition (autonomous, self-determined) or is regulated by internal or external contingencies (controlled). SDT categorises that behaviour regulations into three types, namely intrinsic motivation, extrinsic motivation and behaviours guided by no clear regulation (amotivation).

Intrinsic motivation represents the most autonomous form of motivation, and reflects an inherent tendency possessed by all humans to seek out novelty and challenges, to explore and to learn. When intrinsically motivated, individuals will pursue a goal or activity because the pursuit is enjoyable or intrinsically captivating, and satisfaction experienced is inherent in the activity. Extrinsic motivation refers to behaviours conducted to obtain outcomes unrelated to the activity itself and is conceptualised to be a multidimensional construct, incorporating external, introjected and identified regulations. External regulation can be defined as behaviour regulated by extrinsic, instrumental reasons (e.g. to attain an external reward and/or to avoid punishment). With introjected regulation, the impetus for action stems from the perceived need to avoid negative emotions, such as anxiety or culpability or to obtain ego enhancement such as pride. Identified regulation, capturing a more autonomous or self-determined form of extrinsic motivation, 'reflects a conscious valuing of a behavioural goal or regulation; such that the action is accepted or owned as personally important' (Ryan and Deci, 2000a: 72). Amotivation exists when individuals passively engage in activities without any sense of intention. Amotivation reflects a lack of any clear reason to engage in the activity and is produced when people feel incompetent, and/or do not value an activity, or do not perceive any contingencies (internal or external) between their actions and the desired outcome(s) (Deci and Ryan, 1985; Ryan and Deci, 2000b).

Deci and Ryan (1985, 2000) have proposed that intrinsic motivation and certain forms of more self-determined extrinsic motivation (primarily identified regulation and, in some rare cases, introjected regulation) enhance psychological functioning (e.g. task absorption, non-contingent sense of self-worth), and thus lead to positive outcomes. On the other hand, it is proposed that types of motivation that are low (e.g. external regulation) or absent (amotivation) in self-determination relate to maladaptive cognitive, affective, and behavioural responses (e.g. burnout) and research in the physical domain supports these propositions (e.g. Balaguer *et al.*, 2011; Standage *et al.*, 2003).

Schwartz's theory of the contents and structure of individual values

In Chapter 5 of this book (Lee *et al.*, 2008) the relationship between motivational processes and values has been explored based on values derived directly from youth sport. In the present chapter we adopt the model of values in the wider context of adult life developed by Schwartz (1992, 2012). In both cases, values are defined as broad, transituational goals that vary in importance and reflect guiding principles in people's lives. More specifically, values are (a) motivational goals that transcend specific situations, (b) inherently desirable and are cognitively represented in ways that enable people to communicate about them, and (c) personal beliefs (Roccas *et al.*, 2002).

As has been identified in the Introduction and is presented in detail by Bardi and Schwartz in Chapter 8 of this book, Schwartz's theory of individual values assumes that people's values are ordered into hierarchies of personal importance and holds that higher values are more likely to guide people's life. In his theory, Schwartz has distinguished between the *content* and *structure* of the values and argued that the former creates the latter. With respect to the *content of values*, in Table 7.1 we can see the ten basic values defined by Schwartz (1992) according to the motivational content that underlies them. Each basic value is defined by a number of items that represent actions contributing to the central goal of the basic value in question. Although there is variation in the importance individuals may place on the different values, there are also near-universal similarities in value importance (see Chapter 8). It is understandable then why Schwartz (1992) argues that these basic values play a guiding role in how individuals process and respond to various salient contexts in their life (e.g. sport).

Regarding the *structure of values*, Figure 7.1 presents the ten motivationally distinct values and their circular motivational structure ordered according to the motivation that undergirds each one of them. Every two adjacent values in the circle share a common motivation. Schwartz and his colleagues have developed a theoretically-based values taxonomy based on a circumplex structure. More highly correlated values are situated closer together, while lower correlations between values are reflected via greater distance between the points. In contrast,

Table 7.1 Definitions of Schwartz's basic values

Value	Definition	Single values
Power	Social status and prestige, control of dominance over people and resources	Social power, authority, wealth, protecting my public image
Achievement	Personal success through demonstrating competence according to social standards	Successful, capable, ambitious, influential
Hedonism	Pleasure and sensuous gratification for oneself	Pleasure, enjoying life
Stimulation	Excitement, novelty, and challenge in life	Daring, a varied life, exciting life
Self-direction	Independent thought and action-choosing, creating, exploring	Creativity, freedom, independent, curious, choosing own goals
Universalism	Understanding, appreciation, tolerance and protection for the welfare of all people and for nature	Broadminded, wisdom, social justice, equality, a world at peace, a world of beauty, unity with nature, protecting the environment
Benevolence	Preservation and enhancement of the welfare of people with whom one is in frequent personal contact	Helpful, honest, forgiving, loyal, responsible
Tradition	Respect, commitment and acceptance of the customs and ideas that traditional culture or religion provide the self	Humble, accepting my portion in life, devout, respect for tradition, moderate
Conformity	Restraint of actions, inclinations, and impulses likely to upset or harm others and violate social expectations or norms	Politeness, obedient, self-discipline, honouring parents and elders
Security	Safety, harmony and stability of society, of relationships, and of self	Family security, national security, social order, clean, reciprocation of favours

Source: Adapted from Bardi and Schwartz (Chapter 8, this book)

values that are across from one another on the circumplex will tend to conflict and are therefore in opposing positions in the circle. Bardi and Schwartz point out (see Chapter 8) that it is quite difficult, and sometimes impossible, to pursue conflicting values. The structure proposed by Schwartz and colleagues has been confirmed in many studies undertaken in more than 50 countries (e.g. Schwartz, 1992, 1994; Schwartz and Sagiv, 1995).

The circle of values can also be viewed as being composed of four higher order basic values that form two bi-polar orthogonal dimensions: *self-enhancement* (power, achievement) versus *self-transcendence* (universalism, benevolence), and *conservation* (security, tradition, conformity) versus *openness to change*

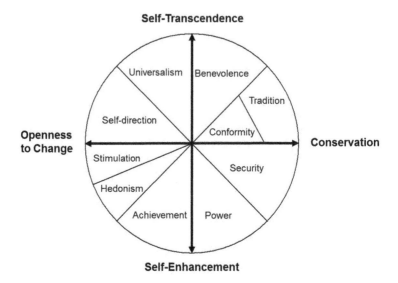

Figure 7.1 Structure of values representing the ten basic values and their motivational
structure

Source: adapted from Schwartz (1992)

(self-direction, stimulation). See Chapter 8 for a more detailed description of
these dimensions. In our work, these four second-order dimensions have been
supported in data from 505 Spanish students between the ages of 15 and 19 years.
Confirmatory factorial analyses of a Spanish version of the questionnaire
provided evidence for the validity of the theoretical typology of the ten values and
the assumed 4 second-order factors (Balaguer *et al.*, 2006).

Achievement goals, self-determination and values

As has been pointed out previously (e.g. Duda *et al.*, 2005), there are a number of
commonalities between the self-determination (Deci and Ryan, 1985, 2000) and
achievement goal (Dweck, 1999; Nicholls, 1989) frameworks. Both centre on variations in the meaning of the achievement-related behaviour, and more specifically
the two frameworks hold that these differences in meaning have important implications for the quality of the motivational processes operating and the quality of the
sport experience. The postulates of, and the empirical evidence supporting, AGT
and SDT point to the benefits of adopting more personally controllable, task-
centred, and self-referenced motivational approaches to sport engagement. Previous
research has found that a task orientation corresponds to greater intrinsic motivation and other more self-determined regulations (e.g. Kavussanu and Roberts,
1996). Ego orientation and perceptions of an ego-involving climate are more
strongly and positively associated with external motivation than with other types of
regulation (Balaguer *et al.*, 2011; Petherick and Weigand, 2002).

Objectives of the current study

Personal values are assumed to be more global guiding principles which have a motivational function, thereby potentially influencing why people engage, how people act and what is important to them in particular situations. In this work, we examined how athletes' personal (life) values are related to motivational variables (achievement goals and motivation regulations) for sport engagement as emphasised within the achievement goal and self-determination theories. Specifically, we conducted: (1) descriptive analyses of athletes' basic values, second order value dimensions, goal orientations (task and ego) and motivation regulations (intrinsic motivation, identified regulation, introjected regulation, external regulation and amotivation) and (2) regression analyses of basic values and second order value factors on goal orientations and the five types of motivation regulations.

Methodology of the current study

Participants and procedure

A total of 277 adolescent athletes from different sports (163 boys and 114 girls) from the Comunidad Valenciana (Spain), ranging in age from 15 to 18 years (mean = 15.9; SD = .83), participated in this study. All participants had been practicing sport at least 2–3 days per week (mean = 4.15, SD = .75), for over five hours per week (mean = 5.78, SD = .64).

Participation in the study was voluntary and anonymous. After one of their training sessions, the athletes completed a battery of scales (taking approximately 20 minutes). Instructions on how to fill in the multi-section questionnaire were provided by the researcher, emphasising that the athletes should respond as honestly as possible, that there were no right or wrong answers, and that their responses would be kept confidential.

Instruments

Values were assessed by responses to the Spanish adaptation (Balaguer *et al.*, 2006) of the 45-item Schwartz Value Survey (SVS; Schwartz, 1992) which taps ten basic values: conformity, tradition, security, benevolence, universalism, self-direction, stimulation, hedonism, achievement and power (see Table 7.1). When completing the scale, the participants were requested to think about how important these values are for them as guiding principles in their life. Following the listing of each value, there was an explanation to help participants better understand its meaning. Responses were provided on a nine-point asymmetric scale with the following response labels: 'opposed to my values' (–1), 'not at all important' (0), 'slightly important' (1), 'fairly important' (2), 'quite important' (3), 'moderately important' (4), 'very important' (5), 'extremely important' (6), and 'central in my life' (7).

To assess their task and ego orientation in the sport setting, the athletes responded to the 13-item (task: seven items; ego: six items) Spanish version of the Task and Ego Orientation in Sport Questionnaire (TEOSQ; Duda, 1989; Balaguer *et al.*, 1996). Athletes were requested to think of when they felt most successful in their major sport and then indicate their agreement with items reflecting task- and ego-oriented criteria. Responses were indicated on a five-point Likert scale ranging from 'strongly disagree' (1) to 'strongly agree' (5).

To measure the types of motivation underlying their sport participation, we adapted (and translated to Spanish employing the back translation procedure) SDT-grounded sub-scales that have been used to tap reasons for physical activity/sport engagement (see http://selfdeterminationtheory.org). The final scale was composed of 18 items that reflect five different types of regulation: Intrinsic motivation, identified regulation, introjected regulation, external regulation and amotivation. The items are preceded by the question, 'Why do you participate in your sport?' Participants responded to the items on a seven-point scale ranging from not at all true (1) to very true (7). To examine the factor structure of the types of motivation, we carried out confirmatory factor analysis. The examination of the goodness of fit of the model showed an adequate fit to the data (χ^2 (109) = 265.21, $p < .01$, RMSEA = .08, CFI = .99, NNFI = .99).

Reliability analyses indicated that, in general, internal consistency coefficients were greater than .70. However, the alpha values observed for tradition ($\alpha = .67$), security ($\alpha = .60$), self-direction ($\alpha = .66$), and achievement ($\alpha = .66$) values and identified regulation ($\alpha = .64$) were marginal (see Table 7.2).

Results and conclusions

The results of the present research extend current understanding of the relevance of values to motivational processes in sport (see Chapters 5 and 8). In our research, athletes attributed high importance to hedonism, benevolence and self-direction basic values and low importance to power. The other basic values (conformity, universalism, stimulation, security, achievement and tradition) were rated as moderately important to the athletes in our study. With respect to second-factor value dimensions, athletes attributed moderate importance to all of them. In relation to the goal orientations, athletes scored moderately high in task orientation and relatively low in ego orientation which is consistent with what is observed in the literature (Duda and Whitehead, 1998). In terms of the different motivation regulations assessed, athletes scored high in intrinsic motivation and identified regulation, and low in introjected regulation, external regulation and amotivation (Table 7.2).

As values are considered as guides of action in people's life, we hypothesised that values are best conceptualised as potential predictors of goal orientations and motivation regulations in the specific domain of sport. Therefore we conducted a series of regression analyses centred on the prediction of the two goal orientations and the five types of motivation as a function of the athletes' overriding life values.

Table 7.2 Descriptives and internal consistency of each variable in the study (*n* = 277)

Variables	Range	Mean	SD	Alpha
Basic values				
Conformity	–1–7	4.89	1.13	.71
Tradition	–1–7	4.04	1.06	.67
Security	–1–7	4.79	1.08	.60
Benevolence	–1–7	5.06	.99	.76
Universalism	–1–7	4.82	1.09	.81
Self-direction	–1–7	5.06	.98	.66
Stimulation	–1–7	4.58	1.34	.76
Hedonism	–1–7	5.17	1.33	.42[a]
Achievement	–1–7	4.49	1.29	.66
Power	–1–7	3.60	1.76	.73
Value dimensions				
Conservation	–1–7	4.55	.93	.81
Self-transcendence	–1–7	4.94	.94	.87
Openness to change	–1–7	4.94	.98	.82
Self-enhancement	–1–7	4.05	1.29	.75
Goal orientations				
Task orientation	1–5	3.97	.65	.85
Ego orientation	1–5	2.69	.86	.85
Motivation regulations				
Intrinsic Motivation	1–7	5.36	.96	.71
Identified Regulation	1–7	4.74	1.26	.64
Introjected Regulation	1–7	2.30	1.31	.80
External Regulation	1–7	2.00	1.28	.81
Amotivation	1–7	2.24	1.47	.84

Note: [a] Hedonism is composed of two items, so Pearson correlation is presented.

Basic values, value dimensions, and goal orientations

Broadly speaking, sport-related goals have traditionally been understood to inter-relate with values to determine the meaning behind and the behaviours adopted by athletes in pursuit of success (see Chapter 5). The present study revealed conceptually coherent relationships between particular basic values and values dimensions and task and ego goal orientations.

Basic values and goal orientations

Specifically, task orientation was positively predicted by three close values in the circle, that is, benevolence (β = .21, p < .01), universalism (β = .21, p < .05) and self-direction (β = .15, p < .05), and negatively related to power (β = –.15, p < .05). Benevolence is described as helping to preserve and enrich the experiences of those within whom one is in close proximity, and universalism reflects an understanding, appreciation and tolerance of and desire to protect the welfare of all people and of nature. It makes sense that those athletes who hold these life values are more likely to view others in their sport team as comrades and collaborators not competitors, characteristics of a task orientated perspective on how sport success is pursued. Finally, self-direction, which entails exploration for the purposes of self-development and creativity, was also positively related to pursing sport goals centred on demonstrating self-referent competence and the provision of effort. On the other hand, task orientation was negatively predicted by power, which means that athletes with a strong task orientation were less invested in realising social status and prestige, or control and dominance over other people. This makes sense when one considers the self-referenced and inherent task mastery (i.e. more process- than outcome-oriented) emphasis endemic in a strong task orientation.

Ego orientation in sport was positively predicted by opposing values to what we observed for task orientation; namely, power ($\beta = .21$, $p < .01$), achievement ($\beta = .17$, $p < .05$) and hedonism ($\beta = .20$, $p < .01$). Valuing power suggests that one values dominating others which is aligned with the need to demonstrate superiority within a strong ego orientation. Placing importance on the value of achievement means that the athletes cared about reaching socially-defined achievement standards. The point that this value was positively associated with ego orientation suggests that, in sport, these standards tend to be normatively based or ego-involved. Ego orientation also linked to the value of hedonism in our sample (i.e. obtaining pleasure and sensuous gratification for oneself). This finding reinforces the self-absorption and self-consciousness which could epitomise someone who is strongly focused on ego-involved goals (Duda and Hall, 2001). Furthermore, our results suggest that a strong ego orientation corresponded to less interest in doing things to enhance the welfare of people with whom one is in frequent personal contact (in other words, the benevolence value; $\beta = -.38$, $p < .01$). Again, we have a conceptual consistency between an overarching life value and how this group of athletes is defining success and judging their own capabilities in the specific context of sport. When there is a concern with demonstrating that one is 'the best' or superior, it is more difficult to care about whether others are feeling and doing well.

Value dimensions and goal orientations

The observed relationships between the value dimensions and goal orientations offer a clear picture of which values and orientations hold potential for young people's positive development in sport and which ones are disruptive (see Figure 7.2). The bipolar dimension of self-transcendence versus self-enhancement is the one that presents the clearest pattern of relationships with goal orientations in our study. Task orientation was predicted by self-transcendence ($\beta = .25$, $p < .05$) in a positive manner and negatively by self-enhancement ($\beta = -.16$, $p < .05$). That is, when athletes are concerned with the welfare of others in life in general, their goals are more likely to be directed to developing their skills, mastering the task demands and giving their best effort (i.e. task oriented). When the life value of self-enhancement holds more importance, athletes are less likely to centre on

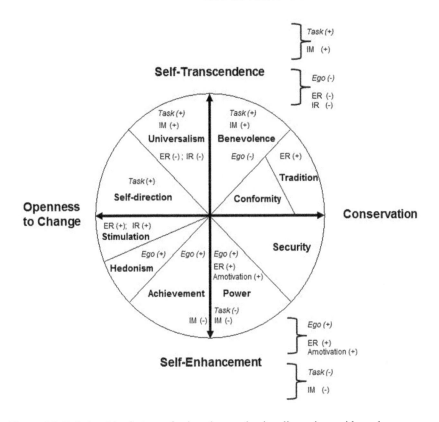

Figure 7.2 Relationships between basic values and value dimensions with goal orientations and motivational regulations

Notes: IM = Intrinsic Motivation; IR = Introjected Regulation; ER = External Regulation

such task-involved criteria for defining success and judging their capabilities. On the other hand, and aligned with what was observed for the first order values, ego orientation was predicted negatively by self-transcendence ($\beta = -.40$, $p < .01$) and positively by self-enhancement ($\beta = .18$, $p < .05$). This finding indicates that when athletes confess to having self-interest (and less concern for the welfare of others) in their overall life values, their sport goals are more likely to revolve around the demonstration of superiority.

AGT research in sport has frequently argued that holding a pronounced ego orientation (particularly without a robust task orientation) is not a healthy perspective to have and that these motivational characteristics are especially maladaptive for low ability athletes (Duda, 2001). This is because failure becomes inevitable when athletes constantly use other, higher ability athletes to set the yardstick for success that remains more out of their control than their own performance and effort. With this outlook, these athletes are unlikely to sustain effort and engagement in sport for the long term. It is important to note that the

risks of compromised sport participation remain even in the case of higher ability athletes. These individuals are also at the peril of a fragile and contingent
sense of self that is strongly tied to successful competitive outcomes and
outstanding performances (Duda and Hall, 2001). For these reasons, it is not
surprising that research has consistently demonstrated that ego orientated athletes
exhibit an increased risk of compromised health, cheating and foul play and other
undesirable achievement related characteristics when the possibility of demonstrating superior competence is questionable.

Basic values, value dimensions, and motivation regulations

This study also revealed some interesting associations between personal values
and the motivation regulations that underpin athletes' pursuit of sport.

Basic values and motivation regulations

Specifically, findings indicated that athletes would be more likely to adopt intrinsic reasons to compete in sport when they value universalism ($\beta = .21, p < .01$)
and benevolence ($\beta = .19, p < .01$). Intrinsic motivation can be viewed as the
quintessential representation of self-determined motivation, resulting in behaviours that are freely initiated and regulated by a sense of choice and volition.
When intrinsically motivated, we would expect a greater desire to be at one with
the activity and in harmony with those who are engaging in the activity along
with oneself. On the other hand, we also found that the possibilities of being
intrinsically motivated are compromised when athletes are guided by the values
of power ($\beta = -.17, p < .05$) and achievement ($\beta = -.25, p < .01$). That is, when
athletes centre on realising social prestige and power in their life overall, they are
not especially interested in participating in sport for the inherent interest, enjoyment and potential to develop one's skills and meet the challenges presented.

Going from the most self-determined extrinsic motivation (identified regulation) to the lack of any behavioural regulation (amotivation), we found that
identified regulation was not significantly predicted by any basic value.
Introjected regulation, which reflects engaging in sport for some internalised
contingency (e.g. out of guilt) was negatively predicted by universalism ($\beta = -.19$,
$p < .05$) and positively by stimulation ($\beta = .23, p < .05$). External regulation dupli-
cated this pattern of associations which emerged for introjected regulation but
was also predicted by values situated in different parts of the circle; that is, by
tradition ($\beta = .20, p < .05$) and power ($\beta = .18, p < .05$) in a positive manner.
Finally, amotivation was positively predicted by power ($\beta = .20, p < .01$).

Value dimensions and motivation regulations

A more readily discernable picture of which are the life values that act as predictors of autonomous and controlled sport motivation is revealed when we focus on
the second order value dimensions in the circumplex structure (self-enhancement

versus self-transcendence and openness to change versus conservation). In our study, we observed that self-transcendence values are related to more adaptive and self-determined reasons for sport engagement while self-enhancement values were associated with more controlled regulations as well as athletes indicating that their participation does not seem to have a rationale or reason (i.e. amotivation). Specifically, we found that when athletes encourage and legitimise the pursuit of self-interest (self-enhancement), they report more controlled motivation (external regulation, $\beta = .18$, $p < .05$) and greater amotivation ($\beta = .21$, $p < .05$). Moreover, they indicate less interest in participating in sport for autonomous reasons (intrinsic motivation, $\beta = -.36$, $p < .01$). However, when athletes hold the welfare of the others as a more important life value (self-transcendence), they are more likely to indicate that they participate in sport for intrinsic reasons (intrinsic motivation, $\beta = .23$, $p < .05$) but not for more controlled reasons in which someone or something else is driving the sport engagement (external regulation, $\beta = -.32$, $p < .01$; introjected regulation, $\beta = -.32$, $p < .01$). Finally, we found that the other bi-polar dimension (openness to change versus conservation) did not seem to be relevant to the motivational variables we assessed.

Overall, the observed relationships between motivation (goal orientations and motivation regulations) and basic values indicate that the values that are consistently associated to indicators of high quality/adaptive motivation are benevolence and universalism (positive relationship) and power (negative relationship). Regarding value dimensions, we found that self-transcendence is positively related with markers of quality motivation (task orientation and intrinsic motivation), meanwhile self-enhancement emerged as a negative predictor of this more adaptive motivational perspective. On the other hand, our results revealed that the life value which corresponded to indicators of low quality motivation (ego orientation, external regulation) and amotivation was power. The findings also indicated that the two extremes of the bi-polar dimension *self-enhancement* versus *self-transcendence* are related in a positive and negative direction respectively with the targeted hallmarks of maladaptive motivational perspectives (see Figure 7.2). That is, the athletes who are more ego-oriented and externally regulated were more likely to indicate importance on the overarching guiding principle of self-enhancement. On the other hand, the emphasis placed on self-transcendence life values negatively predicted ego orientation and extrinsic motivation within the sport context.

Summary and conclusion

In summary, the study presented in this chapter has highlighted a number of significant associations between basic values and value dimensions with the key aspects of athletes' motivation as conceptualised in AGT and SDT; namely, the ways in which they tend to define success and judge their competence and also their reasons for participating in sport. Although correlational rather than causal, these findings help to substantiate the perspective that value systems transpose between life and sport, and can impact the meaning of engagement in sporting pursuits.

Importantly, the present work also reveals potential avenues for intervention to optimise motivation in sport and/or use sport as a vehicle to promote adaptive life values. Both AGT and SDT postulate that the social environment operating in achievement contexts such as sport holds implications for the quality of athletes' motivation when they engage in this activity (Duda and Balaguer, 2007). The motivational climate created by others in the sporting social environment was not considered in the present study. However, the findings pointing to the associations between values and motivation quality imply that sport may be a vehicle through which optimal values and the personal growth of young people could be promoted; if we can create sporting environments which are more task-involving and autonomy-supportive (Duda and Balaguer, 2007).

References

Ames, C. (1992) Classrooms, goal structures, and student motivation. *Journal of Educational Psychology*, 84, 261–74.

Balaguer, I., Castillo, I. and Tomás, I. (1996) Análisis de las propiedades psicométricas del Cuestionario de Orientación al Ego y a la Tarea en el Deporte (TEOSQ) en su traducción al castellano [Analyses of psychometrical properties of the task and ego orientation in sport questionnaire]. *Psicológica*, 17, 71–81.

Balaguer, I., Castillo, I., García-Merita, M., Guallar, A. and Pons, D. (2006) Análisis de la estructura de valores en los adolescentes [Analyses of the structure of values in adolescents]. *Revista de Psicología General y Aplicada*, 59(3), 345–58.

Balaguer, I., Castillo, I., Duda, J.L., Quested, E. and Morales, V. (2011) Predictores socio-contextuales y motivacionales de la intención de continuar participando: Un análisis desde la SDT en danza [Social-contextual and motivational predictors of intentions to continue participation: A test of SDT in dance]. *Revista Internacional de Ciencias del Deporte*, 25, 305–19.

Bardi, A. and Schwartz, S.H. (2013) How does the value structure underlie value conflict? Chapter 8, this book.

Deci, E.L. and Ryan, R.M. (1985) *Intrinsic Motivation and Self-Determination in Human Behavior*. New York: Plenum Press.

Deci, E.L. and Ryan, R.M. (2000) The 'what' and 'why' of goal pursuits: Human needs and the self-determination of behaviour. *Psychological Inquiry*, 11, 227–68.

Duda, J.L. (1989) The relationship between task and ego orientation and the perceived purpose of sport among male and female high school athletes. *Journal of Sport and Exercise Psychology*, 11, 318–35.

Duda, J.L. (2001) Achievement goal research in sport: pushing the boundaries and clarifying some misunderstandings. In Roberts, G.C. (ed.) *Advances in Motivation in Sport and Exercise*. Champaign, IL: Human Kinetics, pp. 129–82.

Duda, J.L. and Balaguer, I. (2007) The coach-created motivational climate. In Lavalee, D. and Jowett, S. (eds) *Social Psychology of Sport*. Champaign, IL: Human Kinetics, pp. 117–38.

Duda, J.L. and Hall, H. (2001) Achievement goal theory in sport: Recent extensions and future directions. In Singer, R.N., Hausenblas, H.A. and Janelle, C.M. (eds) *Handbook of Sport Psychology*, 2nd edn. New York: John Wiley, pp. 417–43.

Duda, J.L. and Whitehead, J. (1998) Measurement of goal perspectives in the physical domain. In Duda, J.L. (ed.) *Advances in Sport and Exercise Psychology Measurement.* Morgantown, WV: FIT Press, pp. 21–48.

Duda, J.L., Cumming, J. and Balaguer, I. (2005) Enhancing athletes self-regulation, task involvement and self-determination via psychological skills training. In Hackfort, D. Duda, J.L. and Lidor, R. (eds) *Handbook of Research in Applied Sport Psychology.* Morgantown, WV: FIT Press, pp. 159–81.

Dweck, C.S. (1999) *Self-Theories: Their Role in Motivation, Personality, and Development.* Philadelphia, PA: Psychology Press.

Kavussanu, M. and Roberts, G.C. (1996) Motivation in physical activity contexts: The relationships of perceived motivational climate to intrinsic motivation and self-efficacy. *Journal of Sport and Exercise Psychology*, 18(3), 264–80.

Lee, M.J, Whitehead, J., Ntoumanis, N. and Hatzigeorgiadis, A. (2008) Relationships among values, achievement orientations, and attitudes in youth sport. *Journal of Sport and Exercise Psychology*, 30(5), 588–610.

Nicholls, J.G. (1989) *The Competitive Ethos and Democratic Education.* Cambridge, MA: Harvard University Press.

Parks, L. and Guay, R.P. (2009) Personality, values, and motivation. *Personality and Individual Differences*, 47, 675–84.

Petherick, C.M. and Weigand, D.A. (2002) The relationship of dispositional goal orientations and perceived motivational climate on indices of motivation in male and female swimmers. *International Journal of Sport Psychology*, 33, 218–37.

Roberts, G.C. (2012) Motivation in sport and exercise from an achievement goal theory perspective: After 30 years, where are we? In Roberts, G.C. and Treasure, D.C. (eds) *Advances in Motivation in Sport and Exercise.* Champaign, IL: Human Kinetics, pp. 1–58.

Roccas, S., Sagiv, L., Schwartz, S.H. and Knafo, A. (2002) The big five personality factors and personal values. *Personality and Social Psychology Bulletin*, 28, 789–801.

Rokeach, M. (1973) *The Nature of Human Values.* New York: Free Press.

Ryan, R.M. and Deci, E.L. (2000a) Self-determination theory and the facilitation of intrinsic motivation, social development, and well-being. *American Psychologist*, 55(1), 68–78.

Ryan, R.M. and Deci, E.L. (2000b) Intrinsic and extrinsic motivations: Classic definitions and new directions. *Contemporary Educational Psychology*, 25, 54–67.

Schwartz, S.H. (1992) Universals in the content and structure of values: theoretical advances and empirical tests in 20 countries. In Zanna, M.P. (ed.) *Advances in Experimental Social Psychology*, 25, 1–65. New York: Academic Press.

Schwartz, S.H. (1994) Are there universal aspects in the structure of human values? *Journal of Social Issues*, 50, 19–45.

Schwartz, S.H. (2012) Values and religion in adolescent development: Cross-national and comparative evidence. In Tromsdorff, G. and Chen, X. (eds) *Values, Religion, and Culture in Adolescent Development.* New York: Cambridge University Press, pp. 97–122.

Schwartz, S.H. and Sagiv, L. (1995) Identifying culture-specifics in the content and structure of values. *Journal of Cross-Cultural Psychology*, 26(1), 92–116.

Standage, M., Duda, J.L. and Ntoumanis, N. (2003) Predicting motivational regulations in physical education: The interplay between dispositional goal orientations, motivational climate, and perceived competence. *Journal of Sport Sciences*, 21, 631–47.

Part II

Value transmission and value change

8 How does the value structure underlie value conflict?

To win fairly or to win at all costs?
A conceptual framework for value-
change interventions in sport

Anat Bardi and Shalom H. Schwartz

Values are a key motivational basis for decision making and for behaviour (see Rokeach, 1973; Schwartz, 1992). This includes the sport context, where competitors often have to resolve a value-based conflict – to do whatever it takes in order to win or to play fairly and perhaps reduce the chances of winning. An established theory of value conflicts and compatibilities can explain the basis for such conflicts in sport. The aim of this chapter is to present this theory, locate values specific to the sport context within the structure of basic values, and therefore provide a better understanding of value conflicts in sport. Theory and knowledge on value change is then used to provide a basis for value interventions in order to promote fair play values and behaviours.

The chapter begins with a description of the general features of the Schwartz (1992) value theory, the relations of values to behaviour, and value change. We then present the application of the value theory to values specific to sport, and use the value theory to provide a better understanding of the common conflict of winning versus fair play in competitive sport. Finally, theory and findings on value change are used as a possible basis for resolving this conflict and for encouraging more desirable values and behaviour in sport.

Schwartz's theory of the contents and structure of individual values

Following Kluckhohn (1951) and Rokeach (1973), Schwartz defined values as desirable goals that transcend specific situations (Schwartz, 1992). These goals serve as guiding principles in people's lives. That is, they are general principles that people apply to help decide which attitude or behaviour to prefer over another. Because these goals are perceived as generally desirable in society, they also serve as a basis for justifying behaviours. Values exist in hierarchies of personal importance. That is, for one person status may be more important than fairness while for another person fairness may be more important than status. The more important the value in the personal hierarchy, the more it is likely to guide a person's life. Indeed, many studies have found that values predict perceptions, goals, attitudes, and behaviours (see recent reviews in Bardi *et al.*, 2008; Maio, 2010; Roccas and Sagiv, 2010).

The contents of values

Schwartz (1992) defined ten basic values according to the motivational content underlying them. That is, each basic value expresses a different motivational goal. Each basic value is measured by a number of single value items, chosen because actions that follow from these single value items promote the central goal of the basic value. The ten values and their definitions are presented in Table 8.1, and value items that represent each basic value appear in brackets. Although people differ in the importance they attribute to different values, there are also near-universal similarities in value importance. Using samples from all inhabited continents including representative samples from 13 nations, teacher samples from 56 nations, and university student samples from 54 nations, Schwartz and Bardi (2001) found striking similarities in value hierarchies. More specifically, benevolence values are consistently at the top of the hierarchy as the most important values to people across countries. Self-direction values tend to be second in importance and universalism values tend to be third in importance. Conformity and achievement values tend to be around the middle of the hierarchy, and hedonism values are consistently in the seventh place. Finally, power values are consistently at the bottom of the value hierarchy.

The structure of conflicts and compatibilities among values

In addition to the content of values, the theory is also concerned with the compatibilities and conflicts among values. Two values are considered as compatible if they lead to compatible attitudes and behaviours. Similarly, two values are said to be in conflict if they lead to opposing attitudes and behaviours. Values can also be independent of one another if pursuing one value does not have clear implications for pursuing the other value. We next elaborate on this argument with an example, using values that are particularly relevant for sport behaviour.

Benevolence values are concerned with preserving and enhancing the welfare of the people with whom one is in daily contact, that is, one's group members. Universalism values are concerned with preserving and enhancing the welfare of all people. Both these values promote the interests of others – they imply behaviours and attitudes which transcend selfish interests. These are therefore prosocial values. Hence, benevolence and universalism values are compatible with one another.

Achievement values are concerned with personal success. They focus on obtaining admiration from others. But the pursuit of fame and glory sometimes comes at the expense of others. High achievement strivers are so focused on their own success that they may find little time and have little readiness to make the effort required to help others. In addition, sometimes helping others can come at the expense of one's own achievement. Therefore, achievement and benevolence are conflicting values.

Self-direction values are primarily concerned with independent, active efforts to create, to explore new ways of doing and understanding things, and to improve

Table 8.1 Definitions of motivational types of values in terms of their goals and the single values that represent them

Value type	Goal	Single values
Power	Social status and prestige, control or dominance over people and resources	Social power, authority, wealth, preserving my public image
Achievement	Personal success through demonstrating competence according to social standards	Successful, capable, ambitious, influential
Hedonism	Pleasure and sensuous gratification for oneself	Pleasure, enjoying life, self-indulgent
Stimulation	Excitement, novelty, and challenge in life	Daring, a varied life, exciting life
Self-direction	Independent thought and action-choosing, creating, exploring	Creativity, freedom, independent, curious, choosing own goals
Universalism	Understanding, appreciation, tolerance and protection for the welfare of all people and for nature	Broadminded, wisdom, social justice, equality, a world at peace, a world of beauty, unity with nature, protecting the environment
Benevolence	Preservation and enhancement of the welfare of people with whom one is in frequent personal contact	Helpful, honest, forgiving, loyal, responsible
Tradition	Respect, commitment and acceptance of the customs and ideas that traditional culture or religion provide the self	Humble, accepting my portion in life, devout, respect for tradition, moderate
Conformity	Restraint of actions, inclinations, and impulses likely to upset or harm others and violate social expectations or norms	Politeness, obedient, self-discipline, honouring parents and elders
Security	Safety, harmony and stability of society, of relationships, and of self	Family security, national security, social order, clean, reciprocation of favours

Source: adapted from Schwartz (1996)

one's skills and ideas. Although people who emphasise self-direction express their own interests, they don't necessarily do so at the expense of others. There is therefore no inherent conflict between pursuing self-direction values and performing actions intended to benefit the in-group. Hence, self-direction values do not conflict with benevolence values, but they are not especially compatible either.

The entire set of relations among the values is represented in Figure 8.1. Compatible values are represented in adjacent regions. The more different the

Figure 8.1 Circle organized by motivational congruence and opposition

motivational goals of two values are, the greater the distance between them, going around the circle. Conflicting values are located in polar positions in the circle.

The ten basic values can be further combined into four higher order motivations, ordered on two bipolar dimensions: self-enhancement versus self-transcendence, and conservation versus openness to change. Self-enhancement values (achievement and power) are primarily concerned with enhancing one's own selfish interests; self-transcendence values (benevolence and universalism) aim at enhancing and protecting others, whether they are close (in benevolence) or distant (in universalism). Hence, these higher-order values are based on conflicting motivations.

Conservation values (security, tradition, conformity) aim at preserving the status quo of behavioural conventions (conformity), practices and beliefs (tradition), or social order (security). The pursuit of conservation values controls unpredictability. In contrast, the pursuit of openness to change values (self-direction and stimulation) increases unpredictability because it exposes the person to new activities and challenges. These values emphasise intrinsic motivation for mastery. Hedonism shares the motivational goals of both self-enhancement and openness to change.

Because pursuing two conflicting values can be difficult and is often impossible, it is likely that as people's value systems develop, they resolve possible value conflicts by deciding which one of two conflicting values is more important to them. Therefore, the theoretical expectation is that the more a person values benevolence, for example, the more this person is likely to value universalism and the less he or she is likely to value power and achievement. When all the specific expectations for each of the values are combined together, a structure of the circle portrayed in Figure 8.1 is expected.

The theory is examined with multi-dimensional scaling, which maps all values in a two dimensional space by taking into account all possible correlations among values. The higher the correlation between the two values, the closer they are in the spatial representation. The two dimensional mapping is therefore expected to be similar to the theoretical circle in Figure 8.1. This theory has been examined in 75 nations worldwide (Schwartz, 2011). The distinction of the 10 values and their structure of relations appears to be universal or nearly so (Schwartz, 2011). The comprehensive fit of data to the theory suggests that the ten basic values reflect fundamental contents of values.

The circular structure of motivations implies that any behaviour may be based not only on the value that it directly expresses, but on the entire system of values. For example, the behaviour of playing fairly directly expresses universalism values, as it is based on a prosocial motivation towards people outside the person's group (the opponents in a game). Hence, this behaviour should correlate most positively with universalism values. However, as benevolence values are also based on a prosocial motivation, this behaviour should also be somewhat positively related to benevolence values. In contrast, power and achievement values are based on a motivation that conflicts with universalism values. Hence, they should be negatively related to the behaviour of playing fairly. That is, the more a player values power and achievement the less he or she is likely to be motivated to play fairly.

More generally, relations between playing fairly (and most other behaviours) should have meaningful links with the entire system of values. That is, behaviours should relate most positively to the value that they directly express, and their correlations with other values should become less and less positive as one goes around the circle of the values. Indeed, such relations between values and behaviours have been found for a wide range of behaviours (e.g. Bardi and Schwartz, 2003). This pattern of relations should be expected, and indeed was found, with other variables as well, such as needs (e.g. Calogero *et al.*, 2009), goals (e.g. Levontin and Bardi, submitted), attitudes (e.g. Sagiv and Schwartz, 1995) and demographic variables (e.g. Schwartz, 2005).

Value measurement

Different value questionnaires have been developed to measure the values of this theory. The original questionnaire, the Schwartz Value Survey (SVS; Schwartz, 1992), consists of a list of value items, each one selected to represent one motivation. Each value item is labelled and followed by a definition. For example, one of the value items measuring universalism values is 'EQUALITY (equal opportunity for all)'. Respondents rate how important each value is to them, as a guiding principle in their life. They answer on a scale of nine points, ranging from –1 (opposed to my values) via 0 (not important) and 3 (important) to 7 (of supreme importance). The original version of the questionnaire included 56 value items (Schwartz, 1992), and a later version included 57 value items with the addition of a third item to the hedonism value index (Schwartz *et al.*, 2000). Forty-six of these values were found to have near-universal meanings and are therefore used in the indexes of the basic values, listed in Table 8.1 above. Most of the cross-cultural research has been done using this value questionnaire.

The SVS items are abstract and are therefore less suitable for non-educated respondents and for adolescents. As a result, Schwartz and his colleagues developed a more concrete value questionnaire for these populations, called the Profile Values Questionnaire (PVQ; Schwartz *et al.*, 2001). In this questionnaire, each item describes a person in terms of a value that is important to this person. For example, a parallel item to the SVS item of equality is: 'He thinks it is important that every person in the world be treated equally. He believes everyone should have equal opportunities in life.' Participants rate how similar the person described is to them on a 6-point scale from 'not like me at all' to 'very much like me'. The full version of this questionnaire includes 40 items, and a shortened version includes 21 items (see Schwartz, 2012). Research with this questionnaire has yielded a similar structure of relations among values and similar correlations to other variables across many nations around the world (Schwartz, 2005). This version has also been used successfully with adolescents (see Schwartz, 2012). A new instrument that builds on the PVQ is now being developed together with a refinement to the theory, dividing some of the ten broad values into narrower values (see Schwartz *et al.*, 2012).

Recently, a pictorial measure of values has been developed to be used with younger children (Döring *et al.*, 2010). Each of the ten basic values is portrayed by two pictures that show a child doing something that expresses one of the values. The children indicate the importance of what is portrayed in the picture to them by placing stickers with the pictures in different boxes. For example, a picture that measures universalism values shows children of different races holding hands. Using this measure, the circular structure of values according to the Schwartz value theory (1992) has been found with 9–10-year-olds (Döring *et al.*, 2010), indicating that these values indeed reflect very basic motivations.

Value change

Values have been expected (e.g. Rokeach, 1973) and found (e.g. Bardi *et al.*, 2009) to be quite stable. Once values are developed, they are expected to change little and usually only as a response to a significant life change. Indeed, Bardi *et al.* (2009) found greater value change the more people experienced life-changing events that require adjustment. Because of the structure of conflicts and compatibilities of values, it makes sense that values will change according to the circle in Figure 8.1. For example, if power values become more important, achievement values should also become more important to the person whereas benevolence and universalism values should become less important. Indeed, this pattern of change has been found both in a laboratory experiment that employed a value-change intervention (Maio *et al.*, 2009) and in longitudinal studies in real life (Bardi *et al.*, 2009). In addition, because the system of values is interlinked with other aspects of the self, such as beliefs, attitudes, goals, and behaviour, it is likely that a change in one of these aspects will lead to a compatible change in the other. And indeed, a longitudinal study has found that a change in values predicted a later compatible change of beliefs and vice versa (Goodwin *et al.*, 2012). As values predict behaviour, a change in values is likely to lead to a change in compatible behaviours. Hence value change can be a driver for behaviour change.

Bardi and Goodwin (2011) have offered a theoretical model of value stability and change. Because values function just as any other established cognitive schema does, they automatically affect which stimuli people attend to, how they perceive situations, and therefore how they behave. These automatic processes make values difficult to change, because any one-time action to change values, if successful, is likely to have only a momentary effect. As people go on about their lives, their established schemas (including values) are likely to continue to operate automatically and affect their behaviour. Hence, any value-changing action must be repeated and ongoing in order to lead to a gradual long-term change in schemas and therefore values.

The most straightforward way to change values is through *persuasion*. However, such attempts often fail (reviewed in Bardi and Goodwin, 2011). Other ways are likely to be more successful. As values can be activated automatically by cues in the environment, cues that apply to the desired values (e.g. fairness) can be activated, for example, by slogans and other symbols. Bardi and Goodwin (2011) also proposed that *identification* with a group or a significant person (e.g. a coach, a fellow player) can be a facilitator of value change, when the person or group display behaviours that express particular values. This, indeed, is used in the Football for Peace programme (see Chapters 9 and 10 by Lambert), in which coaches display the desired behaviour of fairness and respect for others. Additionally, in Chapter 11 of this book, Freeman and colleagues detail the importance of significant others in transmission of sport values from physical education teachers to their pupils.

In our analysis below, we use another facilitator of value change, one that has been identified by Bardi and Goodwin (2011) as the most prominent in the literature, namely the facilitator of *adaptation*. Schwartz and Bardi (1997) suggested that people acclimate their values to reinforcement contingencies in their environment. For most values, when pursuit of a certain value leads to positive consequences the value is likely to increase in importance, and vice versa: when pursuit of this value leads to negative consequences it is likely to decrease in importance. For example, if playing fairly is followed by acknowledgement and praise, it is likely to increase in importance. But if playing fairly is not acknowledged while at the same time reducing the person's chances of achieving a desired outcome such as winning, it is likely to decrease in importance. We use this idea as well as the rest of the knowledge above to apply values to the sport context, identifying the location of values specific to sport within the basic value theory (Schwartz, 1992) and proposing a basis for value intervention in sport.

Application of the value theory to values specific to sport

As the value theory reflects fundamental value systems, it can be applied to various areas of life, including sport. Values specific to sport (such as sportsmanship) can be viewed as specific expressions of basic values in the area of sport. By locating the values specific to sport in the general structure of values, a fundamental value conflict inherent to competitive sport can be understood better. We begin by locating some of the key values specific to sport within the Schwartz (1992) value theory, drawing on research on values in sport.

Lee and Cockman (1995; Chapter 2), in one the earlier studies of values in youth sport, studied adolescent team members in tennis and football. They presented sport dilemmas to their participants, in a form similar to that of Kohlberg (see Colby and Kohlberg, 1987). They recorded both the choices respondents made in the dilemmas and their justifications. The justifications revealed the values respondents used as criteria for decisions. These values are naturally specific to sport situations. This work was followed by the development of questionnaires measuring values in sport contexts. The Youth Sport Values Questionnaire (YSVQ; Lee *et al.* 2000; Chapter 3) was developed to assess the importance of 18 sport-specific values extracted from the discussions in Lee and Cockman's study. We locate some key values from this questionnaire within the Schwartz (1992) value theory. The location of the other values in this questionnaire as well as additional information about them can be found in Appendix 1 of this book. A revised questionnaire was later developed and validated based on accumulated knowledge and with the aim of focusing on a smaller number of key broad values relevant to sport, each measured with multiple items. This questionnaire is the Youth Sport Values Questionnaire–2 (YSVQ-2; see Chapter 5).

The relative importance of sport values

Consistently, the most important value to young athletes was enjoyment (Chapter 3). This value stems from the motivation underlying hedonism values. It can be part of the broader motivation to enhance oneself alongside achievement and power values or part of the motivation for openness to change alongside stimulation and self-direction (see Figure 8.1). Its location at the top of the hierarchy of values in sport is incompatible with its location as seventh out of 10 in the universal hierarchy of basic values (see above; Schwartz and Bardi, 2001), but it is compatible with value hierarchies of adolescents (see Schwartz, 2012). This suggests that it is a particularly important value in the sport context for adolescents and that their main motivation to play sport is to have fun rather than to acquire prestige in winning. This value is therefore normative in adolescents' sport and is not involved in frequent conflict, as in most sport situations people can enjoy sport.

Achievement, or personal achievement, was consistently found to be the second in importance in the sport context (Chapter 3). It was later included within the broader concept of competence measured in the YSVQ-2 (Chapter 5). This value focuses on improving one's competence in the relevant sport. Although in its initial version it was called achievement, this value does not stem from achievement values in the Schwartz (1992) value theory. This is because Schwartz's achievement values are based on the motivation for socially approved success, whereas in the YSVQ and YSVQ-2 this value is based on the motivation for challenge and personal definition of what constitutes success. It stems more clearly from Schwartz's self-direction values (see Figure 8.1), which are based on the motivation for freedom of action and thought. Its high ranking in the sport values hierarchy is compatible with the high ranking of self-direction values in the near-universal hierarchy of basic values (see above; Schwartz and Bardi, 2001). As with enjoyment, this value is not part of frequently experienced conflicts in sport, as in most situations, athletes can strive to improve their performance.

The YSVQ-2 (Chapter 5) focused on three broad values in the sport context: competence (discussed above), moral values, and status values. Moral values include items that express values in the Schwartz (1992) theory that were indeed found to be perceived by student participants as moral values (Schwartz, 2007). Specifically, the value items 'I do what I am told' and playing properly express conformity values; 'I help people when they need it' expresses benevolence values; and 'I try to be fair' expresses universalism values (see Figure 8.1). The last item in the moral values category in the YSVQ-2, 'I show good sportsmanship', is broader, and probably expresses conformity, benevolence, and universalism. Moral values are typically important to adolescent athletes, but less important than competence and enjoyment values (see Chapters 3, 5, and 6 Whitehead and Gonçalves).

The third and last broad value in the YSVQ-2 is status. This is a competitive value that is aimed at demonstrating dominance over others, and includes items pertaining to winning, outperforming others, and looking good. They are based on the broad motivation of self-enhancement in the Schwartz (1992) value theory and particularly on power values (see Figure 8.1). These are the least important values for young athletes (see Chapters 5 and 6). Moreover, winning was consistently the least important of the 18 values in the YSVQ (Chapters 3 and 6). This is compatible with the robust finding that power values are rated as the least important across cultures (see above; Schwartz and Bardi, 2001). Although winning and status are rated as the least important values when athletes are faced with a list of values in a value questionnaire, these values are still sufficiently important to be part of common conflicts in sport. This was revealed in Lee and Cockman's (Chapter 2) study that focused on moral dilemmas in sport. In this study, winning was one of the most frequently mentioned values. It was reflected by propositions such as 'I go out to win'.

Another value that was spontaneously mentioned frequently was fairness (Chapter 2), defined as not allowing an unfair advantage in the contest or judgment. This value was reflected in statements such as 'You have to let people have a fair game'. As stated above, this value expresses universalism values in the Schwartz (1992) theory. It stems from a basic motivation for social justice, or protecting the welfare of in-group as well as out-group members, by allowing all to have an equal opportunity to succeed.

Conflict and compatibility in sport values

As can be seen in Figure 8.1 above, universalism and power values are based on conflicting motivations. This means that there are many situations in which these values conflict. In the sport context, power and universalism values conflict when a player increases his or her chances of winning by violating principles of universalism values in playing unfairly (by cheating, by annoying the opponent, etc.). The stronger the motivation to win, the more players are likely to be tempted to violate values of fairness by cheating and gamesmanship. If players want to win and play fairly at the same time, they are repeatedly faced with this conflict.

For example, a young football player in the Lee and Cockman study (Chapter 2) expressed his preference for the value of winning over the fairness value by stating: 'I would commit a foul to make sure we won'. This action violates an implicit contract to play by the rules and not spoil the game, thereby being unfair to competitors (this is the value of contract maintenance). This boy may have experienced no conflict because he prefers power and achievement to universalism values. But what if both values were highly important to him? Whichever decision he makes would leave him with a problem of self-dissatisfaction, because he would violate one of his most important values. Engaging repeatedly in situations that require one to make self-dissatisfying decisions can be quite intolerable. To avoid repeated self-dissatisfaction, he is eventually likely to attribute more importance to one of the competing values and to reduce the importance of the other value.

As young athletes become more successful, the pressures and expectations of them to achieve and contribute to winning increase. There are direct as well as indirect pressures. Direct pressures come from their friends on the team and their coaches and sport teachers. Indirect pressures are exerted by the wider social system of their school and school friends. Teams that are more successful are accorded higher status and schools that are successful in sport are perceived as more prestigious. School friends admire the status of the team, because they make them feel more proud of their school. In other words, pursuing power and achievement values leads to positive consequences, and through the process of adaptation explained above (Bardi and Goodwin, 2011; Schwartz and Bardi, 1997), power and achievement values are likely to increase in importance. Hence, if there is a conflict between power/achievement and universalism values, the pressure from the social environment is to solve it by increasing power and achievement values. However, the studies cited above regarding the structure of value change (Bardi *et al.*, 2009; Maio *et al.*, 2009) suggest that an undesired side effect is likely to be decreasing the importance of universalism values of fairness as well as benevolence values of being helpful and responsible.

With regard to benevolence values, the more successful a competitor becomes, the more social esteem he or she receives from the social surroundings. As one becomes more focused on his or her personal success, one is less likely to pay attention to the needs and requests of others, thereby reducing prosocial behaviours toward in-group members. In terms of values, this process is likely to reduce the importance attributed to benevolence values.

Avoiding conflict

Presenting the situation as we have, it seems like an inherently unsolvable conflict. However, according to the theory, there is another possible motivation to perform well in sport, other than achievement values. This is the will to excel out of intrinsic motivation, without seeking social rewards. This motivation underlies self-direction values and competence values in the YSVQ-2. It was expressed spontaneously in the Lee and Cockman study (Chapter 2).

One example of a self-direction value related to sport and physical education is self-actualisation. It is defined as experiencing the activity for its own sake and accompanying transcendent feelings. It is drawn from statements such as 'If you've done your best it gives a great feeling, there's nothing like it'. In terms of the YSVQ-2, this quote also expresses competence values. As shown in Figure 8.1, self-direction values are compatible with universalism values. Furthermore, they are not in conflict with benevolence values, which are important for responsible behaviour, cooperation, and loyalty to the team. Therefore, a motivation to excel based on self-direction values rather than on power and achievement values is likely to reduce behaviours that violate standards of fairness. In addition, self-direction values tend to be highly important to people (see above; Schwartz and Bardi, 2001); and their sport-specific counterpart, competence values, tend to be highly important to young athletes (see above; Chapter 5). This suggests that encouraging these values further is achievable as the foundation for the importance of these values already exists.

Both Schwartz's (1992) achievement and self-direction values imply working to improve one's performance. The key difference between them is that in achievement values the motivation for self-enhancement stresses social superiority and prestige. Therefore, achievement values motivate improving performance in order to gain social esteem. And indeed, achievement values were found to be positively related to performance-approach goals, the goal to outperform others and obtain social esteem (Levontin and Bardi, submitted). They are likely to enhance performance efforts in settings that promise an external reward. Similarly, status values in the YSVQ-2 positively predicted ego orientation in sport among adolescent athletes (Chapter 5). In contrast, self-direction values express the motivation for challenge, growth, and change. Here the motivation to improve performance is intrinsic, and does not depend on social rewards. The reward one gets is a sense of self-worth and growth. The expression of self-direction values depends on a feeling that one has chosen independently to engage in the activity. And indeed, self-direction values were found to be positively related mainly to mastery goals, the goals to develop one's competence (Levontin and Bardi, submitted). Similarly, competence values in the YSVQ-2 positively predicted task orientation in sport (Chapter 5). To conclude, while achievement and self-direction values might lead to similar behaviour, both the conditions under which they motivate this behaviour and the nature of the motivation are quite different.

Possible interventions for sport educators

As young athletes are in the phase of developing their value systems (e.g. Schwartz, 2012), sport educators can play a role in encouraging self-direction (or competence) values as the basis for strong performance rather than achievement and power values, focusing more on intrinsic motivation for excellence and mastery instead of the extrinsic motivation for social rewards. They can emphasise improving performance as part of self-actualisation, according to challenges chosen personally, rather than improving performance in order to be superior to others. This should be an ongoing process on the part of coaches, teachers and parents; as any one-time action is not likely to lead to permanent change in values (see analysis above). Strengthening self-direction values also has the benefit that strong values affect behaviour automatically, without conscious thought (see above). This means that even in the heat of the competition, when players are likely to make rapid rather than careful decisions, self-direction values would operate automatically and militate against an unethical behaviour that would undermine attainment of excellence. This could also be communicated to players, i.e., that winning through cheating and gamesmanship means that winning does not reflect competent performance or excellence. Similarly, strengthening fairness values is likely to promote automatically behaving fairly in competitions. In addition, based on the findings regarding the structure of value change (see above; Bardi *et al.*, 2009; Maio *et al.*, 2009), strengthening fairness values is also likely to lead to a reduction in the importance of status-seeking values, thereby weakening their automatic activation in competitions.

However, it would be naïve to think that such actions by sport educators are easily undertaken or that they are sufficient. One has to take into account the values implicitly emphasised by the entire reward system of youth sport. As long as social prestige and rewards are accorded to individuals and schools/clubs on the basis of winning alone, it will be difficult to shift value emphases away from achievement and power. In addition, according to the understanding of the adaptation facilitator of value change (see above, Bardi and Goodwin, 2011; Schwartz and Bardi, 1997), values are likely to change in accordance with reinforcement contingencies through discouraging demonstration of power (such as the over-zealous joy of winning), reducing the magnitude of rewards for winning, and acknowledging in certificates etc. behaviours that express values of fairness, helpfulness and responsibility. The coaching manual of the Football for Peace programme already employs these principles (see Chapter 9). In addition, many schools now award certificates for helpfulness, and in physical education and sport programmes certificates can be awarded also based on sportsmanship indicators, such as least number of rule violations, and being courteous to opponents. It is important to keep these certificates and awards at quite a modest level, as the more prestigious they become, the more they are likely to encourage players out of extrinsic motivation (i.e. for the prize itself). This has the danger of competitors displaying fairness and sportsmanship only when coaches, teachers and judges are watching. Instead, such certificates should be portrayed more as acknowledgement of desired behaviour and less as a prize. This is, of course, a fine balance not easily achieved, and requires careful attention from coaches and teachers. Most importantly, rewards should be based on improvement over one's past performance and of personal excellence rather than outdoing others. That is, teachers and coaches could set objective targets of personal improvement and personal excellence. Together, such emphases on self-direction, universalism, and benevolence values may reduce the temptation to behave in an anti-social way and increase levels of sportsmanship in youth sport.

Conclusions

This chapter presented the main features of the Schwartz (1992) value theory and its applications to values specific to sport. The basic nature of values and their universality mean that context-specific values, such as values in sport, can be located within the structure and contents of the value theory and understood in terms of basic motivations. Using theory and knowledge on basic values and their change, we have shown that a common conflict in competitive situations in sport and physical education can be understood better by showing its origins in basic values. Specifically, the understanding of the conflict between winning and fairness is enhanced by the knowledge that winning stems from self-enhancement values which are in conflict with universalism values, the latter including fairness. The chapter used theory and knowledge on value change to suggest a shift in the motivation to perform well from self-enhancement values of winning and status to self-direction values of improving competence. As self-direction values are compatible with prosocial values they are not likely to lead to conflict and to unethical behaviour in sport and physical education. These principles can therefore serve as a conceptual basis for value interventions in sport to ensure that both sport and physical education has a positive influence on youngsters' development.

References

Bardi, A. and Goodwin, R. (2011) The dual route to value change: Individual processes and cultural moderators. *Journal of Cross-Cultural Psychology*, 42, 271–87.

Bardi, A. and Schwartz, S.H. (2003) Values and behavior: Strength and structure of relations. *Personality and Social Psychology Bulletin*, 29, 1207–20.

Bardi, A., Calogero, R.M. and Mullen, B. (2008) A new archival approach to the study of values and value–behavior relations: Validation of the value lexicon. *Journal of Applied Psychology*, 93, 483–97.

Bardi, A., Lee, J.A., Hofmann-Towfigh, N. and Soutar, G. (2009) The structure of intraindividual value change. *Journal of Personality and Social Psychology*, 97(5), 913–29.

Calogero, R. M., Bardi A. and Sutton, R. (2009) A need basis for values: Associations between the need for cognitive closure and value priorities. *Personality and Individual Differences*, 46 (2), 154–59.

Colby, A. and Kohlberg, L. (1987) *The Measurement of Moral Judgement*. New York: Cambridge University Press.

Döring, A. K., Blauensteiner, A., Aryus, K., Drögekamp, L. and Bilsky, W. (2010) Assessing values at an early age: The Picture-Based Value Survey for Children (PBVS-C). *Journal of Personality Assessment*, 92(5), 439–48.

Freeman, P., Leslie, A., Leger, H. and Williams, C. (2013) How important are the values of significant others? Chapter 11, this book.

Goodwin, R., Polek, E. and Bardi, A. (2012) The temporal reciprocity of values and beliefs: A longitudinal study within a major life transition. *European Journal of Personality*, 26(3), 360–70.

Kluckhohn, C. (1951) Values and value-orientation in the theory of action. In T. Parsons and E. Shils (eds) *Towards a General Theory of Action*. Cambridge, MA: Harvard University Press.

Lambert, J. (2013) How can we teach values through sport? Chapter 9, this book.

Lambert, J. (2013) How does coach behaviour change the motivational climate? Chapter 10, this book.

Lee, M.J. and Cockman, M. (1995) Values in children's sport: spontaneously expressed values among young athletes. *International Review for the Sociology of Sport*, 30(3/4; Special Issue: Ethics in Sport), 337–52.

Lee, M.J., Whitehead, J. and Balchin, N. (2000) The measurement of values in youth sport: development of the Youth Sport Values Questionnaire. *Journal of Sport and Exercise Psychology*, 22(4), 307–26.

Lee, M., Whitehead, J., Ntoumanis, N. and Hatzigeorgiadis, A. (2008) Relationships among values, achievement orientations and attitudes in youth sport. *Journal of Sport and Exercise Psychology*, 30, 588–610.

Levontin L. and Bardi A. (Submitted) *Amity Goals: Unveiling a Missing Achievement Goal Using Values*. Manuscript submitted for publication.

Maio, G.R. (2010) Mental representations of social values. In M.P. Zanna (ed.) *Advances in Experimental Social Psychology*, 42, 1–43. New York, NY: Academic Press.

Maio, G.R., Pakizeh, A., Cheung, W.-Y. and Rees, K. (2009) Changing, priming, and acting on values: Effects via motivational relations in a circular model. *Journal of Personality and Social Psychology*, 97, 699–715.

Roccas, S. and Sagiv, L. (2010) Personal values and behavior: Taking the cultural context into account. *Social and Personality Psychology Compass*, 4, 30–41.

Rokeach, M. (1973) *The Nature of Human Values*. New York: Free Press.

Sagiv, L. and Schwartz, S.H. (1995) Value priorities and readiness for out-group social contact. *Journal of Personality and Social Psychology*, 69, 437–48.

Schwartz, S.H. (1992) Universals in the content and structure of values: theoretical advances and empirical tests in 20 countries. In M.P. Zanna (ed.) *Advances in Experimental Social Psychology*, 25, 1–65. New York: Academic Press.

Schwartz, S.H. (1996) Value priorities and behavior: Applying a theory of integrated value systems. In C. Seligman, J.M. Olson and M.P. Zanna (eds) *The Psychology of Values: The Ontario Symposium*, 8, 1–24. Hillsdale, NJ: Erlbaum.

Schwartz, S.H. (2005) Robustness and fruitfulness of a theory of universals in individual human values. In A. Tamayo and J.B. Porto (eds) *Valores e comportamento nas organizaç Atoes [Values and Behaviour in Organisations]*. Petrópolis: Vozes, pp. 56–95.

Schwartz, S.H. (2007) Universalism values and the inclusiveness of our moral universe. *Journal of Cross-Cultural Psychology*, 38, 711–28.

Schwartz, S.H. (2011) Values: Individual and cultural. In F.J.R. van de Vijver, A. Chasiotis and S.M. Breugelmans (eds) *Fundamental Questions in Cross-Cultural Psychology*. Cambridge: Cambridge University Press, pp. 463–493.

Schwartz, S.H. (2012) Values and religion in adolescent development: Cross-national and comparative evidence. In G. Tromsdorff and X. Chen (eds) *Values, Religion, and Culture in Adolescent Development*. New York: Cambridge University Press.

Schwartz, S.H. and Bardi, A. (1997) Influences of adaptation to communist rule on value priorities in Eastern Europe. *Political Psychology*, 18, 385–410.

Schwartz, S.H. and Bardi, A. (2001) Value hierarchies across cultures: Taking a similarities perspective. *Journal of Cross Cultural Psychology*, 32, 268–90

Schwartz, S.H., Sagiv, L. and Boehnke, K. (2000) Worries and values. *Journal of Personality*, 68, 309–46.

Schwartz, S.H., Melech, G., Burgess, S., Harris, M. and Owens, V. (2001) Extending the cross-cultural validity of the theory of basic human values with a different method of measurement. *Journal of Cross Cultural Psychology*, 32, 519–42.

Schwartz, S.H., Cieciuch, J., Vecchione, M., Davidov, E., Fischer, R., Beierlein, C., Ramos, A., Verkasalo, M., Lönnqvist, J.-E., Demirutku, K., Dirilen-Gumus, O. and Konty, M. (2012) Refining the theory of basic individual values. *Journal of Personality and Social Psychology*, 103, 663–88.

Whitehead, J. and Gonçalves, C.E. (2013) How similar are sport values in different nations? Chapter 6, this book.

9   How do we teach values through sport?

A values-based approach to coaching sport in divided societies

John Lambert

Football 4 Peace (F4P) is a co-existence project for Jewish and Arab children in Israel which teaches peace-related values through sport. The project annually brings together Arab and Jewish children at various locations within Israel for six days in July with the intention of improving community relations through physical activity and sport. One of its distinguishing features has been the development of a specialist football (soccer) coaching manual. Through a carefully designed series of practical coaching activities, this manual animates and exemplifies a series of values that promote fair play, cooperation, mutual understanding, and aid the cause of conflict prevention and co-existence. This chapter first identifies the five values that underpin the project then describes the development of the F4P coaching manual, driven by an action research paradigm, and presents a pedagogical model that is exigent to achieving the project's objectives. It then locates the five central values within the global value structure of Schwartz (1992), and considers the wider potential of teaching for value transmission. The chapter is principally concerned with identifying the key features of F4P coaching manual and, drawing upon empirical studies carried out in the UK and Israel between 2004 and 2010, describing its application and discussing its efficacy.

The previous chapter discussed relations between values and offers a theoretical framework within which we can understand the conflicting and congruent nature of values. The critical narrative now focuses around how certain learning theories are applied in order that the values most conducive to conflict prevention and co-existence can be transmitted in opposition to power and security values. The purpose of Chapter 10 (Lambert) is to then demonstrate how a motivational climate conducive to teaching values through sport may be facilitated and, again drawing upon reflective practice, identify specific coach behaviours which are advocated within the F4P coach education programme that are contributory factors to creating such an environment.

The Football 4 Peace values

The Football 4 Peace project which began in 2001 involves 1000 Arab and Jewish children aged between 11 and 14 and uses football as a medium through which to promote conflict prevention and co-existence. In 2004, for pragmatic and educational reasons, a dedicated football coaching manual (Lambert, 2006) was written which integrated football and community relations activities as a guide for coaches. The primary rationale for producing the coaching manual was that more needed to be done to ensure that the contents of that football programme were clearly underpinned by values and principles that fed a broader community relations agenda and that those values and principles were understood and accepted by the local coaches and experienced by the children in practice (Sugden, 2006). There was a need for a coherent and relevant set of values that could be accepted by all partners across the project.

Through selected practices and games, the manual accentuates the core values of the project: *respect, responsibility, equity and inclusion, trust,* and *neutrality.* These values which are the foundation stones of this project were not clarified or articulated until January 2004, three years after the initiative was founded. Now they are such an important part of the project that they are frequently referred to in every F4P context, on and off the field. They are listed in Table 9.1.

If one follows the principle that values are motivational concepts that have their roots in basic human needs (Rokeach, 1973; Schwartz, 2005) then *neutrality* is not a value. One cannot be motivated by merely being impartial and not voicing opinion. Nevertheless, it is a principled stance that is so important to the F4P project that it has been adopted as a fundamental value. These five items are not intended to be a definitive list of the values that might be adopted by all sport for development and peace projects but a selective set of values which embody the spirit of F4P and best relate to its main objectives:

- provide opportunities for social contact across community boundaries;
- promote mutual understanding;
- engender in participants a commitment to peaceful coexistence; and
- develop football skills and games sense.

The project's core values relate to the first three aims and guide decisions that shape the intervention. The last aim is the least important and is not an explicit focus in the sessions. The F4P values exist in order to offer the young participants an alternative way to view their choice of behaviour and to empower them in this choice.

The Football 4 Peace coaching manual

The F4P coaching manual is a dedicated curriculum which offers guidance for coaches to teach values which promote peace-building through football. The development of the manual has been guided by reflective practice based upon action research principles. Action research is a form of enquiry that enables practitioners to investigate and critically evaluate their work as it unfolds in the field (McNiff and Whitehead, 2006; Reason and Bradbury, 2001). These developmental accounts of practical engagement and on-going teaching and learning modification reveal how action researchers are trying to improve their own

Table 9.1 The Football 4 Peace values from the F4P Coaching Manual

Value	What it is	What it looks like
Respect	Appreciation of one's own individuality and the dignity and worth of others in a context of social diversity.	Respect for oneself, respect for team mates and opponents, respect for coaches and parents, and respect for the laws of the game and those that administer them.
Responsibility	Understanding that individual behaviour in practice sessions and in games influences and has impact upon the performance and experience of others.	Working with and for others are key aspects of the F4P project. Success in sport, particularly team sport, relies upon mutual aid and self-sacrifice.
Equity and inclusion	Making every aspect of F4P accessible to all and valuing each participant equitably is a principle that permeates the coaching. Recognition that games that are played fairly are the most fun for everyone.	Within F4P all participants are treated equally and the commitment to equality is recognised in the way that practices and games are organised and run. Those who want to play can play regardless of ethnicity, race, religion, gender, and ability.
Trust	Mutual reliance on the integrity and commitment of each fellow participant in the project.	Players that trust one another play well together. Learning to have faith in the capacities of others to carry out their roles and responsibilities dutifully and mutually, in ways that also contribute to the well-being of team-mates, is an essential ingredient of good sportsmanship.
Neutrality	An absence of prejudice against any class, ethnic group or religion. There is no room for political bias. Impartiality should be shown when dealing with each individual irrespective of their ethnic, political and religious identity.	F4P is a politics-free zone. Those who participate in F4P, players, coaches, parents, administrators, leave their political views and ideological positions outside. This does not mean changing political and ideological standpoints, this is not our business, but we do require that such positions are not expressed in and around the F4P experience.

learning, and progressively influence the learning of others (Coughlan and Brannick, 2005). These accounts come to stand as fluid theories of professional practice, upon which others can build and improve. Based on this paradigm, this chapter draws conclusions about the coaching environment that needs to be nurtured which will most effectively allow values transmission to occur through sport.

During the early stages of planning the manual Beedy's (1997) Sports Plus model had a strong influence on both its composition in terms of content and pedagogy and the understanding of the potential for coaching in the social and affective domains (Krathwohl, 2002; Laker, 2000) through sport. The Sport Plus structure of goal setting, coach facilitation and observation, and a period of reflection is based on sound social, cognitive and behavioural learning theories. Put simply, children learn from what the coaches say and what they do as they translate the values into reality. The holistic approach to coaching and humanistic view of the role of the coach along with the recognition that children can learn values which influence attitudes in a physical setting through modelling, rewards and consequences, and dialogue (Beedy, 1997) are prominent characteristics of the model. The adaptation of the Sport Plus theory to the practice of coaching in Israel with its sport for community relations agenda would offer a challenge but one worth accepting.

Facilitating teachable moments

An important principle that governed the development of the manual was to choose football-related practices and games that would facilitate the 'teachable moments' (TMs); those situations where player behaviours can be related to the chosen F4P core values: *respect, responsibility, trust, equity and inclusion,* and *neutrality.* Positive examples of concrete behaviours that exemplified the more abstract values could then be reinforced through peer and coach feedback. For example, a player who helps the coach set up equipment at the start of the session without being previously asked is demonstrating *responsibility* and this can be recognised and rewarded with praise during the cool down (period of reflection) at the end. The choice of learning activities, whether competitive or co-operative skill practices, football games or trust games, were chosen in order to facilitate 'teachable moments' and thus provide prime opportunities for teaching values by reflecting on significant situations within each session. A prime learning activity might be that the players would be given responsibility for running their own substitutions in a game and the coach could later facilitate discussion on whether this was conducted in an equitable way. There would inevitably be some learning of football skills taking place in each session but this would be of secondary, implicit importance.

The four-phase session structure

Each session plan from the manual is divided into four phases as shown in the exemplary plan (Table 9.2). The session begins with a *warm up*, which does not follow a traditional format of pulse-raiser and progressive stretching to prepare physically for the activity. It includes a trust or teambuilding activity to introduce the values followed by an introductory football activity which is aimed at developing group amity and cohesion. During the ensuing *technical* (skill learning) and *games* phases the coach observes for teachable moments where he/she can draw

Table 9.2 An exemplary coaching plan from the Football 4 Peace Coaching Manual (age group: under 12; Session 4: heading)

Phase	Activity	Teachable moments
Warm-up 20 mins	*Fox and hen*: Played in groups of 8/9. Six people hold hands to form a tight circle. One 'fox' starts outside of the circle and a 'hen' is inside. The circle must work to protect the hen from the fox by tightening the circle to create a barrier and loosening it to allow the hen to be released from the centre or enter it from outside when appropriate. The game is over when the fox tags the hen. Allow each person to experience both roles.	*Responsibility/equity and inclusion/trust* Each member of the team has an important role in protecting the hen. Group bonding activity.
	Head to head: In pairs, the players balance a ball between their foreheads while racing each other over a set distance. If they drop the ball they must go back to the start. Progression: join up pairs and run a relay race.	*Equity and inclusion/ neutrality/respect* Encourage them to pair up with a partner that they do not know very well. Observe for cheating.
Technical phase 40 mins	*Over and under*: In pairs with one ball per pair. Players start by taking turns to juggle the ball with the head. They then progress to head to one another. To emphasise attacking play, head the ball through your partner's legs to score a point.	*Responsibility* Your feed needs to be accurate if your partner is to head effectively. Are the groups scoring correctly?
	Headers: Four players in two pairs. Players from each pair stand on adjacent sides of a 10 × 10 yard square. X1 throws an underarm pass to X2 who tries to head the ball past the Os. If one of the defending team (Os) manage to head the ball back past the Xs they get a double goal. Adjust the size of the area according to the ability of the group.	*Respect/responsibility* Observe for disputes over 'goals'. How are these resolved? Conflict or compromise?

Table 9.2 continued

Phase	Activity	Teachable moments
	Head for goal: Set up two goals and divide the players into pairs. Each team complete the sequence throw–head–catch to move towards goal. Finish with a header into empty goal and then move across to attack the other goal. Progression: add goalkeeper	*Responsibility/equity and inclusion/respect* Encourage the players to pair up with people that they are not already friendly with.

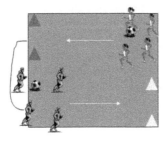

Phase	Activity	Teachable moments
Game phase 40 mins	*Throw–head–catch*: Divide the players into 2 equal teams. Each team complete the sequence throw, head, catch to score one point. The other team can intercept the ball using their hands. They will referee their own games without coach intervention. Progression: no interception out of the throw–head–catch sequence and add goals (only score with a header).	*Respect/responsibility/ equity and inclusion* Look for fair play and, conversely, players claiming points when out of sequence. Are the strongest players involving their whole team? Who are the players showing good leadership from a F4P values perspective?

Phase	Activity	Teachable moments
Cool-down 20 mins	Each team lines up in two lines facing each other. A tennis ball is thrown to somebody in the opposite line. When that player catches it they must give an example of good play (1 point) or good behaviour (3 points) from the session. The first team to 10 points are the winners. If a player cannot think of a teachable moment he/she can pass the ball on without scoring. The coach listens in and shares the best examples with the whole group.	*Responsibility/respect/ equity and inclusion.* A game that involves everyone taking responsibility for recognising and praising the actions of others.

attention to situations when one of the F4P values is either violated or exemplified in a positive way. The technical phase typically includes some collaborative games or practices that necessitate players from different communities working together to either play as a team or develop a skill. The game phase is a competitive element when the children are placed into situations where they work collectively with others against an opposing team composed of both Jewish and Arab players. Both phases will facilitate the type of interactive behaviour that provides a rich source of TMs.

The *cool-down* consists of a combination of gentle physical activity based around the values theme of the day and some discussion on the teachable moments. The coach asks 'What? So what? Now what?' (Beedy, 1997). It is a plenary phase that consolidates the players' understanding of the notion that each abstract value can be attached to specific behaviours and attitudes that may be exhibited in the session. Ultimately, the aim is that these behaviours and attitudes are internalised by the children and transferred to life back in their respective communities. For example, any cheating out on the field is compared to deception in everyday life in terms of the lack of *respect* and *responsibility* that it demonstrates and the conflict that it can cause. The behaviour during the off-pitch cultural programme, which includes reciprocal visits to communities, is often an indicator of the progress made over the week in respect of values being internalised by the children and whether they transcend situations. Although the manual includes some guidance for coaches on where particular activities might elicit certain TMs from the children, coaches are given autonomy to observe for TMs relating to any F4P value at any time.

The F4P pedagogy

The reflective approach places a special demand on coaches as they are asked to coach football using a format and a divergent style (Mosston and Ashworth, 2002) that may be alien to them. They are expected to adapt from a traditional technocratic approach which places an emphasis on learning football skills to a *facilitate–observe–reflect–reinforce* approach. The training of coaches that takes place on and off the field is based upon the principles that are set out in the manual. The aim is to develop the shared values in all the players through competition, learning, co-operation and reflection with an emphasis on fun and enjoyment. The coaching that takes place is based on players being able to recognise the value concepts in action and learning to model them. By the end of the programme the young people involved should be able to attach each value to specific behaviours and attitudes and have the motivation to transfer these behaviours to life beyond the football pitch.

Due to the nature of F4P coaching, the values being developed go beyond those that are typically taught through sport. *Trust* and *neutrality* are rarely key explicit elements of any sport programme. *Equality* is fundamental to all F4P coaching and teams are selected by the coach or the players in order to be fair and equal. Elitism is replaced by *inclusion*. The coaching is based around the values rather than the sport so that values are central to the teaching and are not just a by-product of what might happen on the field. Situations are facilitated where issues of *respect, responsibility, equity and inclusion, neutrality*, and *trust* are going to emerge and will need to be resolved by the players. Hellison and Templin (1991) incorporate similar scenarios into their responsibility model referring to them as 'built-in dilemma dialogues'. For example, the children are asked to select their own teams on the basis of fairness and equality. The teams would, therefore, be expected to have equal number of Arab and Jewish children and be equal in numbers and ability. For this to occur the children will need to demonstrate their *neutrality* (within the F4P project), *respect* one another and justify the *trust* that the coach has invested in them. Observations and evaluations have repeatedly shown this to happen when the children are delegated this *responsibility* with minimal coach intervention (Lambert and Gardiner, 2010).

The F4P pedagogy deliberately facilitates situations where the ability to co-operate and compromise, (values concerned with the welfare of others), is tested. For example, where there is a game with no referee the players have to agree an outcome from every contentious decision which may not be to the liking of some players but it is necessary to compromise for the game to run smoothly. A tournament involving all project clusters, the F4P Festival of Football, takes place after the coaching programme on day six. The removing of referees was extended to all F4P games including those in the Festival and, by and large, this move has proved a success leading to children taking *responsibility* for the administering of the laws. Reflecting with the players on such situations by asking people to explain the rationale behind their behaviour decisions can provide a basis of cognitive support which is a factor in inducing value change. Positive reinforcement is regarded as preferable to aversive control of behaviour (Smith *et al.*, 2007) as it has consistently been demonstrated to be most effective, especially with young people.

Football is a sport that is often synonymous with incidences of unethical behaviour but there are a number of reasons why it is such a suitable activity for the development of personal, social and moral values. One such reason is that it is a universally popular game. 'The people's game' as it has been branded, is the most popular game in the world, cutting across nationality, gender, social and class boundaries (Ben-Porat and Ben-Porat, 2004). It is not only relatively easy to organise and facilitate but most children love playing it. This is a crucial point to make in that the young people involved in F4P first and foremost are there to play football. Many of the situations set up deliberately in the practices within the manual are expected to lead to possible disagreements, cheating and intense competition between individuals and teams. The role of the coach is to observe, highlight and help the protagonists resolve these situations in a way that will impact on all of the young players involved in the session. Without these intense rivalries there would be limited opportunity to teach the behaviours attached to each value. Not only is football the 'hook' but it provides fertile ground for values teaching.

Value theory and value change

Football 4 Peace is fundamentally concerned with a set of core values, related to peace-building, being transmitted to young people using sport as a medium. In order to shed further light on this process it is expedient to explain an underpinning conceptual framework which links theories of value structure (Schwartz, 1992) and value change (Bardi *et al.*, 2009, Bardi and Goodwin, 2011) with the practice of values-based coaching methods. It is not uncommon for sport interventions to fall into a 'practice to theory' (Hellison and Doolittle, 2000) category where, although a conceptual framework has progressively emerged, it is primarily informed by practice that has been subjected to cycles of evaluation and adaptation over a number of years. In other words, through identifying good practice it has been possible to make sense of established value theories and to demonstrate their application. In the case of F4P a deeper understanding of the nature and structure of human values extends the significance of the work and illustrates the synergy between the progressive coaching methods, drawn from action research, and value theory.

According to the value theory developed by Rokeach (1973) and Schwartz (e.g. 1992), and outlined in previous chapters of this book, values are an individual's enduring beliefs that certain forms of behaviour, or long-term outcomes, are more personally or socially desirable than their opposing alternatives. Individual values are relatively few in number, and the same values are found world-wide, although their relative priorities differ in nations and individuals. People develop an individual *value system* in which their values become ordered by importance, and these priorities then guide their decisions and behaviour, and serve as standards for evaluation and justification of actions. These personal values transfer across situations, and it is this key characteristic of values that underpins the aim of the F4P programme to teach values through sport that will transfer to other life contexts.

Whereas value priorities differ among individuals and groups, the structural relationship between basic values is unchanging. Figure 9.1 presents a simplified version of the Schwartz circular continuum of values described in Chapter 8 of this book. Within this *value structure* the adjacent values have much in common, but values which are diametrically opposed in the circle are in conflict in daily life. The F4P values focus on *concern for others*, rather than *self-interest*. *Responsibility* represents benevolence or the *welfare of friends and team-mates*, while *equality* represents universalism or the *welfare of all*. This bi-polar axis of the model was discussed by Bardi and Schwartz in Chapter 8 where they contrasted the value of fair play (concern for others) with winning at all costs (self-interest).

However, F4P values also relate to the second bi-polar axis of the model and focus on *openness to change* rather than *stability*. The value of *independence* (or self-direction) contrasts *security* values, and the *excitement* and *pleasure* values which are intrinsic in all activities contrasts values of *tradition* and *conformity*. These structural relationships among values are important because *value systems* interact with *value structure*, such that when a particular value becomes more

Figure 9.1 A model of value relationships
Source: adapted by Lee (2003) from Schwartz (1992)

important in an individual's value system the opposing value becomes less important. The figure therefore demonstrates that the focus of F4P on values in the
shaded area of the figure are ideally selected to reduce the impact of the opposing values, such as *power, tradition,* and *security* which serve to perpetuate
conflict in divided societies.

Mechanisms of value change

Because values are enduring and trans-situational, they cannot be changed
rapidly. Five facilitators of change are proposed by Bardi and Goodwin (2011),
three of which are relevant to F4P.

Adaptation

People tend to adapt their values to reinforcement contingencies in the environment (see Chapter 8). Their dominant values may be frustrated if their situation
changes which may lead to questioning of those values and, if occurring repeatedly, could lead to the diminishing of importance of that value. Behaviour allied
to power and security values is not surprisingly prevalent in Israeli's divided society where a 'zero sum' mentality leading to intransigence is common. It is not
unusual for disagreements or even fights to break out between the Arab and
Jewish children on day one of the coaching but, if the learning environment and
coaching practice nurtures the F4P values effectively, by the last day this animosity can be transformed into group cohesion.

The continuous recognition and reinforcement of the five core F4P values through reflection and praise acts as a stimulus for value change. For example, throughout the coaching each child is treated on an equal basis irrespective of background or skill level and there is an emphasis on mutual *respect* that permeates through all activities. Arabs and Jews play together in teams coached by both Arab and Jewish coaches. By repeatedly presenting through carefully designed activities and values-based coaching methods an alternative set of values to those previously dominant the coach aims to alter the value priorities of the children. Only when certain values are repeatedly challenged and other diametrically opposed values are frequently reinforced will a change in the thoughts that affect perception and behaviour occur (Bardi and Goodwin, 2011). Young people may question their existing value systems if they consistently conflict with the values of a significant other (the coach) and the institutional (the project) value priorities.

A child who has only been subjected to prejudiced opinions against people from 'rival' communities is likely to feel uncomfortable and challenge these thoughts if they are continually put into situations where they find that they can work perfectly well with people from 'the other side'. Both Arab and Jewish communities share responsibility for hosting each coaching day which necessitates travelling between communities and the F4P off-pitch programme typically involves activities like traditional dance or orienteering where Arab and Jewish children share culture or work together to solve problems in each other's neighbourhood. Barriers are gradually broken down as previously accepted prejudices are challenged through natural social integration.

Consistency maintenance

The theory that changes in behaviour can lead to a reappraisal of values and consequent changes in attitudes informs much of the coaching F4P pedagogy. The process of consistency maintenance is when one is motivated to put right inconsistencies in self-concept resulting from incongruity between one's values and one's behaviour (Rokeach, 1973). It involves self-dissatisfaction which is a consequence of inconsistencies in the self-concept. The self-persuasion process (Aronson, 1999) relies on principles of cognitive dissonance where people realise that their expressed value may not be the one that drives their behaviour making the latter value salient. By reinforcing behaviour related to F4P values through teachable moments coaches are getting the children to question some deep-seated values that are antagonistic to their newly-adopted fair play approach. This disjuncture (Jarvis, 1987) has varying levels of impact depending on the effectiveness of the intervention or the person's openness to change.

Group identification

When somebody joins a new group or team the values of that group may differ from their own values. Changes in identification can lead to value change as joining a new group or team may well lead to adoption of their values which may differ from previous values (Bardi and Goodwin, 2011). F4P coaches instigate group bonding based on shared values which supersede religious or racial group-ings. This is symbolised by the new mixed Arab and Jewish team adopting the name of a European football club for the duration of the project. Alternative values may be used to interpret situations which replace previously dominant schema due to the switch in identification. By the time Real Madrid play Ajax in the F4P Festival differences in race, religion or culture are overridden by shared team goals.

Summary

Depending what values it is laden with, sport can either foster harmonious rela-tions between peoples or generate conflict. Thus, in deeply divided societies, simply getting rival communities to play more sport does not guarantee that social cohesion will follow (Coalter, 2010; Kay, 2009; Sugden and Bairner, 1995). To achieve the latter, the meanings attached to sport and the teaching and learning styles used need to be appropriate to peace related objectives. With due regard for this, a pedagogical model based upon using football as a tool for peaceful co-existence and conflict prevention has been devised. Its key characteristics are:

- An underpinning set of values that best relate to the F4P peace-building aims. *Respect, responsibility, equity and inclusion, trust and neutrality* are the core values which are modelled by the coaches and guide their work
- A four-phase format for each coaching session which includes a warm up, technical phase, game phase and cool down. Within each stage learning activities are facilitated which provide prime competitive or collaborative situations for values teaching.
- Coaches who are trained to implement a divergent coaching style distin-guished by a facilitate-observe-reflect-reinforce approach.
- Teachable moments are identified followed by reflection on and discussion of participants' behaviour by their peers. Positive examples of behaviour relating to the F4P values are recognised and reinforced through praise.

If coaching strategies that can affect value change are used in practice and rigor-ously evaluated then it opens up the possibility for sport interventions in different settings to decrease the importance of values that are associated with anti-social behaviour (power values) and increase the individual's adherence to values that lead to prosocial behaviour (universalism, benevolence).

One's values transcend situations and guide decision-making (Schwartz, 1992) and this has particular significance for F4P. The premise that positive values and attitudes learned on the sports field can be taken with the children into their community and exhibited there (Beedy, 1997) is worthy of further investigation. Society is in need of a cultural medium like sport through which young people are encouraged to replace anti-social with prosocial values. This chapter is concerned with illustrating the application of the F4P coaching manual which has developed through several action research cycles in order to improve its efficacy with respect to teaching values conducive to harmonious community relations. The next chapter explores how a motivational climate might be created which facilitates such learning in the affective and social domains.

References

Aronson, E. (1999) The power of self-persuasion. *American Psychologist*, 54, 875–84.

Bardi, A. and Goodwin, R. (2011) The dual route to value change: individual processes and cultural moderators. *Journal of Cross-Cultural Psychology*, 42(2), 271–87.

Bardi, A. and Schwartz, S.H. (2013) How does the value structure underlie value conflict? Chapter 8, this book.

Bardi, A., Lee, J., Hofman-Towfigh, N. and Soutar, G. (2009) The structure of intra-individual value change. *Journal of Personality and Social Psychology*, 97(5), 913–29.

Beedy, J.P. (1997) *Sports Plus: Positive Learning Using Sports*. Hamilton: Project Adventure.

Ben-Porat, G. and Ben-Porat, A. (2004) (Un)bounded Soccer: Globalization and Localization of the game in Israel, *International Review for the Sociology of Sport*, 39(4), 421–36.

Coalter, F. (2010) The politics of sport for development: limited focus programmes and broad gauge problems. *International Review of the Sociology of Sport*, 31, 295–314.

Coughlan, D. and Brannick, T. (2005) *Doing Action Research in Your Own Organization*. London: Sage.

Hellison, D. and Doolittle, S. (2000) Moral education in the practice of sport and physical education. In C.E. Gonçalves, S.P. Cumming, M.J.C e Silva and R.M. Malina (eds) *Sport and Education: Tribute to Martin Lee*. Coimbra: University of Coimbra.

Hellison, D. and Templin, T. (1991) *A Reflective Approach to Teaching Physical Education*. Champaign, IL: Human Kinetics.

Jarvis, P. (1987) *Adult Learning in a Social Context*. London: Croom Helm.

Kay, T. (2009) Developing through sport: Evidencing sport impacts on young people. *Sport in Society: The Impact of Sport*, 12(9), 177–91.

Krathwohl, D.R. (2002) A revision of Bloom's Taxonomy: An overview. *Theory into Practice*, 41(4), 212–18.

Laker, A. (2000) *Beyond the Boundaries of Physical Education: Educating Young People for Citizenship and Social Responsibility*. London: Routledge Falmer.

Lambert, J. (2006) The Football for Peace coaching manual: A values-based approach to coaching sport in a divided society. In Sugden, J. and Wallis, J. (eds) *Football for Peace? Teaching and Playing Sport for Conflict Resolution in the Middle East*. London: Meyer & Meyer.

Lambert, J. (2013) How does coach behaviour change the motivational climate? Chapter 10, this book.

Lambert, J. and Gardiner, J. (2010) Teaching and learning citizenship through physical education. In Hayes, S. and Stidder, G. (eds) *The Really Useful Book of Teaching Physical Education*. London: Routledge Falmer.

Lee, M.J. (2003) Values: Physical education and sport – a conflict of interests? The Physical Association Fellows' Lecture, December, London.

McNiff, J. and Whitehead, J. (2006) *Action Research*. London: Sage.

Mosston, M. and Ashworth, S. (2006) *Teaching Physical Education*. 5th edn. San Francisco, CA: Benjamin Cummings.

Reason, P. and Bradbury, H. (2001) *Handbook of Action Research*. London: Sage.

Rokeach, M. (1973) *The Nature of Human Values*. New York: Free Press.

Schon, D. (1983) *The Reflective Practitioner: How Professionals Think in Action*. London: Temple Smith.

Schwartz, S.H. (1992) Universals in the Context and structure of values: theoretical advances and empirical tests in 20 countries. In M.P. Zanna (ed.) *Advances in Experimental Social Psychology*, 25, 1–65. New York: Academic Press.

Schwartz, S.H. (2005) Robustness and fruitfulness of a theory of universals in individual human values. In Tamayo, A. and Porto, J. (eds) *Values and Behavior in Organizations*, pp. 56–95. Petrópolis: Vozes.

Schwartz, S.H. and Bardi, A. (2001) Value hierarchies across cultures: Taking a similarities perspective. *Journal of Cross-Cultural Psychology*, 32, 268–90.

Smith, R., Smoll, F. and Cumming S. (2007) Effects of a motivational climate intervention for coaches on young athletes' sport performance anxiety. *Journal of Sport and Exercise Pyschology*, 29, 39–59.

Sugden, J. (2006) The challenge of using a values-based approach to coaching sport and community relations in multi-cultural settings. The case of Football for Peace (F4P) in Israel. *European Journal for Sport and Society*, 3(1), 7–24.

Sugden, J. and Bairner, A. (1995) *Sport and Sectarianism in a Divided Ireland*. Leicester: Leicester University Press.

10 How does coach behaviour change the motivational climate?

The creation of a learning environment conducive to the transmission of prosocial values

John Lambert

This chapter describes how certain coach behaviours are critical to developing an environment conducive to the transmission of the five key Football 4 Peace (F4P) values that were described in Chapter 9 (Lambert). A coaching model is presented which is characterised by a learning climate where 'everyone is a winner' as psychomotor performance is replaced as the criterion for success by a range of values-based behaviours which can be demonstrated by everybody irrespective of their sporting ability. The process of training coaches will be explained, identifying the teaching styles and specific behaviours of the coach which are critical to fostering an atmosphere in which learning in the affective and social domains (Krathwohl, 2002; Laker, 2001) takes precedence within a sports coaching context.

The programme will be described in relation to the three environmental influences in Lee's (1995) interactionist model (Figure 10.1), notably an institutional value system, a significant others value system, and a motivational climate. In this context, the institutional value system is represented by *Football 4 Peace International*, a non-governmental organisation (NGO) for sport development (see www.football4peace.eu) which for several years was run in partnership between the University of Brighton, the German Sport University Cologne, and the British Council. The F4P values are embedded in its coaching manual. The aim of the project is to transmit values based upon co-existence and conflict resolution to influence the *personal value system* of each participant through the intervention of a team of trained coaches, who fill the role of *significant others*. In turn, the coaches' behaviour creates a *motivational climate* where prosocial values, attitudes and behaviour are salient. This manipulation of the learning environment leads to *consequences* for participants in terms of (a) perceptions of self and others in relation to competence, (b) enhanced positive emotions, and (c) increased prosocial behaviour.

The institutional value system

The F4P programme and the values it promotes were described in Chapter 9. The five values of *respect*, *responsibility*, *equity and inclusion*, *trust*, and *neutrality* fit the circular value structure of Schwartz (1992) and represent values

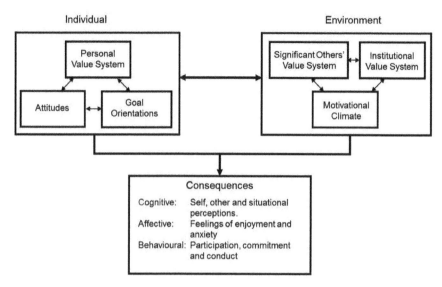

Figure 10.1 An interactionist model for research development
Source: adapted from Lee (1995)

demonstrating concern for the welfare of others in contrast to personal power and achievement. The programme also supports values of openness to change in opposition to values of security and tradition. These values are not considered as a value system with hierarchical priorities, and are promoted as of equal importance. However, they do take priority over values of showing skill or winning. Although not named in the peace-building values, the value of enjoyment is considered essential to the effective operation of the project.

The coaches' values

The coaches are the significant others in F4P. They have to meet the challenge of coaching sport in a tri-lingual environment within a society that is divided across religious, social, political, and cultural boundaries. They are also expected to change the emphasis of their coaching from the psychomotor to the social and affective domains and to embrace the F4P philosophy and methodology. This requires a diverse range of personal skills and attributes and frequently a change in the coaches' own value system before they can deliver F4P effectively in Israel. This may be a particular problem for Israeli coaches for whom power and security values typically have a high priority (Kaufmann and Galily, 2009).

This section on coaches' values will first summarise how the programme operates in Israel and then describe the coach recruitment process and the coach training camp that prepares coaches to meet the demands they will find there.

The coaching is delivered by coaches from the UK, Germany and Israel in partnership. In Israel the coaching staff consists of one European Union (EU) coach and a coach/translator from each Arab and Jewish community. This triad of coaches works with approximately 16 children aged 11–12 from both local communities for two hours and then a similar-sized group of 13–14-year-olds for the same length of time. When the children are not involved in on-pitch activities they are participating in off-pitch trust games, problem-solving and teambuilding with local youth workers. This pattern is replicated four times at each local project so that in total approximately 128 children, 12 coaches and 4 youth workers are involved at each venue. Additionally, an extra EU head coach with F4P experience oversees the programme liaising with local people in key leadership roles.

The coach recruitment process

Applicants for coaching positions are selected for interview using the following criteria: (a) their openness to 'new' coaching methods and reflective practice (b) whether their values appear to reflect those of the project and (c) their football coaching experience and/or qualifications. The reality is that many of the young coaches enlisted to work within the F4P ethos need to transform their practice from a didactic, technocratic coach to a facilitator–observer–reflector. This demands that the recruitment process be rigorous enough to identify those individuals who have the willingness, confidence and skills to make that often seismic shift in coaching style. At interview each EU applicant is asked to present a coaching scenario aimed at teaching a specific F4P value to their fellow applicants and, after taking part in several hours of practical values-based sessions, the candidates who model the requisite values and aptitudes are invited on the training camp. Lee (1993) was rightly concerned that coaches examine their own values and motivations as well as understanding those of their athletes (see Appendix 3). Not only must F4P coaches embrace the core values of the project, they are required to understand the F4P pedagogy and apply it in a challenging, tri-lingual situation (Lambert, 2006a).

The coach training camp

A coach training camp is held in the UK ten weeks before the project begins in Israel and lasts one week. It serves to demonstrate the values to the coaches and to introduce the pedagogical model. The week is critical to instilling the project's values into the EU and Israeli coaches and sports leaders, and their consequent actions are of considerable importance to transmitting the values thereafter.

The training is attended by a cohort of more than 100 young volunteer coaches from university sports courses in the UK and Germany and similarly inexperienced Arab and Jewish coaches from local sports clubs in Israel. A group of EU and Israeli coaches who have a background of values-based coaching at varying levels through contact with F4P are also invited. Each F4P coach has been selected on the basis of their ability to use football as a medium through which to teach values. While a basic experiential knowledge of football is required, it is equally important that the coaches are able to recognise how children learn values and are capable of creating an engaging, fun environment within which children can be taught them.

In Israel the 'twinned' Arab and Jewish communities are allocated a team of five EU coaches who work alongside their local counterparts. On the first day of the training camp the participants are put into groups with those that they will be working with in Israel. They then take part in off-pitch teambuilding, problem-solving and trust games activities that focus on the five core values and develop group identity. From day two they conduct on-pitch sessions with their coaching peers, using activities from the F4P coaching manual (Chapter 9) designed to transmit the values. By the end of the week each group has developed into a cohesive unit and is able to reflect and implement the values that permeate the F4P project.

Embracing a facilitate–observe–reflect approach

During the coach education programme the F4P coaches are given examples of how they can use positive reinforcement and dialogue as strategies to teach values. The initial coach education sessions are conducted in a similar format as the sessions in Israel but with peers instead of children. By taking the role of the children the young coaches are recipients of the values-based teaching and gain an insight into the various aspects of this pedagogical approach in order to better understand the issues when transferring this approach to children.

The coaches are introduced to the concept of 'teachable moments' (TMs), where actions are observed that offer tangible expressions of those otherwise abstract value concepts (Beedy, 1997). For example, the coach may illustrate respect by recognising and praising a player who shakes the hand of opponents directly after the match. As the players, in this case the coaches, become familiar with reflecting on their own and other's behaviour they will be able to recognise TMs for themselves, recall them and relate them to the core values. This form of learning places prosocial behaviour as the criterion for achieving competence and this form of competence is accessible to everyone at a self-referenced level. The coach acts as a facilitator for a reflective discussion about the TMs, their significance for that session and future behaviour goals.

Coaches are trained in how to positively reinforce the core values through private and public praise. Punishment is also occasionally used to discourage antisocial behaviour, for example when a player is cheating in a competitive drill, and they are either denied attention or reprimanded, but this approach is discouraged as it is rarely as effective as the player's response is less predictable and aversive methods tend to undermine the positive atmosphere that is being nurtured. On the occasions that this strategy is used the child is provided with an explanation of how this type of behaviour impacts on others and creates conflict. The coaches learn that by reinforcing certain behaviours they help to generate the cognitive dissonance that many of the children will feel as recognition for winning football games becomes of secondary importance. The children instead begin to seek social approval for their behaviour which is instrumental in altering personal value priorities (Schwartz, 1992).

The pedagogy goes beyond passive observance of the behaviours of significant others to intervening to change values by drawing attention to behaviours and discussing them. For example, players are progressively introduced to the concept of respect and what it looks like through TMs, it is discussed with them, transferred to them and ultimately demonstrated by them. One representation of this is that coaches are encouraged to observe for the way the children behave after their team scores a goal. They should note which children quietly shake the goal scorer's hand rather than run around punching the air in an over-zealous celebration which is provocative to the opposing team. The coach is then expected to facilitate a reflective dialogue which addresses why the more respectful response is deemed appropriate. This form of social learning requires the coach to model values and to encourage observational learning in a social context (Bandura, 1986).

While practice and guided discovery are advocated and used, the prevailing teaching style used in the F4P coaching is divergent (Mosston and Ashworth, 2002). The coach is taught to place the players into games or situations where the outcome cannot always be predicted. For example, the players may be given responsibility for deciding the rules of the games and the composition of each team within the parameters that they must be inclusive and fair. Contrary to some people's expectation, the young players in F4P thrive on responsibility and relish the autonomy that is afforded them. This coaching style would be seen by some coach educators as risky and discouraged by some national governing bodies (NGBs) as it deviates from a hegemonic, standardised coaching model that their accredited coaches are encouraged to follow (Cushion, 2011). This leads to problems of adaptation and resistance from some NGB-trained coaches to the progressive methods presented in F4P.

Cascade training

Initially the coach education was organised such that a few experienced UK coaches delivered exemplar sessions to the remaining EU and Israeli coaches. Over the past couple of years there has been a shift in approach towards a three-tier model of cascade training and mentoring which allocates coach education roles according to different levels of involvement and experience in F4P practices. The tier 1 coaches, usually the largest group, are those new to the project; tier 2s have at least one year of F4P experience; and those in tier 3 have enough expertise in values-based coaching to take a major leadership role in coach education. Tier 3 present the pedagogical model to the whole cohort, tier 2 work with tier 1 under the guidance of tier 3, and finally tier 1 deliver sessions from the F4P Manual with groups of children on the final day. As each coach gains more experience of values-based coaching and becomes more adept at the coaching methods their role in the coach education grows so that they assume increasing responsibility for passing on pedagogical skills and there is a permeation of the values among the coaches.

In accordance with principles of self-determination theory this has increased the autonomy, competence and relatedness (Deci and Ryan, 2000a) of all coaches and improved sustainability as the local Arab and Jewish coaches now have more responsibility for and ownership of the on-field activities through their coach training responsibilities. The coach educators on F4P are using similar methods to educate the coaches as the coaches are with the children; the development of self-autonomy supported by reciprocity, positive feedback and reinforcement (Smith and Smoll, 1996). There is now a strong impression that the local coaches could continue F4P without the support of the EU group which was not the case two years ago.

Creating a learning environment to promote values

A learning climate is created both by the nature and structure of the activities in the programme, and by the actions of the teachers or coaches within this structure. The next section will first summarise how the five F4P values are encouraged by the activities of the coaches. It will contain a description of how competitive activities are used to create the rivalries that produce the antisocial behaviour and the teachable moments through which values can be exemplified.

Establishing group identity

Identification with a group can lead to value change (Bardi and Goodwin, 2011) and this is a deliberate strategy in the project. A key task on the first day is to put the children into equal groups of mixed Arab and Jews and to give them F4P T-shirts to wear. They have to symbolically discard their local football shirts and replace them with F4P shirts to reinforce the feeling of equity and group identity. They are introduced to their EU coach and two Arab and Jewish coach–translators who work with them throughout the project so that relationships have time to build and typically a bond is created across the whole group. When this is achieved through the team-building and trust games facilitated by inclusive coaching practices the group's shared identity is stronger by the end of the week. Coaches were asked to keep reflective diaries and one young EU coach had written:

> It was an amazing week. The children arrived as two groups and went home as one. The communities that I worked in were only a few miles apart but most of the children had never experienced 'the other.' I felt proud at the tournament seeing my teams sitting together chatting to each other regardless of belief; the way all kids should!

Bearing in mind the divisions in Israeli society it is not surprising that there is initial resistance to building mixed community teams but gradually the coach is able to break barriers by employing activities that are fun and engendering an engaging learning environment. By the end of the programme the group had adopted an alternative set of values, including equality and respect, so huddles, high fives and other physical displays of friendship without boundaries were habitual and widespread.

Teaching values through competitive situations and moral dilemmas

A particular feature of F4P is the use of activities that will create conflict, in order that players can learn how to respond constructively. Intense rivalry is a common element in sport which makes it rather a surprising choice as a 'tool' for building community relations. It is precisely because of football's propensity to cause conflict and rivalry that makes it so suitable an activity for values-based peace-building work. The behaviours that are a product of this fierce competition provide opportunities for TMs in abundance.

Amid all the over-zealous rivalry that can lead to anger, cheating and aggression, there are always examples of *respect, responsibility, equity, inclusion* and *trust* being demonstrated which can be observed, reflected upon and reinforced. For example, when using cones for goals there will inevitably be some contentious decisions over whether a shot has gone inside or outside the cone. This is likely to lead to arguing between the teams especially as referees are rarely used. The coach is trained to stand back and observe for the children who mediate and encourage compromise. During the Cool Down the coach will reflect on the incident asking the players to identify any peers whose actions helped to minimise conflict and how they had acted to resolve it.

Moral dilemmas are commonplace in sport (Lee, 2004; Hellison and Templin, 1991) and are utilised within the F4P teaching strategy. A dilemma may be created by the coach if they leave the group to run their own substitutions as their chances of winning the game may be diminished if they give the less accomplished players equal game time to the most proficient players (see Chapter 12 Telfer and Knowles). However, the children are also aware that equity and inclusion are central to the ethos of the project. The resultant dissonance may lead to a questioning of their value priorities. It is imperative that coaches resist the temptation to intervene in any intra- or inter-group disputes that take place (unless it escalates to violence) and merely stand back, observe and be ready to reflect on behaviours witnessed later in the session.

Developing the values

Opportunities for learning through reinforcement are commonly facilitated by the coach within the reflective 'cool-down' phase at the end of the day. The coaches are guided to ask the children to reflect on peer behaviours observed and then ask them to think in a more abstract way in order to generalise from one experience to another. Finally, they broaden the intellectual exercise by expecting them to apply what they have learned to other situations. For example, a player may offer to leave the field so that one of the substitutes can get some playing time. The children may be able to compare that selfless attitude to somebody who offers to start on the bench then, in a different context, to somebody in their community who voluntarily gives up their time to do charity work. To facilitate learning through this cognitive process requires skill and practice in order for questions to be crafted at an appropriate, progressive level. In respect of each value the coach prompts the children to ask themselves What does this mean? What does it look like in action? (Beedy, 1997).

Behaviours are more likely to become habitual if the children not only know what to do and how to do it but why they are doing it (Covey, 1989; Smith *et al.*, 2003). This contextualisation is what gives them a rationale for their behaviour and a conviction to sustain it beyond the football field. The process is enhanced if the coach relates the behaviours to situations in the outside world. By comparing playing fairly on the field to adhering to laws in the community children can learn that in both contexts it will lead to a more just, cohesive and satisfying situation. Conversely, not playing to the rules will lead to conflict and animosity. By facilitating transfer of learning the coach has 'encapsulated the profound metaphors of life that lie just under the surface of the games we play' (Beedy, 1997: 114).

Achievement goal theory

The coaching philosophy extolled within the project illustrates some elements of Achievement Goal Theory (AGT). There is abundant empirical evidence to suggest that a young person who plays sport within a mastery climate where the coach rewards them for effort, improvement and co-operation in order to develop a self-referenced concept of ability will experience greater enjoyment, be more intrinsically motivated to participate and is more likely to exhibit prosocial behaviours than someone who plays in a performance climate (Duda and Balaguer, 2007). A performance climate, by contrast, develops a comparative concept of ability. The coach reinforces superiority over others and gives more attention and recognition to the talented and successful.

F4P promotes values related to equality, not power and status, hence it seeks to develop a self-referenced view of success rather than a comparative view, which can lead to anxiety and fear of failure in those with low ability. An environment of emotional safety where fear of failure is eliminated and positive feedback is available to everyone irrespective of their football skills can be attractive to all children whatever their personal motivational disposition.

Research evidence from Lee *et al.* (2000) demonstrates that enjoyment is valued most highly by young athletes. Enjoyment is an outcome of the task-involving goal state activated by the mastery climate created. It is accompanied by low levels of anxiety hence the fun that children have in a non-threatening setting leads to a positive affective response and a desire to participate due to intrinsic motivation (Deci and Ryan, 2000a). As the Jewish and Arab children mix and play together gradually they begin to associate co-existence with enjoyment, put divisions to one side and realise that they have a great deal in common. The collaborative activities within the F4P coaching manual, such as ball juggling as a trio linked by hands, offer prime opportunities to co-operate in helping others to succeed and this amity goal is particularly significant to the people of their age (Levontin and Bardi, submitted).

Self-determination in practice

The F4P coaching formula as set out in the coaching manual has synergy with the tenets of self-determination theory (SDT) which is built on the notion of autonomy support through a democratic coaching style which includes listening to the athletes and providing positive feedback (Ntoumanis, 2012). The F4P coach education programme espouses the gradual devolvement of responsibility to the players within a climate of emotional safety where coach-athlete mutuality rather than controlling methods are predominant (Potrac and Barrett, 2011). The F4P coaching manual is designed to be used alongside athlete-centred, autonomy-supportive methods and the consequent autonomy, competence and relatedness (Amorose, 2007) that the children feel can provide the intrinsic motivation to embrace the prosocial values and the behaviours attached to them as legitimate goals hence all elements in Lee's consequences box (Figure 10.1) are enhanced. Practitioners trained in the F4P pedagogic model, although equipped with the basic organisation and communication skills, are encouraged to give responsibility to the children and listen to their viewpoints in order to empower them in their choices of behaviour. The cool-down is a case in point as in this concluding reflective phase to the coaching session responsibility is gradually devolved to the players by the coach. The coach is delegated initially with the task of reflecting on, articulating, and reinforcing prosocial behaviours before progressively transferring this responsibility to the children on the second or third day of the project by which time they will be able to recognise and describe TMs for themselves. Coach feedback has suggested that the children respond positively to being given responsibility and to receiving approval from their peers.

In the spirit of equity the aim is to create an inclusive environment as the coach makes little reference to football prowess and rejects elitism in favour of switching the focus to prosocial behaviour and valuing everyone's efforts in this regard. Children judge a coach on how they are treated and, as Beedy (1997: 64) puts it, 'Children may forget what you say but will never forget how you make them feel.'

Putting the values to the test

The project concludes with a Festival of Football which is a competitive tournament where some of the five core F4P values come into direct conflict with strong power and achievement values related to winning matches in a performance climate and ultimately a trophy for best team or fair play. This puts the previous values learning to the test as the players are separated from their regular coaches in this highly charged situation.

There has been debate within F4P about whether there should be any prizes awarded at the Festival with persuasive arguments for and against. One argument for retaining the trophies is to provide a test situation. However, when positive reinforcement takes the form of prizes it can lead to an artificial motivational climate where the behaviour desired by the coach is exhibited for the wrong reasons (Kohn, 1993). For example, a minority of teams were motivated to display the right behaviour principally to win the fair play trophy. As Shields and Bredemeier (1995: 53) put it, 'the rationale behind the choice of behaviour (the process) determines the morality of the behaviour'. If the aim is for the children to internalise the core values and to take them beyond the football field then this is more likely to be achieved through intrinsic goals such as increased self-esteem.

The rationale for removing extrinsic motivation in the form of prizes from youth sport is a strong one because extrinsic motivation often undermines intrinsic (De Charms, 1968) but that would necessitate a significant shift in coaching culture. In the context of F4P there would be a stronger case for awarding a prize to the winning team than a fair play trophy as this would test whether the players are intrinsically motivated to play fair.

There are some local coaches who during the festival of football have got caught up in the competitive atmosphere and forget that they should be modelling the F4P values but fortunately these are a small minority. Competition is a feature of sport just as it is a constituent of society in general and young people need to understand how to deal with competition without being divisive. One UK coach observed,

> I feel the festival is a good idea, however, from my experience a lot of the values were lost. Coaches were yelling from the sideline, parents were provoking the players and a sense of fair play was lost. However, it was clear that some teams had embraced the values and displayed them in the games. That was really inspirational to see.

While many of the children had internalised the F4P values enough to consistently exhibit moral attitudes without their coaches at the festival, for some the adaptation had been more temporary and superficial. If a whole team scored consistently high or low on sportsmanship then that may reflect on the effectiveness of the coach.

Conclusion

The narrative in Chapter 10 has described how a set of values have been promoted by the people involved in the delivery of football for peace by utilising a pedagogical model within a motivational climate that they have created. The teaching of the values and the fostering of the learning environment are dependent on the actions of the coaches who promote the project's transcending value system and may undergo changes to their own value system. They adopt a facilitative coaching style which reflects values of responsibility and equality in contrast to traditional didactic methods which reflect power and security (Cushion, 2010). The recruitment and training of these coaches is critical to the whole process.

A key legacy of F4P has been the values-based pedagogical paradigm which invites coaches to take an alternative, humanistic view of their role (Hellison, 1995) and provides them with the knowledge and skills to create a climate where young people whose value systems are taking shape can learn positive values.

References

Amorose, A.J. (2007) Coaching effectiveness. In M.S. Hagger and N.L.D. Chatzisarantis (eds) *Intrinsic Motivation and Self-Determination in Exercise and Sport*. Champaign. IL: Human Kinetics, pp. 209–27.

Bandura, A. (1986) *Social Foundations of Thought and action: A Social Cognitive Theory.* Englewood Cliffs, NJ: Prentice-Hall.

Bardi, A. and Goodwin, R. (2011) The dual route to value change: individual processes and cultural moderators. *Journal of Cross-Cultural Psychology*, 42(2), 271–87.

Beedy. J.P. (1997) *Sports Plus. Positive Learning Using Sports*. Hamilton: Project Adventure.

Covey, S. (1989) *The Seven Habits of Highly Effective People*. London: Simon and Schuster.

Cushion, C. (2010) Coach behaviour. In J. Lyle and C. Cushion (eds) *Sports Coaching: Professionalisation and Practice*. Edinburgh: Elsevier.

Cushion, C. (2011) Coach and athlete learning: a social approach. In R.I. Jones, P. Potrac, C. Cushion and L.T. Ronglan (eds) *The Sociology of Sport Coaching*. Abingdon: Routledge.

De Charms, R. (1968) *Personal Causation*. New York: Academic Press.

Deci, E.L. and Ryan, R.M. (2000a) The what and why of goal pursuits: Human needs and the self-determination of behaviour. *Psychological Inquiry*, 11, 227–68.

Deci, E.L. and Ryan, R.M. (2000b) Self-determination theory and the facilitation of intrinsic motivation, social development, and well-being. *American Psychologist*, 55, 68–78.

Duda, J.L. and Balaguer, I. (2007) The coach-centred motivational climate. In S. Jowell and D. Lavalee (eds) *Social Psychology of Sport*. Champaign, IL: Human Kinetics.

Hellison, D. (1995) *Teaching Responsibility through Physical Activity*. Champaign, IL: Human Kinetics.

Hellison, D. and Templin, T. (1991) *A Reflective Approach to Teaching Physical Education*. Champaign, IL: Human Kinetics.

Kaufmann, H. and Galily, Y. (2009) Sport, Zionist ideology and the state of Israel. *Sport in Society*, 12(4), 1013–27.

Knafo, A. and Schwartz, S.H. (2003) Parenting and adolescents' accuracy in perceiving parental values. *Child Development,* 73, 595–611.

Kohn, A. (1993) *Punishment by Rewards*. Boston, MA: Houghton Mifflin.

Krathwohl, D.R. (2002) A revision of Bloom's taxonomy: An overview. *Theory into Practice*, 41(4), 212–218.

Laker, A. (2001) *Developing Personal, Social and Moral Education through Physical Education*. London: Routledge Falmer.

Lambert, J. (2006a) A values-based approach to coaching sport in divided societies: The Football for Peace coaching manual. In J. Sugden and J. Wallis (eds) *Teaching and Playing Sport for Conflict Resolution in the Middle East*. London: Meyer & Meyer, pp. 13–34.

Lambert, J. (2006b) From Kfar Kara/Menashe to Acco: A comparison of two Football for Peace experiences. In J. Sugden and J. Wallis (eds) *Teaching and Playing Sport for Conflict Resolution in the Middle East*. London: Meyer & Meyer, pp. 35–50.

Lambert, J. (2013) How can we teach values through sport? Chapter 9, this book.

Lee, M. (1993) Why are you coaching children? In M. Lee (ed.) *Coaching Children in Sport: Principles and Practice*. London: E. & F.N. Spon.

Lee, M.J. (1995) Relationships between values and motives in sport. Paper presented at the 9th European Congress in Sports Psychology, Brussels, Belgium, 4–9 July.

Lee, M.J. (2004) The importance of values in the coaching process. In M.Silva and R. Malina (eds) *Children and Youth in Organized Sports*. Coimbra: Coimbra University Press, pp. 82–94.

Lee, M.J., Whitehead, J. and Balchin, N. (2000) The measurement of values in sport:Development of the Youth Sport Values Questionnaire. *Journal of Sport and Exercise Psychology*, 22, 307–26.

Levontin, L. and Bardi, A. (Submitted) Amity goals: Unveiling a missing goal orientation using values. Manuscript under review.

Mosston, M. and Ashworth, S. (2002) *Teaching Physical Education*. 5th edn. San Francisco, CA: Pearson Education.

Ntoumanis, N. (2012) A self-determination theory perspective on motivation in sport and physical education: current trends and possible future research directions. In G. Roberts (ed.) *Advances in Motivation in Sport and Exercise*, 3rd edn. Champaign, IL: Human Kinetics.

Potrac, P. and Barrett, S. (2011) Jurgen Habermas: Communicative action, the system and the lifeworld: critiquing social interaction in coaching. In R.L. Jones, P. Potrac, C. Cushion and L.T. Ronglan (eds) *The Sociology of Sport Coaching*. Abingdon: Routledge.

Schwartz, S.H. (1992) Universals in the content and structure of values: theoretical advances and empirical tests in 20 countries. In M.P. Zanna (ed.) *Advances in Experimental Social Psychology*, 25, 1–65. New York: Academic Press.

Schwartz, S.H. (2012) Values and religion in adolescent development: Cross national and comparative evidence. In G. Tromsdorff and X. Chen (eds) *Values, Religion, and Culture in Adolescent Development*. New York: Cambridge University Press.

Shields, D.L.L. and Bredemeier, B.J.L. (1995) *Character Development and Physical Activity*. Champaign, IL: Human Kinetics.

Smith, R.E. and Scholl, F.L. (1996) The coach as a focus of research and intervention in youth sports. In R.E. Scholl and F.L. Smith (eds) *Children and Youth in Sport: A Biopsychosocial Perspective*. Chicago, IL: Brown & Benchmark.

Smith, A., Lovatt, M. and Wise, D. (2003) *Accelerated Learning: A User's Guide*. London: Network Educational Press.

Telfer, H. and Knowles, Z. (2013) How can sport practitioners balance conflicting values? Chapter 12, this book.

11 How important are the values of significant others?

The influence of physical education teachers' values and types of school on youth sport values

Paul Freeman, Alec Leslie, Hannah Leger and Craig Williams

A defining characteristic of personal values is that they are ordered by importance. Therefore they can be considered as hierarchical value systems for individuals or groups. In Chapter 3, Lee and colleagues identified an 18-item hierarchical value system for young athletes. They found that young athletes attached most importance to enjoyment, personal achievement, and sportsmanship. Further, Lee (1996) and Lee and Balchin (1996) asked young athletes which *significant others* most influenced their sport values; coach, club, and teacher were found to be the three most influential significant others. No research, however, has specifically examined the similarity between youth sport values and the value priorities of significant others. Given that values impact upon a range of outcomes such as perceptions, attitudes, goals, and behaviour (see Chapter 8 of this book), it is vital that researchers explore how youth sport values are influenced by the social environment.

In the UK, sport is a component of physical education (PE); hence it is appropriate to study the similarity between the sport values of pupils and their PE teachers. The PE and Sport Survey 2009/10 (Quick *et al.*, 2010) found that pupils in state secondary schools had an average of 107 minutes of PE per week, and that 46 per cent of pupils participated in at least 3 hours of PE and out of hours sport organised by their school per week. Therefore, drawing on social learning theory (Bandura, 1977), teachers, as easily observable and authoritative figures, might be key sources from which their pupils learn sport values. Indeed, researchers have argued that personal values are developed during childhood socialisation via interaction and experience, such that children can learn values by observing their environment and the behaviours of their significant others (Knafo and Schwartz, 2003; Rokeach, 1973). Thus, how PE teachers behave and the values which they display will be observed by their pupils, who might then internalise the values.

If teachers are to effectively transmit values, a crucial requirement may be that pupils accurately perceive those values. In an 18-month longitudinal study with 1,014 German secondary school pupils, Gniewosz and Noack (2012) found that children's perceptions of their parents' values were a key pathway to children sharing those values. Similarly, in sports coaching, Smith and Smoll (1991) outlined the importance of children's perceptions in mediating the impact of coaching behaviours on children's attitudes, and further concluded that children's perceptions are often very accurate. This central role of children's perceptions in the transmission of values from parents and from coaches underpins the need to examine their role in the transmission of values from teachers.

Although values are core beliefs that transcend situations (Schwartz, 1994), Lee (1993; Appendix 3, this book) found that students and coaches expressed different value priorities for sport and for life. This illustrates that some *value differentiation* can occur under strong contextual influences (Daniel *et al.*, 2011). Interestingly, in a review of character development and physical activity Shields and Bredemeier (1995) found a lower level of moral reasoning in sport than in life. They described a special form of 'game reasoning' and a 'bracketed moral-ity' in which the normal standards of daily life are temporarily suspended. In the *sport context* moral values may thus have lower priorities. Therefore in compar-ing the values of pupils and teachers it is important to differentiate between teachers' values when teaching and when playing sport themselves.

In the *teaching context*, teachers may prioritise certain values due to internal and external influences. For example, teachers can feel a personal responsibility to promote respect, cooperation, and social responsibility through their teaching (Ennis, 1994). Further, in state schools the Key Stage 3 and 4 National Curriculum for Physical Education (NCPE; Qualifications and Curriculum Authority, 2007a, 2007b), which provides a framework for PE for pupils aged 11–16 years, high-lights a range of objectives that reflect values such as enjoyment, achievement, overcoming opponents, and promoting fairness, team work and responsible citi-zenship. Independent schools have greater freedom over the content and focus of their sporting activities. In contrast to the range of objectives in the NCPE, researchers have suggested that independent schools often place a key emphasis on competitive sport, high achievement, and developing elite athletes, which are used to promote a school's reputation (Horne *et al.*, 2011; Swain, 2006; Tozer, 2012). Better facilities and more time are directed towards sporting competence, with Saturday morning sport and the employment of specialist sport coaches. Indeed, Swain (2006) observed that the time devoted to sport in one independent school was double that typically allocated within the state sector. As Ennis and Chen (1995) noted, if institutional value systems differ across types of schools, pupils would be exposed to different educational opportunities and therefore the sport values of pupils from state and independent schools might differ.

The aim of the present study was to explore the potential influence of PE teachers' values and type of school on youth sport values. An initial examination was made of the perceived importance of significant others on the sport values of school children. Subsequently four key objectives were set to examine:

1   how similar pupils' sport values were to those of their PE teachers;
2   if the pupils' perceptions of their teachers' values mediated the relationship between the values of teachers and pupils;

3   if teachers' values were consistent across teaching and playing contexts; and
4   if type of school influenced pupil's values.

We hypothesised that there would be a significant positive correlation between pupils' own value systems and the value systems of their PE teachers. We also hypothesised that there would be a significant positive correlation between pupils' perceptions of the teachers' values and the teachers' actual values, and that pupils' perceptions would mediate the relationship between the values of teachers and pupils. Further, we hypothesised that teachers would prioritise different values in teaching compared to playing sport. Finally, we hypothesised that sport values would differ between pupils from state and independent schools.

Method

Participants

A total of 438 school children from the southwest of England participated in the study. After screening for inconsistent responses, 27 participants were removed leaving a final sample of 411 pupils (188 males, 221 females, 2 unreported; age range 11–16 years, mean = 14.0 years, SD = 1.6) and their PE teachers (9 males, 10 females; mean age = 34.7 years, SD = 8.1). All pupils had attended their current school for at least six months, and were at Key Stage 3 ($n = 191$) or 4 ($n = 220$). There were 143 pupils and four teachers from state schools, and 263 pupils and 15 teachers from independent schools. Pupils participated at recreational ($n = 71$), school/club ($n = 236$), county ($n = 64$), and regional ($n = 23$) levels (17 unreported) across team ($n = 240$) and individual ($n = 166$) sports (5 unreported). Teachers participated at recreational ($n = 9$), club ($n = 2$), county ($n = 6$), and regional ($n = 2$) levels across team ($n = 14$) and individual ($n = 5$) sports. They had a mean 11.9 years (SD = 7.7) total teaching experience, and had taught in their current school for a mean 7.5 years (SD = 4.6).

Measures

Youth sport values

The Youth Sport Values Questionnaire (YSVQ) described in Chapter 3 was used in four modified versions. Following an initial stem of 'When I do sport it is important to me that …', the YSVQ asks participants to respond to 18 value statements on a seven-point asymmetric rating scale ranging from –1 ('this idea is the opposite of what I believe') through 0 ('this idea is not important to me') to 5 ('this idea is extremely important to me'). The YSVQ was used to provide group mean scores on each of the 18 values, which were then ranked in order of importance to demonstrate the value systems.

Pupils and teachers each completed two modified versions of the YSVQ. Pupils firstly completed the YSVQ in relation to what was important to them when they played sport. Pupils responded to 20 items on the seven-point asymmetric rating scale. Following Lee *et al.* (Chapter 3), these included two non-scoring items that made conflicting statements and served to identify inconsistent responses. Further, following previous research in general social psychology (e.g. Bardi and Schwartz, 2003) and the recommendation of Lee *et al.* (2008), prior to rating the values, participants were asked to select their most and least important value to anchor their use of the response scale. The second YSVQ completed by pupils assessed their perceptions of the values that were important to their main PE teacher, with the initial stem of 'My PE teacher thinks that when I do sport it is important that …'.

Teachers initially completed the YSVQ in relation to what was important to them when they played sport. The format and instructions were the same as used with pupils. Teachers then completed a second version of the YSVQ in relation to what was important to them when teaching sport, with the initial stem of 'When I teach sport it is important that my pupils …'.

Significant others

Pupils completed the Significant Others Questionnaire (SOQ) used by Lee and Balchin (1996). The measure asked pupils to rate nine significant others on how much each one influenced what they thought was important in their main sport. Pupils responded on a five-point scale ranging from 0 ('does not apply') through 1 ('does not influence you at all') to 4 ('influences you very much indeed').

Procedures

The study was approved by an institutional ethics review committee. All head teachers were provided an information sheet and signed informed consent for their school to be involved in the project. Data were collected anonymously from pupils in class time. The class teacher and a member of the research team were present to guide the pupils and answer questions. Pupils completed demographic information before completing the two versions of the YSVQ and the SOQ. Although not analysed in the present study, pupils then completed the Attitudes to Moral Decision-making in Youth Sport Questionnaire–2 (see Appendix 2).

PE teachers completed their questionnaires in a classroom. Initially, teachers completed demographic information, before completing the two versions of the YSVQ. After all measures were completed, participants were debriefed, and given the opportunity to ask any questions.

Results

Descriptive statistics which relate to the exploration of hierarchical priorities will be presented before the data on correlations and group differences which relate to the examination of hypotheses.

Importance of significant others

Pupils' perceived that the most important influences on their sport values were coach, club and friends; school and PE teacher ranked sixth and seventh respectively (see Table 11.1). However, school ranked last for state pupils but third for independent school pupils. These rankings include only those pupils for whom a particular significant other such as coaches or siblings was applicable. When the ratings were instead analysed from all pupils, friends ranked first and the importance of schools and teachers rose to third and fourth place.

The value systems of pupils and teachers

The hierarchical value systems of pupils and teachers are presented in Table 11.2 alongside the value system found by Lee *et al.* in Chapter 3. Whereas pupils themselves prioritised enjoyment and achievement they perceived their teachers to prioritise achievement and contract maintenance. Teachers themselves prioritised sportsmanship and being fair when teaching but self-actualisation and contract maintenance when playing sport. Nevertheless there was high consistency across those values ranked at the extremes of the hierarchy. In all value systems personal achievement, contract maintenance, and sportsmanship were within the top five ranks whereas conformity and winning were within the bottom three. Pupils perceived their teachers to rank enjoyment lower and obedience higher than their own or the teachers' own ratings.

Relationships between the sport value systems of pupils and their PE teachers

There were strong parametric and non-parametric correlations between the four relevant value systems (see Table 11.3). The correlations between the pupils' own ratings and the values of school children in Lee *et al.* (Chapter 3) were also significant ($r = .93$, $\rho = .95$, $p < .01$), despite the inclusion of recreational participants in the present sample.

   Moreover, a mediation analysis using the PROCESS SPSS custom dialogue (Hayes, 2012) examined if pupils' perception of their teachers' values mediated the relationship between teachers' and pupils' values. After controlling for teachers' values in playing sport, the indirect effect from teachers to pupils' values via pupils' perceptions was significant ($ab = .48$, 95% CI = .05–1.15).

Comparison of teachers' values for playing sport and teaching

There were high correlations between teachers' values in the two contexts, but an examination of Table 11.2 shows that the moral values of being fair, tolerance, obedience, and sportsmanship were ranked higher by teachers when teaching than when playing. Paired samples *t*-tests with Bonferroni correction revealed significant differences between their ratings for three values. Sportsmanship and obedience were higher in teaching compared to playing ($t = -3.77$ to -3.83, $p < .01$); companionship was higher when playing compared to teaching ($t = 4.44$, $p < .01$).

Table 11.1 Perceived importance of significant others on the value systems of youth sport participants

Significant other	Combined sample				State school pupils				Independent school pupils				Overall sample		
	Rank	Mean	SD	n	Rank	Mean	SD	n	Rank	Mean	SD	n	Rank	Mean	SD
Coach	1	3.09	.86	353	1	2.93	.92	85	1	3.13	.83	268	2	2.67	1.32
Club	2	2.94	.93	296	5	2.69	1.01	89	2	3.04	.88	207	7	2.14	1.53
Friends	3	2.74	.87	411	2	2.77	.95	133	5	2.72	.83	278	1	2.72	.92
Sporting hero or role model	4	2.71	1.06	319	3	2.76	1.15	93	6	2.69	1.03	226	8	2.13	1.46
Father	5	2.69	1.00	371	7	2.57	.99	104	4	2.73	1.00	267	5	2.43	1.24
School	6	2.61	1.01	411	9	2.17	1.03	133	3	2.82	.94	278	3	2.56	1.12
PE teacher	7	2.58	.99	410	6	2.58	1.01	132	7	2.57	.99	278	4	2.54	1.07
Mother	8	2.48	1.06	387	4	2.75	1.02	117	8	2.36	1.05	270	6	2.34	1.18
Brother(s) or sister(s)	9	2.24	1.02	349	8	2.32	.98	107	9	2.20	1.04	242	9	1.91	1.23

Notes: With the exception of the overall sample (n = 411), participants who stated that a significant other did not apply to them were removed prior to the calculation of that mean.

Table 11.2 The value systems of pupils and teachers

| | Pupils | | | | | | PE teachers | | | | | | Youths in Lee et al. (2000) | | |
| | Values in playing | | | Perception of teachers' values | | | Values in teaching | | | Values in playing | | | | | |
Value type	Rank	Mean	SD	Rank	Mean	SD	Rank	Mean	SD	Rank	Mean	SD	Rank	Mean	SD
Enjoyment	1	4.04	1.15	8	3.57	1.26	3	4.32	.95	3	3.89	.81	1	4.22	1.02
Personal achievement	2	3.57	1.33	1	4.20	1.03	4	4.26	.87	=5	3.74	1.10	2	4.04	1.02
Contract maintenance	3	3.41	1.41	2	4.13	1.08	5	4.11	1.20	2	4.00	.82	4	3.89	1.11
Compassion	4	3.31	1.28	7	3.60	1.22	=8	3.63	1.07	=5	3.74	.99	6	3.68	1.12
Sportsmanship	5	3.28	1.40	4	4.01	1.09	1	4.63	.76	4	3.79	.98	3	3.90	1.07
Being fair	6	3.27	1.33	6	3.74	1.19	2	4.42	.61	9	3.47	1.47	5	3.73	1.18
Showing skill	7	3.21	1.31	5	3.87	1.09	11	3.53	1.17	8	3.58	.96	8	3.59	1.15
Tolerance	8	3.10	1.37	9	3.52	1.23	=8	3.63	1.01	13	2.84	1.34	7	3.67	1.09
Conscientious	9	3.08	1.32	10	3.28	1.44	7	3.74	1.41	5	3.74	1.15	11	3.47	1.11
Team cohesion	10	3.08	1.36	11	3.20	1.43	14	3.05	1.43	12	3.11	1.28	10	3.50	1.22
Self-actualisation	11	3.06	1.39	13	3.00	1.38	6	4.05	.78	1	4.16	.76	14	3.04	1.45
Health and fitness	12	2.94	1.48	12	3.19	1.34	13	3.11	1.45	10	3.16	1.46	13	3.20	1.46
Obedience	13	2.81	1.45	3	4.07	1.16	12	3.21	1.27	=16	1.79	1.18	9	3.58	1.24
Excitement	14	2.69	1.50	15	2.94	1.34	15	2.61	.98	15	2.16	1.17	12	3.22	1.38
Companionship	15	2.52	1.63	17	1.70	1.67	16	.89	1.24	14	2.26	1.41	16	2.00	1.65
Public image	16	2.28	1.42	14	2.97	1.60	10	3.58	1.30	10	3.16	1.34	15	2.94	1.38
Conformity	17	1.60	1.59	16	2.10	1.83	18	.58	1.68	18	.53	1.12	17	1.86	1.64
Winning	18	1.06	1.74	18	1.19	1.78	17	.68	1.63	=16	1.79	1.93	18	1.27	1.75
Mean		2.91			3.24			3.22			3.05			3.27	

Table 11.3 Correlations between value systems of pupils and PE teachers

	1	2	3	4
1. Pupils' own values		.83**	.85**	.79**
2. Pupils' perception of teacher's values	.81**		.88**	.62**
3. Teachers' values in teaching	.83**	.71**		.85**
4. Teachers' values in playing	.77**	.53*	.83**	

Notes: * $p < .05$; ** $p < .01$. Pearson's r above the diagonal, Spearman's ρ below the diagonal.

Comparing the value systems of youth sport participants from independent and state schools and their perceptions' of PE teachers' values

In order to identify group differences a two-way multivariate analysis of covariance (MANCOVA) was performed on the pupils' value system data with type of school (state, independent) as a between-participants factor, focus of pupils' rating (own values, perceived teachers' values) as a within-participants factor, and mean importance of values as a covariate. Significant main effects were found for school type ($F = 4.09$, $p < .01$, $\eta_p^2 = .17$) and pupils' ratings ($F = 5.01$, $p < .01$, $\eta_p^2 = .21$), along with a significant interaction ($F = 2.58$, $p < .01$, $\eta_p^2 = .12$). Pupils from state schools valued conformity and companionship more highly than pupils from independent schools who valued self-actualisation, personal achievement, excitement, sportsmanship, and showing skill more highly than state school pupils. Pupils valued enjoyment and companionship more highly than they perceived their teachers did, and perceived that their teachers valued public image, personal achievement, obedience, sportsmanship, showing skill, and contract maintenance more highly than they did themselves. Interactive effects showed pupils from independent schools, compared to state schools, valued self-actualisation, personal achievement, health and fitness, sportsmanship, excitement and showing skill more, and also perceived that their teachers valued personal achievement more (see Table 11.4). Compared to the perception of independent school pupils, state school pupils perceived that their teachers valued conscientiousness, compassion and tolerance more highly.

Discussion

This study breaks new ground by directly examining the influence of PE teachers' values and type of school on youth sport values, but results must be interpreted with reference to the relative importance of significant others. Consistent with findings from Lee and Balchin (1996) coaches and clubs were viewed as most influential but, in contrast, friends replaced teachers in third place while schools and PE teachers were ranked sixth and seventh. Since coaches and clubs are voluntarily selected they are naturally important, and the new influence of friends over teachers and schools may in part reflect an increase in social networking among pupils. A greater influence of schools in the independent

Table 11.4 The value systems of state and independent school pupils and their perceptions of their PE teachers' values

Value type	Pupils' own values				Pupils' perception of teachers' values			
	State		Independent		State		Independent	
	Mean	SD	Mean	SD	Mean	SD	Mean	SD
Enjoyment	3.86	1.36	4.13	1.02	3.57	1.35	3.57	1.23
Personal achievement	3.04	1.50	3.82	1.16	3.98	1.15	4.30	.96
Contract maintenance	3.17	1.58	3.53	1.31	4.02	1.11	4.17	1.07
Compassion	3.17	1.40	3.38	1.22	3.78	1.16	3.51	1.24
Sportsmanship	2.78	1.62	3.51	1.22	3.85	1.21	4.08	1.03
Being fair	3.19	1.41	3.31	1.29	3.78	1.27	3.73	1.16
Showing skill	2.63	1.55	3.48	1.08	3.71	1.22	3.94	1.02
Tolerance	2.94	1.53	3.17	1.29	3.69	1.20	3.45	1.24
Conscientious	2.80	1.47	3.21	1.21	3.51	1.48	3.18	1.41
Team cohesion	2.86	1.45	3.18	1.30	3.25	1.53	3.17	1.38
Self-actualisation	2.66	1.53	3.25	1.27	2.92	1.50	3.04	1.33
Health and fitness	2.56	1.61	3.12	1.39	3.28	1.42	3.15	1.31
Obedience	2.56	1.75	2.93	1.27	3.96	1.31	4.11	1.09
Excitement	2.09	1.66	2.97	1.33	2.91	1.47	2.96	1.28
Companionship	2.83	1.52	2.36	1.66	1.85	1.76	1.64	1.63
Public image	2.03	1.50	2.40	1.37	2.97	1.68	2.97	1.57
Conformity	1.88	1.57	1.47	1.58	2.55	1.92	1.89	1.76
Winning	1.11	1.86	1.04	1.68	1.22	1.92	1.18	1.71
Mean	*2.68*		*3.01*		*3.27*		*3.22*	

sector may occur due to independent schools devoting greater time and resources to sport compared to state schools. The relative importance of educational influences rose to third and fourth place, consistent with Lee and Balchin (1996), when ratings disregarded the personal applicability of a particular significant other and showed their average importance across the entire sample.

How similar are pupils' values to those of the teacher?

Social learning theory (Bandura, 1977) and previous values research (e.g. Knafo and Schwartz, 2003; Rokeach, 1973) would suggest that interactions and experiences during childhood may lead schoolchildren to adopt similar values to their significant others. No research, however, has examined this issue in sport and PE. Although no casual links can be inferred strong correlations existed between the pupils' own values, their perception of their teachers' values, and the teachers' actual values. It appears that the amount of sport delivered within both state (Quick *et al.*, 2010) and independent (Swain, 2006) schools is sufficient for a synchronisation of pupils' and teachers' values.

In addition to the correlations between the overall value systems both pupils and teachers consistently ranked personal achievement, contract maintenance, and sportsmanship in the top five places with conformity and winning in the bottom three. These ranks are also consistent with the international youth sport hierarchy presented by Whitehead and Gonçalves in Chapter 6 of this book.

Despite the general congruence between pupils' and teachers' values, there were some notable differences in the rankings of some values. Although based on descriptive statistics rather than inferential tests, the rankings suggest that pupils under-perceived their teachers' valuing of enjoyment, being fair, and self-actualisation. This might indicate that teachers need to express these values more clearly. Further, pupils thought that their teachers placed greater importance on several competence and moral values than they did themselves. If pupils' and teachers' values are incongruent motivation towards sport may be diminished. Overall, pupils considered sport values to be more important to their teachers than to themselves.

Value transmission

If teachers are effectively transmitting values to their pupils, a key question is how does this occur? The mediation analysis indicates that this might operate through the pupils' perceptions of their teachers' values. Values were perceived more accurately in parent-child dyads when parents communicated in a clear and consistent manner over time and in both words and actions (Gniewosz and Noack, 2012; Grusec and Goodnow, 1994; Knafo and Schwartz, 2003). The strong correlation between pupils' perceptions and teachers' actual values in the present study would indicate that teachers do generally express their values clearly.

Stability of teachers' values across contexts

Core values transcend situations (Schwartz, 1994), thus PE teachers' values would be expected to be consistent in playing and teaching sport. The high correlation between the two value systems supports this. Certain values, however, were ranked higher when teaching. Teachers rated two moral values, obedience and sportsmanship, more highly when teaching sport than when competing in it. The relative importance of moral values in teaching may be shaped by various factors ranging from a school's ethos, the NCPE, or teachers' own beliefs. For example, the NCPE notes the role of PE in developing concepts of fairness, personal and social responsibility, and citizenship (Qualifications and Curriculum Authority, 2007a, 2007b). In contrast, when playing sport teachers may place less emphasis on moral values following the development of differences between life reasoning and game reasoning which begin around 12 or 13 years of age (Shields and Bredemeier, 1995). That is, playing sport allows an escape from everyday life and moral responsibilities to a situation in which individuals can exert more freedom and self-interest.

The influence of type of school

The present study could not directly assess and compare the institutional value systems of state and independent schools. However, in independent compared to state schools, pupils thought that their teachers valued achievement, and they themselves valued achievement, skill, fitness, excitement, sportsmanship and self-actualisation, whereas in state schools pupils thought their teachers valued compassion, tolerance, and conscientiousness. This suggests a focus in the independent schools on sport achievement rather than inter-personal relations.

The focus of pupils on success and excitement through sport would inform a recent debate in Great Britain regarding a situation in which more medals were won at the London Olympics by British athletes from independent schools than state schools, and independent schools enjoyed a greater proportional representation in Team GB (e.g. Tozer, 2012). A question is whether such differences in values as those observed in the present study better prepare independent school children for high-level sport.

Lee (2004) highlighted a distinction between PE and sport, in that PE focuses on personal development whereas sport focuses on participation and competition. The importance of achievement values in independent schools may reflect a stronger emphasis generally placed on sport rather than a wider perspective of PE in state schools. Different value priorities across state and independent sectors may also arise if independent school teachers focus on developing skills and notable results to justify fees and attract pupils. Indeed, Horne *et al.* (2011) suggested that the development of highly skilled and successful athletes is used as a marker of quality and a promotional tool by independent schools.

Limitations and future directions

A limitation of this study was the cross-sectional design which prevents causal inferences regarding value transmission over time or stability of values within an individual. Future longitudinal designs would facilitate the examination of value stability across Key Stages 3 and 4 and progressive transmission of values from PE teachers to their pupils. A further limitation was the relatively small sample size of teachers, particularly from state schools which prevented thorough comparisons of teachers' values in teaching and playing and across state and independent schools. Future studies may address this issue by increasing the number of teachers, which would also introduce the possibility of using multi-level modelling to account for nesting within the data. That is, pupils were nested within teachers, who themselves were nested within schools. In a methodological innovation for sport psychology we introduced anchoring of the value scales, and we recommend that this is continued in future values research.

Conclusion

This is the first study to explore the similarity of sport value systems of pupils and their PE teachers. We found that school children's sport values were similar to both their perception of their PE teachers' values and the teachers' actual values and that their perceptions of their teachers' values mediated the relationship between teachers' and pupils' values. This is seen as the first step in value transmission (Knafo and Schwartz, 2003). However, certain values which were highly rated by teachers, including enjoyment, being fair, and self-actualisation, were not accurately perceived by their pupils.

We also found that teachers gave less importance to some moral values when playing sport than when teaching, and that teachers in the independent sector were perceived to value achievement more highly. Their pupils valued achievement, skill, sportsmanship, excitement, fitness, and self-actualisation more highly than state schools pupils. Future research should examine the reasons behind differences in value systems of young competitors and their significant others to enhance effective value transmission.

References

Bandura, A. (1977) *Social Learning Theory*. New York: General Learning Press.

Bardi, A. and Schwartz, S.H. (2003) Values and behavior: Strength and structure of relations. *Personality and Social Psychology Bulletin*, 29, 1207–20.

Bardi, A., and Schwartz, S.H. (2013) How does the value structure underlie value conflict? Chapter 8, this book.

Daniel, E., Schiefer, D., Möllering, A., Weisman, M.B., Boehnke, K. and Knafo, A. (2011) Value differentiation in adolescence: the role of age and cultural complexity. *Child Development*, 83, 322–36.

Ennis, C.D. (1994) Urban secondary teachers' value orientations: Social goals for teaching. *Teaching and Teacher Education*, 10, 109–20.

Ennis, C.D. and Chen, A. (1995) Teachers' value orientations in urban and rural school settings. *Research Quarterly for Exercise and Sport*, 66, 41–50.

Gniewosz, B. and Noack, P. (2012) What you see is what you get: The role of early adolescents' perceptions in the intergenerational transmission of academic values. *Contemporary Educational Psychology*, 37, 70–9.

Grusec, J.E. and Goodnow, J.J. (1994) Impact of parental discipline methods on the child's internalization of values: A reconceptualization of current points of view. *Developmental Psychology*, 30, 4–19.

Hayes, A.F. (2012) PROCESS: A versatile computational tool for observed variable mediation, moderation, and conditional process modeling. White paper. Retrieved from www.afhayes.com/public/process2012.pdf.

Horne, J., Lingard, B., Weiner, G. and Forbes, J. (2011) 'Capitalizing on sport': sport, physical education and multiple capitals in Scottish independent schools. *British Journal of Sociology of Education*, 32, 861–79.

Knafo, A. and Schwartz, S.H. (2003) Parenting and adolescents' accuracy in perceiving parental values. *Child Development*, 74, 595–611.

Lee, M. (1993) Why are you coaching children? In Lee, M. (ed.) *Coaching Children in Sport: Principles and Practice*. London: E. & F.N. Spon, pp. 27–38.

Lee, M.J. (1996) *Young People, Sport and Ethics: An Examination of Fairplay in Sport*. London: Sports Council.

Lee. M. (2004) Values in physical education and sport: a conflict of interests? *British Journal of Teaching Physical Education*, 35, 6–10.

Lee, M. and Balchin, N. (1996) Social influences on values in young athletes. *Journal of Sports Science*s, 15(1), 92–93.

Lee, M.J., Whitehead, J. and Balchin, N. (2000) The measurement of values in sport:

Development of the Youth Sport Values Questionnaire. *Journal of Sport and Exercise Psychology*, 22, 307–26.

Lee, M.J., Whitehead, J., Ntoumanis, N. and Hatzigeorgiadis, A. (2008) Relationships among values, achievement orientations, and attitudes in youth sport. *Journal of Sport and Exercise Psychology*, 30, 588–610.

Qualifications and Curriculum Authority (2007a) Physical education: Programme of study for Key Stage 3 and attainment target. Retrieved from http://media.education.gov.uk/assets/files/pdf/p/pe 2007 programme of study for key stage 3.pdf.

Qualifications and Curriculum Authority (2007b) Physical education: Programme of study for Key Stage 4 and attainment target. Retrieved from http://media.education.gov.uk/assets/files/pe 2007 programme of study for key stage 4.pdf.

Quick, S., Simon, A. and Thornton, A. (2010) PE and Sport Survey 2009/10. Retrieved from www.education.gov.uk/publications/eOrderingDownload/DFE-RR032.pdf.

Rokeach, M. (1973) *The Nature of Human Values*. New York: The Free Press.

Schwartz, S.H. (1994) Are there universal aspects in the structure and content of human values? *The Journal of Social Issues*, 50, 19–45.

Shields, D.L.L. and Bredemeier, B.J.L. (1995) *Character Development and Physical Activity*. Champaign, IL: Human Kinetics.

Smith, R.E. and Smoll, F.L. (1991) Behavioral research and intervention in youth sports. *Behavior Therapy*, 22, 329–44.

Swain, J. (2006) The role of sport in the construction of masculinities in an English independent junior school. *Sport, Education and Society*, 11, 317–35.

Tozer, M. (2012) Contributing to Team GB at London 2012. Retrieved from www.peandsports.co.uk/PE&Sport_chapter34.pdf.

Whitehead, J. and Gonçalves, C.E. (2013) How similar are sport values in different nations? Chapter 6, this book.

12 How can sport practitioners balance conflicting values?

Ethics, values and practice: A reflective dialogue on value dilemmas and coaching practice

Hamish Telfer and Zoe Knowles

This chapter is a reflective dialogue between two practitioners focused on ethical considerations that influence sports practice in relation to coaching values. In particular it explores the interface between coaching those who are deemed 'less talented' with that of the 'more talented' – a common encounter with its own dilemmas for sports practitioners. The dialogue focuses on one of Kant's moral requirements for rational decision-making outlined in his 'categorical imperatives', viz. ensuring that we do not 'use others as a means to an end'. This is of particular importance with regard to the power position inherent within the coach–performer relationship and also highlights the power dynamics and tensions that are at play in the relationship between coach and performer. The chapter starts by outlining some of the key principles being discussed followed by a short section on the nature of reflective practice and in particular the use of dialogue. The reflective dialogue is then reported verbatim.

Values and coaching

Values are subjective in the sense that they can often mean different things to different people even using the same word or words. For practitioners, values should inform the way they conduct their practice though their presence and should be overt or opaque depending on the situation and the individuals. For example, Jenkins discusses the dilemma of espousing 'socially valued statements' such as 'personal growth' of performers through the young person's engagement with sport while exhibiting within their practice, and indeed possibly responding to, an overt outcome orientation culture of winning (Jenkins, 2010: 238).

Brackenridge *et al.* (2007: 199), in their work on child welfare in football, raised the question of whether we see 'children in football as consumers, citizens, workers or players?'. They further questioned the adoption of long-term athlete development (LTAD) as defined by Balyi and Hamilton (2003). While LTAD has been adopted by most British national governing bodies of sport at the behest of organisations such as Sport England and UK Sport, its performance outcome orientation according to Brackenridge *et al.* (2007: 202–3) can be a 'dehumanising practice...focused on "doing" rather than being'. This strikes a chord with Chatziefstathiou, who suggests that sport (with its coaches, officials and volunteers) may be nothing more than 'social marketing' with a reframing 'to embrace the marketing of values and ideas' (Chatziefstathiou, 2012: 27). The relationship (and balance) between altruism and self-fulfilment is nothing new for sport practitioners to grapple with, but this also brings tensions between the values that sport espouses and the inexorable link to the practitioners' personal status dependent on the outcome of their performer(s).

These predicaments are at the centre of value conflict in relation to both the values of sport as well as the values of those who engage in sport. As a result this often generates ethical dilemmas for sports practitioners. Taylor and Garratt (2010) considered these and other challenges inherent in the work of practitioners in their study of 'professionalisation' of coaching, and Telfer and Brackenridge (2011) also outline the issues in attempts to establish coaching standards, specifically with regard to safeguarding and coaching practice. Central to any discussion of the 'duties' implicit in engaging in sports practice professionalised or not, is the principle of 'duty of care'. This principle is at the heart of the UK's Code of Practice for Sports Coaches (Sportscoach UK, 2005). Lyle (2002) argued that sports practice has sets of situationally unique factors with a consequent requirement for degrees of judgement to be exercised relative to each situation. Following from this, Telfer argued that within these situations, these judgements are of necessity nuanced and dependent upon sets of conditions relating to the practice environment 'that may challenge their values and their decision making' (Telfer, 2010: 209). While there may be key ethical principles governing sports practice, the associated moral dilemmas relating to different coaching situations and levels of engagement present challenges for sports practitioners.

The 'craft' of sports coaching (Knowles *et al.*, 2001, 2006) suggests that the experience of coaches is fluid, dynamic and rarely predictable, thus the need to ground sport practice with a set of universal ethical principles is important. Within all levels of sport performance there is an inherent power dynamic in the coach–performer relationship to a greater or lesser extent. This will encompass selection, nature, volume and conduct of training and the establishment of a psychological approach to competition as well as the requirement to often work at the limits of physical capacity. Thus the 'power position' of the practitioner in determining these parameters even with the acquiescence of the performer, is one which must be subject to constant re-examination.

Telfer considered not only *what* practitioners do but *how* they do it and highlighted the importance of being able to discern what a 'good' action is, specifically with regard to being able to 'distinguish between 'good' (for the client) and 'good' (as in virtuous)' (Telfer, 2010: 213). Thus the idea that we can have one set of principles which are universally applied (such as Kant's imperatives) is simplistic, since practitioners are required to exercise moral judgements that are situationally dependent. Brown (2003) argues that moral obligations are a product of conflict, with personal inclination on the one hand and duties on the other. While Lukes (2008) is clear in his view that values are subjective, they should also be recognised as universal, plural and importantly, culturally relative. This leads to both a compliance and divergence of the values that people hold (with a concomitant abstractness of resonance depending on their nature), and lead to the choices people make. This debate about the nature of values and thus how we act as moral agents as practitioners is of particular importance in relation to the claims made that sport is a universal activity which all subscribe to in (more or less) the same way. The interface therefore between the practitioner's and the performer's value systems therefore makes the idea that we can operate by one set or understanding of values, difficult at best. This has significant implications for sport projects used as a means of socialising young people through sport (Houlihan, 2011). Reflective practice is one means for sports practitioners to engage with their practice through self examination aimed at establishing an evidence base to confirm (or otherwise) relevance, efficacy and competence of practice in addition to challenging convention.

Reflective practice/reflective learning

The case for reflective practice as a self appraisal mechanism and learning tool in sports coaching has been actively researched for over a decade (Irwin *et al.*, 2004; Knowles *et al.*, 2001, 2006) and in the allied discipline of sport and exercise psychology where a range of theoretical and applied directions have been discussed relating to process, skills, focus, timing and assessment with reflection (Anderson *et al.*, 2004; Cropley *et al.*, 2010a, b; Knowles and Gilbourne, 2010; Knowles *et al.*, 2011; Martindale and Collins, 2007). Although in essence a cognitive process, reflective practice has typically been documented through a written format akin to journal writing. This can subsequently be used for the purposes of interrogation/assessment/accountability (with relevant permissions). This in turn can contribute to knowledge development of the practitioner or the wider practice field. More recently the appropriateness of such methods have been challenged and sports coaching may in the future be informed by new and innovative reflective methodologies such as narrative, auto-ethnographic approaches or creative non-fiction which are associated with their own subsequent 'markers' or traits (for reviews see Knowles and Gilbourne, 2010; Knowles *et al.*, 2011).

However, for the purposes of this chapter we have used auto-ethnography as a means of embodying the voices of the coaches and to enhance the process of 'storytelling'. The two voices are the coach and his mentor. While the situation and issue has been constructed for the purposes of illustrating the ethical dilemmas that specifically challenge personal values, the dialogue is not in any form scripted and therefore represents a 'real time' discussion between the two 'storytellers'. The dialogue is intended to speak directly to the reader without the requirement for analysis and as such, is a deliberate attempt to ensure that it is not 'theory laden and author evacuated' (Brown *et al.*, 2009: 491). While the text is intended as an example of reflection 'in-action', the reader will hopefully identify with the dilemmas discussed as representative of some of the issues inherent in different ways of their own coaching, and thus will read this as reflection 'on-action'.

Reflective dialogue

The text that follows is a transcript of a bespoke conversation adjacent to the tea urn at a break in morning training with a young squad. The mentor is seen through the text as that of a 'critical friend' offering a combination of reflective responses (offering the coach's words back to them), observations and through these channels an opportunity for staged reflection (Knowles *et al.*, 2007). A narrator has been introduced (italics) to highlight the key issues raised and interjects in the text to take the reader through staged reflection from an objective standpoint (to the mentor and coach), and as such is a prompt for further reflection for the coach at a later time. In the spirit of the chapter no specific conclusion is offered at the end of the transcript. Akin to a process of staged reflection, readers may wish to collect their own thoughts from their engagement in some of the narrator posed questions and compile their own conclusions from this process. Finally, you may wish to consider how this text resonates with your own values, practice and ethical position.

MENTOR: I'm gasping for a brew. How have things been this morning?

COACH: [sounding exasperated] Don't ask! It's just...I'm really getting brassed off...look, we've got a problem and I'm not prepared to play ball anymore.

MENTOR: What's happened? Sounds like it's a big issue. You look pretty irate too.

COACH: Well...you know...people just keep banging on about this 'look after the kids'; the kids are 'the focal point' and yeah they are, but I've got those parents on my back and it's beginning to get me down now because the parents seem to want the team to win every time out. Now, the kids are 11 years of age for goodness sake and I've got a responsibility here, and **you've** told me often enough about the need to include all the kids by rotating the squad. I rotate the squad and we don't win that many matches. The parents are now on my back because they say I'm playing players that actually aren't the best players. They're right, but I need to have all 16 playing because that's what we need for their development and also, they want to be with their mates.

MENTOR: Well...that's what the governing body have asked us to do. We're following this system; we're all part of the system and that's what we've been asked to do. Are you saying that's not what's happening on the ground?

NARRATOR: *At this point the mentor coach tries to establish the nature of the value conflict by clarifying the positions adopted and who holds them, in this case implicitly questioning whether it is a clash between governing body requirements and those values held by the coach.*

COACH: Well, it's happening because I'm holding the line ...

NARRATOR: *Note the coach doesn't state that he agrees, but is perhaps 'tolerating' at best.*

COACH: ...but I don't think it's happening in other clubs, and that's the problem. Because I'll never be evaluated as to whether I'm a good, or at least a half decent coach, if my teams are constantly losing. All people will say is 'don't send your kids to him', because he's not produced a winning team in the last six years or whatever. I exaggerate, but you get the point. So... so... at some point we have to sit down as a club and say look, if we want to have a different take on this from other clubs and our teams to be inclusive, then the parents need to buy into it as well.

MENTOR: As far as I understand it, it's black and white. We're all on this development programme; it's set in stone and we all comply... but are you saying its breaking down? Is it at club level, parent's level, your coaching philosophy? Where is the breakdown happening? I guess if you get one chink in the process it all comes crashing down.

NARRATOR: *The mentor is trying to get the coach to dig deeper for explanations by exploring the nature of the 'breakdown' through considering the relative positions of the club, others or indeed the coach himself.*

COACH: Yeah. No, you're right, you're right. Its challenging me because I bought into this, I had my own kid go through the system and I was really happy with the fact that kids don't develop at the same rate and we all know that, so that's great and I was quite happy to take account ...

NARRATOR: *The mentor has elicited a key response from the coach since the coach needs to understand that it may not be appropriate to value a system because one's own child had a positive experience? Is this a sound basis for 'imposing' this on others? This is a 'particular' view at best.*

COACH: ...you know... that one year the kid wouldn't be so good but the next year they might be a little bit better. But there is a breakdown because despite that this is a club policy and the parents have apparently bought into it, that isn't what I'm getting in my ears week in week out.

MENTOR: So are you saying that what... what they say they buy into and what they actually buy into are two different things?

COACH: Yeah, that's absolutely correct. Yeah. Because when push comes to shove, they don't want **their** kid... [pause]... you know... losing every week. Now, the results aren't quite as bad as that and we're not losing every game but, we're losing substantially more because of the rotation than otherwise we would. Other clubs appear not to be buying into this so I don't know what we do.

NARRATOR: *To reflect you must work with evidence, does the coach have this?*

COACH: Either we need to reinforce this with the parents... we need to reinforce it amongst ourselves or we need to talk to the league and see what they will do. But leagues will just leave it to the clubs, saying well, that's the club's responsibility.

MENTOR: So... in [pause]... in terms of what you can control then... I guess... what... what could you do immediately? If you went back after this cuppa and back to the session, what could you change now.

NARRATOR: *The mentor focuses on immediate control. 'What is under* YOUR *control... ?'*

COACH: [Pause] Well... [pause]... I guess I could focus on telling the kids more... [pause]... how good they are... [pause]... in terms of the process. In other words I could start to say look, let's not focus on what's happening in terms of the result, let's focus on how well we're playing. That holds the line for part of the time but not all the time because they're not daft, they know that if they've only had one win in six weeks, they think they're not playing well. Actually I think they are, so I could reinforce it with the kids.

NARRATOR: *The coach progresses to more rationalised thinking from the emotional, thus switching to what is within his control.*

MENTOR: But... [pause]... but how does that then sit with you, because kids are pretty savvy. You're not convincing and you come across as playing lip service to it in terms of your values ...

NARRATOR: *The mentor challenges the coach's chosen action here.*

COACH: Yeah, yeah ...

MENTOR: ... and living and breathing it.

COACH: Yeah... well... kids aren't daft and they themselves want to win as well and it is becoming more difficult because they are coming to the point where there are two kids in particular when they are introduced into the team for time on the pitch, you can see all the other kids looking at each other, and I don't know what's going to happen here. Either there is going to be a bit of bullying, and I need to watch out for that or... or the better kids are simply going to go other clubs where they say they don't mess around with kids that aren't any good. But I think you're right, there is a fundamental breakdown and I think the club needs to discuss this. What I don't know is, if this is happening with me with this team at eleven years of age and I've had them for two years now, is it happening with the other teams in other age groups? You may have had this conversation as the mentor coach with other colleagues, I haven't.

NARRATOR: *Note the uncertainty on the coach's part as to the scope of the issue here.*

MENTOR: I ask a very simple question in terms of... [pause]... who are you responsible **for** and who are you responsible **to**?

NARRATOR: *This allows the focus to swing to responsibility and its link to values. Hidden within this is the implicit issue of value transmission and the coach power position. How do they link?*

COACH: Yes... [pause]... [thoughtful tone] yeah that's a good point. [Pause]... Well I feel I'm responsible for the kids and I'm responsible to the kids, and to the club because this is where I coach and I bought into this set of values and ethos and I still believe in the ethos but the pressures now are getting to me because I can see the kids suffering and I can see my own reputation being damaged. I think I'm a reasonably good coach and all my colleagues tell me that I'm doing things the right way and the results will come. But they haven't, and I'm beginning to doubt my own confidence in being able to coach.

NARRATOR: *The nature of responsibility and the values implicit within coaching practice start to emerge. The coach is now widening the focus of reflection to that of 'why do I coach' and what is the 'purpose' of my coaching? The coach is now also questioning the consequence of working within a context for such a prolonged period which has given rise to this serious value conflict*

MENTOR: Is your reputation important?

NARRATOR: *Note the mentor here is asking the coach if he would be willing to compromise the values imposed or values held to protect his reputation?*

COACH: [Long pause]...well...nobody likes to keep losing and being known as the coach of the losing team every single week you know. And...my reputation...I think the club maybe has to do more in ensuring my reputation is protected to a degree because I am beginning to hear the comments now about...from the parents...about, well, 'he's not much use' and one actually described me as 'crap'! I'm broad shouldered enough to think...well...that's only your view but...erm...but you can only go so long with that kind of comment.

MENTOR: It sounds like it's getting you down.

COACH: Oh yes! For sure it is. For sure it is. Because I've come from the sport and its difficult for me to shake off the fact that I like winning.

NARRATOR: *Is this therefore a key facet of his coaching values?*

COACH: Everybody likes winning but I'm also sensible enough to know that at eleven years of age we don't know whether ultimately these kids are going to make it or not. It's got be an enjoyable experience, where their skills are enhanced and they're with their friends. We know all of that, but it's just got to be balanced sometimes against being a bit more savvy, so we need to discuss it or I think the club is going to lose kids.

MENTOR: So [pause]...in terms of the compliance issue then, would you say that you comply with the development programme?

NARRATOR: *This is a repeat question and one which is an important facet of the discussion as it allows the practitioner to focus again following a period of deliberation on the issues to hand. This is important in reflective learning as it brings the central issue or question back into focus.*

COACH: I think I do, but I don't think the parents buy into it. I'm beginning to think the kids are not buying into it now and I'm scared of losing the kids. They're with their mates and they are enjoying themselves in training but I can see them bracing themselves each week for the match and that's not good.

MENTOR: So...hypothetically, between you and I, what would you be prepared to do!

NARRATOR: *The role of the mentor in encouraging the coach to engage with change is now explored and deliberated.*

COACH: [Sharp intake of breath]... Well... we need to have a quick fix and I think what we need to do is for me just to put on to the pitch probably the best team that we could put out now and just steady things up a little to begin with and get the confidence back again. I'll need to find ways of reassuring those that aren't going to get much pitch time for a few weeks that they're still valued. While that's going on, we as the coaching team need to talk about this because I want to know if there are similar experiences with other colleagues. The club need to do something about it. There is a 'quick fix' needed otherwise ...

NARRATOR: *This is the start of an action plan under the control of the coach which attempts to try and align values and practice in order to bring the issue within the scope of what the coach considers to be more pragmatic and 'ethical practice'.*

MENTOR: [Interrupting]... Interesting about the order that you put all of that into, in that the quick fix is about winning... so it's winning first, then athlete welfare second?

NARRATOR: *The mentor issues the challenge in relation to the ranges of perspectives at play and to the changing nature of priorities.*

COACH: [Slowly]... But I think... [pause]... I think that's a really good point and you've put me on the spot I guess. Erm... but I think the quick fix is about athlete welfare because I'd keep the squad together by doing it that way for a short period of time. It's about steadying things because the worse position would be if I suddenly found out about a number of kids who were thinking of going to another club. We would be in a difficult position then.

MENTOR: If there was a consistent national system and those kids migrated to another club wouldn't they get exposed to the same thing?

NARRATOR: *This widens the focus of reflection to that beyond the boundaries of local control to give a degree of context.*

COACH: You would hope so, but I'm getting the impression from the teams that I'm playing, and we don't go far as these teams are all local, that these teams are not 'playing to the same rules' we're playing to. You know, I do get the distinct impression that they've got their squad but they play their best players.

MENTOR: So there's a wider issue?

COACH: Yeah I think so. That was my comment about the league, I don't think they would be that sympathetic. They'd leave it to the clubs as to what they did with the kids. I think it's a wider issue.

NARRATOR: *Does the coach have the influence to effect change at this level? Would he be prepared to 'whistle-blow' on those who flout the rules?*

MENTOR: So [pause]... going back to what you can do... erm... what... what are you going to do now?

COACH: Right. What I need to do next I think, is to look at a game that we can realistically win and I need to juggle the 'roll on roll off' substitutions a little bit more... erm... with a little bit more ingenuity if I can put it like that. I'll still attempt to use the squad but if in my judgement one kid isn't used... I just need to say to the kids that we might just try some changes and I might do it by looking at the process rather than the outcome; by saying I'm going to try something new. Therefore over a range of weeks rather than every week, they will all get on the pitch. I think that's probably... [pause]... the best way of dealing with it. They are all still included, but not necessarily on a game by game basis.

NARRATOR: *Mentor and coach discuss an action plan. As the reader, you may have your own solutions. How would you be able to keep all the various interests satisfied? You might now wish to reflect on your own coaching and the dilemmas inherent within your own practice in relation to this and other issues.*

References

Anderson, A.G., Knowles, Z. and Gilbourne, D. (2004) Reflective practice for sport psychologists: Concepts, models, practical implications and thoughts on dissemination. *The Sport Psychologist*, 18, 188–203.

Balyi, I. and Hamilton, A. (2003) Long-term athlete development update: trainability in childhood and adolescence. *Faster, Higher, Stronger*, 20, 6–8.

Brackenridge, C., Pitchford, A., Russell, K. and Nutt, G. (eds) (2007) *Child Welfare in Football*. London: Routledge.

Brown, G., Gilbourne, D. and Claydon, J. (2009) When a career ends: a short story. *Reflective Practice*, 10(4), 491–500.

Brown, W.M. (2003) Personal best. In Boxill, J. (ed.) *Sports Ethics: An Anthology*. Oxford: Blackwell, pp. 144–52.

Chatziefstathiou, D. (2012) Pierre de Coubertin: Man and myth. In Lenskyj, H. J. and Wagg, S. (eds) *The Palgrave Handbook of Olympic Studies*. Basingstoke: Palgrave Macmillan, pp. 26–40.

Cropley, B., Hanton, S., Miles., A. and Niven, A. (2010a) Exploring the relationship between effective and reflective practice in applied sport psychology. *The Sport Psychologist*, 24, 521–41.

Cropley, B., Hanton, S., Miles., A. and Niven, A. (2010b) The value of reflective practice in professional development. An applied sport psychology perspective. *Sports Science Review*, XIX(3–4), 179–208.

Houlihan, B. (2011) Sports development and young people. Introduction: Socialisation through sport. In Houlihan, B. and Green, M. (eds) *Routledge Handbook of Sports Development*. London: Routledge.

Irwin, G., Hanton, S. and Kerwin, D. (2004) Reflective practice and the origins of elite coaching knowledge, *Reflective Practice*, 5, 425–42.

Jenkins, S. (2010) Coaching philosophy. In Lyle, J. and Cushion, C. (eds) *Sports Coaching: Professionalization and Practice*. Oxford: Elsevier.

Knowles, Z. and Gilbourne, D. (2010) Aspiration, inspiration and illustration: Initiating debate on reflective practice writing. *The Sport Psychologist*, 24, 505–20.

Knowles, Z., Gilbourne, D., Tomlinson, V. and Anderson, A. G. (2007) Reflections on the application of reflective practice for supervision in applied sport psychology. *The Sport Psychologist*, 21(1), 109–22.

Knowles, Z., Gilbourne, D., Borrie, A. and Nevil, A. (2001) Developing the reflective sports coach: A study exploring the processes of reflective practice within a higher education coaching programme. *Reflective Practice*, 1, 924–35.

Knowles, Z., Borrie, A. and Telfer, H. (2005) Towards the reflective sports coach: issues of context, education and application. *Ergonomics*, 48, 1711–20.

Knowles, Z., Tyler, G. and Gilbourne, D. (2006) Reflecting on reflection: exploring the practice of sports coaching graduates. *Reflective Practice*, 7, 163–79.

Knowles, Z., Gilbourne, D. and Niven, A. (2011) Outlining concerns and identifying solutions: Steering reflective practice towards the 'narrative turn'. In Anderson, M. and Gilbourne, D. (eds) *Critical Essays in Sport Psychology*. Champagne, IL: Human Kinetics, pp. 59–73.

Lukes, S. (2008) *Moral Relativism*. London: Profile.

Lyle, J. (2002) *Sports Coaching Concepts*. Abingdon: Routledge.

Martindale, A. and Collins, D. (2005) Professional judgement and decision making: the role of intention for impact. *The Sport Psychologist*, 19, 303–17.

Russell, J. (2007) Broad internalism and the moral foundations of sport. In Morgan, J. (ed.) *Ethics in Sport*. London: E. & F.N. Spon.

Sportscoach UK (2005) *Code of Practice for Sports Coaches*. Leeds: National Coaching Foundation.

Taylor, B. and Garratt, D. (2010) The professionalisation of sports coaching: definitions, challenges and critique. In Lyle, J. and Cushion, C. (eds) *Sports Coaching: Professionalization and Practice*. Oxford: Elsevier.

Telfer, H. (2010) Coaching practice and practice ethics. In Lyle, J. and Cushion, C. (eds) *Sports Coaching. Professionalization and Practice*. Oxford: Elsevier.

Telfer, H. and Brackenridge, C. (2011) Professional responsibilities of children's coaches. In Stafford, I. (ed.) *Children in Sport*. London: Routledge.

Telfer, H. and Knowles, Z. (2009) The 'how to' of reflection. In Heaney, C., Oakley, B. and Rea, S. (eds) *Exploring Sport and Fitness: Work-Based Practice*. London: Routledge.

Part III

Overview

13 What questions remain?

Further thoughts and future directions

Editorial team

In this final chapter we present further thoughts to integrate and extend some issues in a way that did not fit easily within existing chapters or within Lee's (1995) interactionist model (Figure 13.1). We also summarise findings and suggest future directions.

Lee's model was intended to generate hypotheses and we first summarise those explored in the book. Within the *Individual* box, Chapter 5 (Lee *et al.*, 2008) confirmed the hypothesis that moral, competence and status values predict prosocial and antisocial attitudes, and that this effect is mediated by goal orientations. Chapter 7 (Balaguer *et al.*) further demonstrated that values predict the motivational components of both achievement goal theory and self-determination theory. Extending to interactions with the *Environment* box, Chapter 11 (Freeman *et al.*) confirmed the hypothesis that personal *value systems* relate to the values of

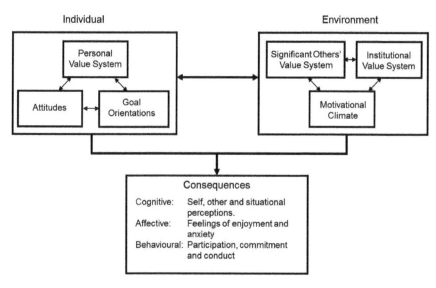

Figure 13.1 An interactionist model for research development
Source: adapted from Lee (1995)

significant others and differ with type of school. Further relationships in the model were examined in the field, as Chapters 9 and 10 (by Lambert) explored how the values of the Football 4 Peace (F4P) programme and its coaches may create a motivational climate to influence both personal *value systems* and behavioural consequences. This chapter concludes with swimming data showing *Consequences* arising from both *Individual* and *Environment*. Many other hypotheses merit exploration and this should include both experimental and longitudinal studies and behavioural variables.

Youth sport value systems and structure

This book has focused particularly on questionnaire studies. An emphasis on questionnaire development is characteristic of a new research field because until a construct is defined and measured, its characteristics and relationships cannot be widely explored. Chapters 2 to 5 described separately the construction of three questionnaires for youth sport values and attitudes. This section clarifies how the two youth sport values questionnaires, YSVQ and YSVQ-2, explore different questions and relate to a measure of adult values in general life.

Value systems in youth sport

Value systems reflect the hierarchical priorities that individuals and groups give to salient values. These subjective rankings are highly important because they influence decisions and behaviour. To identify ecologically valid values the Youth Sport Value Questionnaire (YSVQ) was constructed from spontaneous responses of young competitors in discussions of moral dilemmas in their sport (Chapter 2; Lee and Cockman, 1995). The range of 18 values was considered to be comprehensive and a Canadian replication found no additional values (MacLean and Hamm, 2008). Further research in non-Western nations may be appropriate.

Research with the YSVQ has typically shown that enjoyment ranks highest in youth sport *value systems*, followed by personal achievement and a group of socio-moral values with winning in the lowest position. These six socio-moral values of sportsmanship, contract maintenance (keeping a contract – not spoiling the contest), being fair, compassion, tolerance, and obedience all ranked in the top half of the UK *value system* thus showing a generally high moral standard in young competitors.

Ranks were remarkably consistent across age, gender, sport type, participation level (Chapter 3; Lee *et al.*, 2000), across four of five nations (Chapter 6 Whitehead and Gonçalves) over two decades, and across the values of high school pupils and their PE teachers (Chapter 11). The cross-cultural research showed consistency at the extremes of the hierarchy and cultural variations within it. The universally low placing of winning suggests that, at least in youth sport, the Olympic creed is upheld: it is not the winning that is important but the taking part. Nevertheless winning remains a desirable value in competitive sport, without which it would not be competitive.

Subgroup data (unreported) from some nations described in Chapter 6 also showed high correlations of *value systems* across genders and adjacent age groups, decreasing as the age gap widened. Males gave higher ratings than females to winning and leadership (four nations), and to public image and conformity (two nations), whereas females gave higher ratings than males to compassion (five nations), tolerance (three nations) and sportsmanship (two nations). Future research should explore *value systems* at different competitive levels and in different sports. However, when group comparisons are made the mean importance of sport values should be controlled and advice in Appendix 4 should be noted.

The rankings for youth sport values at the extremes of the hierarchy were consistent with rankings of global adult values for achievement and winning but enjoyment ranked much higher in youth sport (Chapter 6). Self-referenced values, including hedonism, become progressively less important from adolescence to adulthood while other-referenced values become more important (Schwartz, 2012). Sport is a voluntary activity, whereas the global values reflect the needs of humans as biological organisms, requiring social interaction and group maintenance and survival skills (Schwartz and Bardi, 2001).

Value structure in youth sport

The Youth Sport Value Questionnaire–2 (YSVQ-2) was developed by supplementing YSVQ items to assess three higher order value domains, notably moral, competence and status values, by multi-item scales (Chapter 5). It was anticipated that future researchers might similarly derive measures for other value domains but these initial values were selected for the research question posed in Chapter 5, and they matched Webb's (1969) parsimonious categories: playing fairly, playing well, and winning. Moreover they serve as key structural markers in the history of values measurement and the nature of sport.

First, the *moral and competence* value domains represent to some extent the interpersonal and intrapersonal categories of Rokeach (1973), in that the competence values are self-referenced whereas the moral values are not. Second, the *moral and status* value domains represent to some extent the poles of Schwartz's (1992) bi-polar axis from self-transcendence to self-enhancement. This adds *status* as an interpersonal value that is opposed to morality and relevant to winning. Third, sport is a classical achievement situation and *competence and status* values represent intrapersonal and interpersonal views of achievement. Thus they have some relationships with the task and ego orientations of achievement goal theory, a dominant research paradigm in sport psychology.

The Schwartz (1992) *value structure*, described in Chapter 8 (Schwartz and Bardi), shows a circular continuum of basic values based on their motivational content. In Figure 13.2 we have located the YSVQ values in bold italics within the Schwartz circle and the YSVQ-2 values around the periphery. The placement of the 18 YSVQ values is in accordance with locations given to them by Bardi

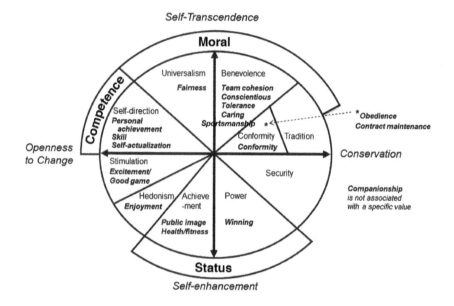

Figure 13.2 Probable location of the youth sport values in the Schwartz (1992) value
structure

in Appendix 1, based on the descriptors and proxy items for the values (see
Chapters 2 and 3), but this has not been empirically verified. Although the
YSVQ-2 values are alongside the areas of the circle where they are relevant, not
all the YSVQ values (e.g. team cohesion) in these areas are in the YSVQ-2, and
some others (e.g. leadership) were added. These are new questionnaires and have
not been developed sufficiently to measure both *systems* and *structure* in the
same instrument. As described above, the YSVQ assesses *value systems*,
whereas the YSVQ-2 begins to explore *value structure* and is appropriate for
studies in which *moral, competence* and *status* values are conceptually relevant
(see Chapter 8).

Values in sport and life contexts

Placement in the diagram assumes that youth sport values are specific exemplars
of globally recognized human values. A more specific examination of sport *value
structure* by multidimensional scaling (MDS) is a topic for future research.
However, the salience and interpretation of youth sport values differ in some
ways from adult life values and we now clarify some different interpretations,
first with reference to the measurement of *achievement* values and then to a recent
refinement of the Schwartz value theory (Schwartz *et al.*, 2012).

The word *achievement* is interpreted differently in the youth sport and life questionnaires. In youth sport, *winning* was the most frequently mentioned value in discussions with young competitors, hence it was taken as a discrete value representing superiority over others. In contrast, self-referenced achievement, such as doing a personal best performance, is represented by the value of *personal achievement*. However, for Schwartz (1992), self-referenced achievement comes within the value of *self-direction* whereas winning is within the value of *power* which represents dominance over others.

The value that Schwartz termed *achievement* focuses more on social approval. It was originally described as the motivation to be judged successful by others through demonstrating competence and was intended to tap normative rather than self-referenced competence. However, some items were ambiguous and the demonstration of competence has been dropped from the refined description which states that the value focuses on approval for socially valued achievement. It is now measured by two items representing self-referenced and comparative achievement but they emerged in the same MDS region.

The refined value theory includes 19 basic values within the circle and three layers of broad categories around the periphery. The rationale of Schwartz *et al.* (2012) is that researchers have tended to treat values as if they are discrete, whereas they lie on a motivational continuum and can be taken in broader or narrower slices for different research questions. Our use of two youth sport value questionnaires to explore different questions is consistent with this refinement.

Enhanced compatibility with YSVQ values is shown in the finer partitioning of Schwartz's 10 values into 19, which names values of *tolerance* and *caring* and subdivides *conformity* to create a value focused on conformity to rules. This relates to the YSVQ value of *contract maintenance* which concerns the implicit agreement, when engaging in sport, to play by the rules. Although rarely named in the book, this value pervades its content. It ranks third in the international youth sport *value system* after enjoyment and personal achievement and is conceptually important because competitive sport would not exist without rules.

However, some values have differential importance in sport and in general life. Whereas adolescence is a time to seek independence, the value of conformity becomes more salient at higher competitive levels, as discussed later. The YSVQ value of obedience ('I do what I'm told') can be assessed by a parallel item ('I follow the coach's instruction'). After winning his first tennis grand slam, Andy Murray paid tribute to the advice of his new coach, Ivan Lendl.

Future research may adapt the YSVQ for disabled or professional sport or create a parallel version for physical education perhaps using initial stimulus material more suitable for dance as an art form and outdoor activities. Values with diverse interpretations (e.g. sportsmanship) may be dropped in favour of less ambiguous values (e.g. fairness) or retained to explore cultural differences. A short form might be useful for sport practitioners to identify key value priorities of participants.

Value theory and achievement goal theory

Values have received scant attention in sport psychology. They have been given some consideration as properties of an achievement task (e.g. utility value; Eccles and Harold, 1991) which influence participation choice. Recently, Sami and colleagues (2013) found that an increase in the subjective task value of physical education was accompanied by increased participation in physical activity. However, they have not been considered from the alternative perspective of value theory (Rokeach, 1973; Schwartz, 1992) which regards values as hierarchical criteria for personal conduct based on a central belief system related to the self concept. Future research should relate these two perspectives in sport.

Achievement goal theory has been a dominant motivational paradigm in sport psychology since the 1980s, but over this time the definition and measurement of achievement goals has changed somewhat. Task and ego orientations represent different *meanings of success* based on differentiated and undifferentiated concepts of ability and are derived from Nicholls' (1989) dichotomous model. Further approach and avoidance goals for mastery (task) and performance (ego) concern different *levels of competence* and are based on Elliot's (2005) trichotomous and 2 × 2 models. A review by Papaioannou and colleagues (2012) outlines conceptual differences and argues that Nicholls' model has greater explanatory power in sport. It implies that values may have a closer conceptual relationship with goal orientations than with approach and avoidance goals.

Values as antecedents of achievement goal orientations

Here we summarize evidence that values predict achievement goals and goal orientations in sport, report a related non-sport study, and extend the discussion to conceptual issues. We mostly refer to relationships with Schwartz's (1992) orthogonal axes, from self-enhancement to self-transcendence and from conservation to openness to change rather than with his individual values.

Goal orientations

In Chapter 5, using a youth sport values questionnaire (YSVQ-2), Lee and his co-workers found that competence and status values predicted task and ego orientations, respectively. The findings were replicated using a different measure of goal orientations (Whitehead *et al.*, 2003).

In Chapter 7, using a life values questionnaire (Schwartz's SVS) Balaguer and co-workers found that self-transcendent and self-enhancing values predicted task and ego orientation, respectively. Task orientation was additionally predicted by self-direction, a value at the openness pole of the second axis. Findings were parallel to a previous study in which task orientation was predicted also by openness (Balaguer *et al.*, 2004).

Approach and avoidance goals

Also using the SVS, Papaioannou and Karakanta (2010, cited by Papaioannou *et al.* 2012) found self-transcendent and self-enhancing values predicted mastery approach and performance approach goals respectively. The second axis was not included in this study hence it is pertinent to note that in academic and work situations performance avoidance goals have been associated with the conservation pole of this axis (Levontin and Bardi, submitted). These researchers also found mastery goals to be associated with the opposing openness pole of the second axis, not with the self-transcendent pole of the first axis. At that self-transcendent pole, using MDS, they discovered a new amity goal, characterised by the motivation to help others succeed.

Further research

At the present stage there is a need to identify which values predict which goals in which circumstance and with which questionnaires. In sport, for example, three 'global level' goal orientations have been identified by Papaioannou *et al.* (2009), notably an ego-enhancing goal, a personal improvement goal, and an ego-protection goal. Levontin and Bardi's (submitted) mainstream study implies that the first would be predicted by self-enhancement, and the next two by the openness and conservation poles of the second axis. The study of values on the second axis opens new research questions. For example, Roberts (2012) reports that a performance avoidance goal has been related to fear of failure in sport, and Chapters 9 and 10 show that security values are important in divided societies.

Conceptual and structural relationships

Both values and goal orientations are cognitive schema that serve as organizing constructs. Each basic value or goal orientation sets up a logical pattern of cognitive, affective, and behavioural consequences that is distinct from that of other values or goal orientations. However, values cover a wider motivational spectrum than achievement goals which focus on achievement situations and thus form a subset of human values. There are more basic values than there are achievement goals, thus some values will predict achievement goals and others will not (see Chapters 5 and 7). However, when values do predict goal orientations these orientations may mediate the effect of values on other variables (see Chapter 5).

Values are organized on a circular motivational continuum, whereas goal orientations are discrete. Schwartz (2012) demonstrated that those values which have the same meaning around the world form a coherent system such that relationships of a salient variable with any one value have implications for its relations with adjacent and opposing values. Figure 13.3 displays data from the correlation matrix of Chapter 7 as a sinusoid curve to show that task and ego orientation had systematic relationships with the basic values on Schwartz's (1992) motivational continuum.

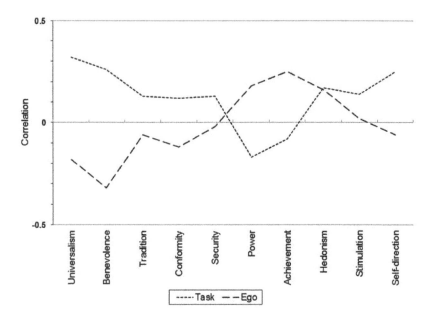

Figure 13.3 Correlations between values and goal orientations
Source: based on data from Balaguer *et al.* (Chapter 7)

Achievement goal orientations, on the other hand, are predicted to have orthogonal (Nicholls, 1989) or bi-polar (Dweck, 1986) relationships. If two values or goals lie on orthogonal axes they are independent of each other and their joint influence can be examined, whereas if they are bipolar their reciprocal relationship precludes the study of this joint influence. The orthogonality of the task and ego orientations conceived by Nicholls has facilitated a search for the most motivationally effective goal profiles, in which the influence of both goal orientations are considered simultaneously. In a recent review Roberts (2012) explains that high task orientation combined with low or moderate ego orientation has adaptive outcomes. Similarly, in a study of value profiles in an academic task, Levontin and Bardi (submitted) found that mastery goals (at the openness pole) enhanced performance after failure when combined with amity goals at the self-transcendent pole of the orthogonal axis but not when combined with performance approach goals at the opposing self-enhancement pole.

An integration of goal profile research from sport psychology with the circular values model and its inherent conflicting, neutral and compatible values might guide interventions for different circumstances. In Chapter 8 Bardi and Schwartz described how the conflict between the bi-polar values of winning and fairness might be remedied by re-focusing achievement on self-direction which is on an orthogonal axis. It would be expected that values associated with an orthogonal axis to that of a target value should be more compatible with it than the values associated with the opposite pole. However, for effective intervention, any alternative value should be high in the *value system* for the target population.

Value hierarchies

In Chapter 8 Bardi and Schwartz maintain that, regardless of the (structural) value conflict between winning and fairness, in a specific situation it is the relative importance of these values (in an individual's stable *value system*) that determines the outcome. Chapters 9 and 10 illustrate how individuals differ in the values and behaviour they express in the same conflict situations. Little has been done in sport regarding priorities of achievement goals, but Papaioannou *et al.* (2012) identified the priority of the dominant goal in relation to others when exploring relationships between values and achievement goals.

Value hierarchies might be considered as antecedents of goal states as well as of goal orientations. The transitory *goal states* of task and ego *involvement* are thought to be mutually exclusive, although goal *orientations* are not, because a performer has limited attention capacity under time stress and emotional arousal. They relate to what the performer is totally involved in at a particular moment and Roberts (2012) views them on a continuum from task to ego involvement. Given that values are central trans-situational beliefs about what is most important to an individual, and that Nicholls (1989) thought it strange to describe people as task-involved if a task was unimportant to them, it is logical to consider *value systems* alongside dispositional and situational triggers of goal involvement.

Values, attitudes and behaviour

Whereas the structural model of Schwartz (1992) illustrates inherent conflicting, compatible and neutral relationships among values the path model of Lee *et al.* (Chapter 5) adds further insight by suggesting means by which moral, competence, and status values can influence attitudes and behaviour in youth sport. This model (Figure 5.2) tested the value-expressive theory of attitudes (using prosocial and antisocial attitudes) and the mediating role of achievement orientations. It has been extended to predict cheating behaviour in a self-refereed international tennis tournament for young elite players in Italy (Lucidi *et al.*, 2013). The YSVQ-2 moral values have been found in Lithuania to positively predict prosocial behaviour towards team mates and opponents and negatively predict antisocial behaviour to opponents (Šukys, 2010). Moral values also negatively predicted moral disengagement (Šukys and Jansonienė, 2012).

Aggression was not included in the path model because the AMDYSQ questionnaire (Chapter 4 Lee *et al.*, 2007) was constructed to focus instead on ethical attitudes. AMDYSQ has nevertheless been used as an index of acceptance of sport aggression in a model to predict moral disengagement in Italy, China, and the USA (Appendix 2). Moral disengagement has been shown recently (Kavussanu *et al.*, 2013) to be a partial mediator of the bracketed morality effect, that is it can in part explain why antisocial behaviour is higher in sport than in university life. The path model gave better prediction of prosocial than antisocial attitudes, hence moral disengagement and performance avoidance goals could be explored as potential mediators, alongside ego orientation, of the effect of values on antisocial attitudes and behaviour.

Focusing on ethical attitudes and fair play

Lee's adoption of a values paradigm was to better understand children's moral decision making and encourage fair play (Lee, 1997). Thus the items for the YSVQ were drawn from discussions with young competitors about moral dilemmas in their sport. Six socio-moral values were found in the top half of the UK value system (p. 204) thus showing relatively high moral values in young competitors. Similarly, research findings with the AMDYSQ questionnaire typically show the greatest endorsement for keeping winning in proportion followed by gamesmanship then cheating, thus demonstrating positive moral attitudes in young competitors alongside their relatively high ranking of moral values.

Despite these positive moral values and attitudes, unethical practices in adult sport can permeate into youth sport. In the USA, for example, children as young as 10 were paid to injure opponents after the Super Bowl champions were found to have done so (Hughes, 2012). As the book goes to press a UK survey of 1102 children aged 8 to 16, conducted in partnership with a national governing body of sport, has found that 75 per cent believed their teammates would cheat if they could get away with it, and a charity has consequently arranged sportsmanship lessons in 4500 schools (MCC and Cricket Foundation, 2013a, 2013b). Most parents (65 per cent) thought cheating in high profile sport added pressure, although both parents and children thought the pressure came from other children wanting to win, rather than from adults. To counter an over-emphasis on winning the path model implies that teachers and coaches should encourage moral and competence values and task orientation to promote prosocial attitudes, and discourage status values and ego-orientation to reduce antisocial attitudes, and cheating and gamesmanship behaviours.

Clifford and Feezell (2010) argue sportsmanship is no longer demonstrated to young competitors and there is a need to regain respect for others and for sport itself. Lee argued for research to identify the extent of unethical behaviour in sport and the attitudes of significant others towards it, then to identify the processes by which children make instrumental or altruistic decisions under the influence of the significant others. The next section explores some of these issues.

Value transmission and change

The chapters in Part 2 presented a framework for understanding value conflict (Chapter 8) and focused on value transmission and change. Chapters 9–11 concerned value transmission from significant others (teachers and coaches) in PE and sport contexts. Chapter 12 (Telfer and Knowles) adds that parental values and league policy can indirectly influence the values of a coach. We relate here to components in the *Environment* box.

Significant others

The values of significant others must be accurately perceived before they can be accepted or rejected. In Chapter 11, Freeman's team found the high similarity in the sport values of pupils and teachers was mediated by the pupils' perception of their teachers' values. This corresponds with the findings of Knafo and Schwartz (2003) who showed that adolescents' accurate perception of their parents' values depended on three processes: the availability of values information; the under-standability of this information; and the adolescents' motivation to attend to it. These processes are illustrated by coaches in the F4P programme (Chapters 9 and 10). They draw attention to values information, explain its importance, make it understandable by asking players for their own examples, and motivate them in an atmosphere of enjoyment and unconditional support. A daily cool down phase provides in depth reflective discussion about behaviour, which is rarely included in mainstream coaching or PE sessions. From a value-transmission perspective, F4P is particularly interesting because coaches must change their own values to adopt coaching styles based on equality rather than power before they can promote equality rather than power values in the children.

To create a change in values is difficult, requiring repeated exposure to the new values, and the effects may be short term (see Chapter 8). In his foreword to this book Don Hellison forcefully rejects claims of automatic transfer. Any transfer of values must be carefully prepared and planned. Three facilitators of value change described in Chapter 8 are illustrated in Chapters 9 and 10, notably identification with a group, adaptation to reinforcement, and management of consistency between actions and behaviour.

The studies in this book did not examine value changes specifically. However, some incidental indicators of the impact of the F4P intervention are shown in the changes in player behaviour observed during the week and recorded in coaching diaries, and the 'end of project' evaluation. The return of players in successive years, as players and then coaches, is evidence that the programme has impact. Longitudinal monitoring of the values and attitudes of players and coaches is desirable but attitudes are more likely than values to show short term change, hence the AMDYSQ scale for keeping winning in proportion may be appropriate.

Institutions

The effect of type of school on pupils', but not teachers', values was examined in Chapter 11. Although the specific values expressed by state and independent schools were not formally assessed Lee (1995) argued that the 'institutional value structure' is manifested in institutional patterns of reinforcement. For example, the funding of elite performers by National Governing Bodies of Sport prioritises the value of winning. The Council of Europe Code of Sports Ethics made recommendations for governments, sport institutions and individuals to promote fair play in children (Council of Europe, 1992).

In Chapter 1, Devine and Telfer explored a range of values held by a variety of physical activity providers and extended the discussion to include government policy and cultural differences. All these 'institutional' agencies will impact the values of young participants through adult intermediaries who provide youth sport and physical education. Research could identify the most common value conflicts, their frequency of occurrence and their specific consequences, in particular the vexed question of dropout. Communication between different levels of involvement is often poor. A Canadian study of a life skills and values development programme found that coaches, parents, and participants had progressively less awareness of the objectives of administrators (Formeris *et al.*, 2012).

Motivational climate

Actions of significant others and the institutions they serve create learning environments that promote different values. Chapters 9 and 10 describe this in the Football 4 Peace programme. In a physical education study which focused more specifically on achievement goal theory Vatali (2011) found perceptions of a task-involving climate positively associated with competence and moral values and negatively associated with status values, while perceptions of an ego-involving climate were positively associated with status values.

It would be expected that the values of significant others (coaches, parents, peers) would relate to the motivational climates they are perceived to create but research is lacking. In a sequel to the study of teachers' and pupils' values (Chapter 11) data is being gathered for parents' and children's values and also perceptions of the parent-initiated motivational climate (L. Goggins, University of Exeter, personal communication, 2013). Parallel data will be collected later for coaches.

Many intervention programmes to teach values through sport are emerging around the world but few specify their methods or have a robust research and evaluation programme. One exception is The Real Madrid Foundation 'Basketvalues' programme, which integrates values education within a mastery climate whilst encouraging player autonomy. Its coach and player education booklet sets out a clear framework and methods (Vila *et al.*, 2012).

The Empowering Coaching™ programme, tested via the European-wide PAPA project (Duda, 2013), is designed to facilitate an autonomy and socially supportive, mastery-focused climate which may also promote prosocial values, but this has not been monitored.

Consequences

Parts 1 and 2 of this book explored individual and environmental variables respectively. We conclude with an illustration of the combined influence of both types of variable on the commitment and performance of young swimmers. These variables represent the behavioural components in Lee's (1995) *Consequences* box.

In swimming, world-class performances can be produced by adolescents who form a sub-culture of elite swimmers, committed to the demands of high performance training. Aplin and Saunders (2009) showed how the mean importance of values of committed Singaporean and Australian swimmers differed systematically from sub-specialist to elite levels (Figure 13.4). They also described how personal values interact with other variables to guide decision-making at each lower transitional stage of engagement as values are re-prioritised for the next level.

At the entry level, described as *experimentation* (with sport and non-sport activities) cultural beliefs about the importance of sport and parental valuing of other activities were influential. The bi-polar axis from openness to conservation in the Schwartz (1992) *value structure* was salient and values of stimulation, in contrast to security, identified the participants. At the next stage of *probation* (an apprenticeship involving willingness to adapt and share values) the axis from self-enhancement to self-transcendence became more important with a need to stabilise motivation to achieve higher performance. At the third stage of *confirmation* (total commitment) there was dedication to values linked to performance criteria and group affiliation.

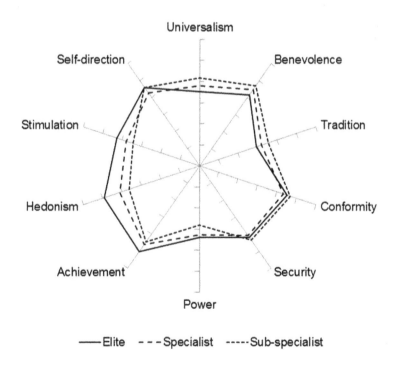

Figure 13.4 Mean importance of values in committed groups of swimmers.
Source: based on data from Aplin and Saunders (2009)

Values were also significantly associated with an index of swimming performance, computed as the ratio of world record time to personal best performance, but the salient values differed with nationality. In Australia, values had a greater role at higher achievement levels and the transmission of sport-related values was more effective than in Singapore. These studies demonstrate that the development and change of personal values interacts with values of significant others, group *value systems* and the national culture.

There is a need to explore values in the context of different sport performance levels in order to improve the coach–performer interface and understand how sport practitioners could engage better with performers. In the UK the training programmes of sports practitioners (coaches) still tends to follow a performance model despite the fact that much of the time of most coaches is at participation level. Within education the obverse tends to be the case.

The discussion in Chapter 1 related to a further need to understand interacting values of sport participants and sport providers. Specifically, (a) the implicit and explicit values of physical activity providers and policymakers have not been examined in relation to the values of participants, (b) teachers' values and those of coaches, particularly those trained from a sport performance model, may be the source of potential dissonance, and (c) the role of teachers and coaches in providing potential 'good' experiences through value transmission needs further examination.

Concluding thoughts

This book has provided a range of perspectives on the nature and influence of values both of and in sport and physical education. The scene was set by exploring the values *of* these activities from the perspective of their providers and policy makers. This approach considers the ends that can be achieved and the services provided to individuals and society by sport and physical education. The focus then changed to explore values *in* sport and physical education from the perspective of participants. This approach considers values as beliefs that certain actions or objectives are preferable to others and thus provide the basis for selection and evaluation of personal behaviour across all situations. Hence an individual's *value system* provides criteria which are the foundation for conduct in sport (Lee, 2001).

Research on this second perspective has been lacking and we have provided an initial Schwartz-based analysis of youth sport *value systems* and of the motivationally based *value structure* within which they operate. This shows a conflict between the self-enhancing values focused on winning, and the self-transcendent values of fair play. Lee (2007) observed that this presents a challenge for adults to encourage both competition and fairness in working with children and young people.

This book has focused on youth sport with the clear understanding that children are not mini-adults. Their social psychological development and processing of issues relating to competition is not mature. As sport has become more professionalised and commercialised and children experience adult sport models at younger ages, interpersonal values of social and moral conduct can be subjugated to personal values of competence and achievement. Choices can be increasingly made on instrumental grounds with decisions delegated to officials. However, adults can transmit values of responsibility and fair play, as illustrated in the F4P programme, by a better understanding of both their own values and those of young competitors.

Involvement in sport and physical activity today encompasses different values across the spectrum of engagement. A clearer understanding of the dynamics of how value priorities 'work' in practice should help adults to provide more positive experiences for children. We hope that this book has value for you as an 'object' and will also prompt you to examine your values as 'personal criteria'.

References

Aplin, N. and Saunders, J. (2009) *Values and the Pursuit of Sports Excellence: Swimmers from Singapore and Australia*. Saarbrücken: VDM Verlag.

Balaguer, I., Castillo, A., Quested, E. and Duda, J.L. (2013) How do values relate to motivation? Chapter 7, this book.

Balaguer, I., Duda, J.L. and Castillo, I. (2004) Achievement goals and values in sport. In *AAASP Conference Proceedings*. Denton, TX: RonJon Publishing, p. 11.

Bardi, A. and Schwartz, S.H. (2013) How does the value structure underlie value conflict? Chapter 8, this book.

Clifford, C. and Feezell, M. (2010) *Sport and Character: Reclaiming the Principles of Sportsmanship*. Champaign, IL: Human Kinetics.

Council of Europe (1992) *Code of Sports Ethics*. Strasbourg: Council of Europe (CDDS).

Devine, C. and Telfer, H. (2013) Why are youth sport and physical eduction valuable? Chapter 1, this book.

Duda, J.L. (2013) The conceptual and empirical foundations of Empowering Coaching™: Setting the scene for the PAPA project. *International Journal of Sport and Exercise Psychology*, 11(4). The article can be retrieved on http://dx.doi.org/10.1080/1612197X.2013.839414

Dweck, C.S. (1986) Motivational processes affecting learning. *American Psychologist*, 41, 1040–8.

Eccles, J.S. and Harold, R.D. (1991) Gender differences in sport involvement: Applying the Eccles expectancy-value model. *Journal of Applied Sport Psychology*, 3, 7–35.

Elliot, A.J. (2005) A conceptual history of the achievement goal construct. In A. Elliot and C. Dweck (eds) *Handbook of Competence and Motivation*. New York: Guildford Press, pp. 52–72.

Formeris, T., Camiré, M. and Trudel, P. (2012) The development of life skills and values in high school sport: Is there a gap between stakeholder's expectations and perceived experiences? *International Journal of Sport and Exercise Psychology*, 10(1), 9–23.

Freeman, P., Leslie, A., Leger, H. and Williams, C. (2013) How important are the values of significant others? Chapter 11, this book.

Hughes, M. (2012) Youth American football team paid to injure opponents. *The Telegraph*, 7 August, retrieved from www.telegraph.co.uk/news/worldnews/northamerica/usa/9577442/Youth-American-football-team-paid-children-to-injure-opponents.html.

Kavussanu, M., Boardley, I., Sagar, S.S. and Ring, C. (2013) Bracketed morality revisited:

How do athletes behave in two contexts? *Journal of Sport and Exercise Psychology*, 35, 449–63.

Knafo, A. and Schwartz, S.H. (2003) Parenting and adolescents' accuracy in perceiving parental values. *Child Development*, 74, 595–611.

Lambert, J. (2013) How can we teach values through sport? Chapter 9, this book.

Lambert, J. (2013) How does coach behaviour change thee motivational climate? Chapter 10, this book.

Lee, M. (1997) Moral well-being: The role of Physical Education and Sport. In N. Armstong, B. Kitty, and J. Welsman (eds) *Children and Exercise*, XIX, 542–62. London: E & F Spon.

Lee, M.J. (1995) Relationships between values and motives in sport. Paper presented at the 9th European Congress in Sport Psychology, Brussels, Belgium, 4–9 July.

Lee, M.J. (2001) Values of sport or values in sport: What does youth sport offer? Paper presented at the International Congress on Bridging Sport, Exercise, and Lifestyle Activity for Health, Finnish Society for Research in Sport and Physical Education, Lahti, Finland, 13–15 February.

Lee, M.J. (2007) Sport, education and society: The challenge. In C.E. Gonçalves, S.P. Cumming, M.J.C. Silva and R. Malina (eds) *Sport and Education: Tribute to Martin Lee*. Coimbra: University of Coimbra, pp. 197–207.

Lee, M.J. and Balchin, N. (1996) *Young People, Sport and Ethics in Sport: An Examination of Fairplay in Youth Sport*. London: The Sports Council.

Lee, M.J. and Cockman, M.J. (1995) Values in children's sport: Spontaneously expressed values among young athletes. *International Review for the Sociology of Sport*, 30(3/4), Special Issue: Ethics in Sport), 337–52.

Lee, M.J., Whitehead, J. and Balchin, N. (2000) The measurement of values in youth sport: Development of the Youth Sport Values Questionnaire. *Journal of Sport and Exercise Psychology*, 22, 307–26.

Lee, M.J., Whitehead, J. and Ntoumanis, N. (2007) Development of the Attitudes to Moral Decisions in Youth Sport Questionnaire. *Psychology of Sport and Exercise*, 8(3), 369–92.

Lee, M.J., Whitehead, J., Ntoumanis, N. and Hatzigeorgiadis, A. (2008) Relationships among Values, Achievement Orientations, and Attitudes in Youth Sport Questionnaire. *Journal of Sport and Exercise Psychology*, 30(5), 588–610.

Levontin, L. and Bardi, A. (Submitted) Amity goals: unveiling a missing achievement goal using values. Manuscript submitted for publication.

Lucidi, F., Mallia, L., Zelli, A., Nicolais, G. and Badacci, A. (2013) Cheating and games-manship in youth Italian players: From attitude to behaviour. Paper presented at the 13th World Congress of the International Society of Sport Psychology, Beijing, China.

MacLean, J. and Hamm, S. (2008) Values and sport participation: Comparing participant groups, age, and gender. *Journal of Sport Behavior*, 31(4), 352–67.

MCC and Cricket Foundation (2013a) *Team Work*. London: Opinion Matters.

MCC and Cricket Foundation (2013b) *Child's Play*. London: Opinion Matters.

Nicholls, J.G. (1989) *The Competitive Ethos and Democratic Education*. Cambridge, MA: Harvard University Press.

Papaioannou, A.G., Simou, T., Kosmidou, E., Milosis, D. and Tsigilis, N. (2009) Goal orientations at the global level of generality and in physical education: Their association with self-regulation, affect, beliefs, and behaviours. *Psychology of Sport and Exercise*, 10, 466–80.

Papaioannou, A.G., Zourbanos, N., Krommidas, C. and Ampatzoglou, G. (2012) The place of achievement goals in the social context of sport: A comparison of Nicholls' and Elliots' models. In G.C. Roberts and D.C. Treasure (eds) *Advances in Motivation in Sport and Exercise*, 3rd edn. Champaign, IL: Human Kinetics, pp. 59–90.

Roberts, G.C. (2012) Motivation in sport and exercise from an achievement goal theory perspective: After 30 years, where are we? In G.C. Roberts and D.C. Treasure (eds) *Advances in Motivation in Sport and Exercise*, 3rd edn. Champaign, IL: Human Kinetics, pp. 5–58.

Rokeach, M. (1967) *Value Survey.* Sunnyvale, CA: Halgren Tests.

Rokeach, M. (1973) *The Nature of Human Values.* New York: The Free Press.

Sami, Y-P., Jaakkola, T., Liukkenen, J. and Nurmi, J-E. (2013) The effects of physical education students' beliefs and values on their physical activity: a growth modeling approach. *International Journal of Sport and Exercise Psychology*, 11(1), 70–86.

Schwartz, S.H. (1992) Universals in the content and structure of values: theoretical advances and empirical tests in 20 countries. In M.P. Zanna (ed.) *Advances in Experimental Social Psychology*, 25, 1–65. New York: Academic Press.

Schwartz, S.H. (2012) Values and religion in adolescent development: Cross-national and comparative evidence. In G. Tromsdorff and X. Chen (eds) *Values, Religion, and Culture in Adolescent Development.* New York: Cambridge University Press.

Schwartz, S.H. and Bardi, A. (2001) Value hierarchies across cultures: Taking a similarities perspective. *Journal of Cross-Cultural Psychology*, 32, 268–90.

Schwartz, S.H., Cieciuch, J., Vecchione, M., Davidov, E., Fischer, R. Beierlein, C., Ramos, A., Verkasalo, M., Lönnqvist, J., Demirutku, K., Dirilen-Gumus, O. and Konty, M. (2012) Refining the theory of basic individual values. *Journal of Personality and Social Psychology*, 103(4), 663–88.

Šukys, S. (2010) Adaptation and validation of the Prosocial and Antisocial Behavior in Sport Scale and Youth Sport Scale for Lithuanians. *Education, Physical Training, Sport*, 78(3), 97–104.

Šukys, S. and Jansonienė, A.J. (2012) Relationship between athletes' values and moral disengagement in sport, and differences across gender, level and years of involvement. *Education, Physical Training, Sport*, 84(1), 55–61.

Telfer, H. and Knowles, Z. (2013) How can sport practitioners balance conflicting values? Chapter 12, this book.

Vatali, D. (2011) Relationship among values and motivational climate in physical education students. Paper presented at the 3rd International Conference of the Psychological Society of Northern Greece.

Vila, G.O., Gimenez Fuentes-Guerra, F.J., Jimenez Sanchez, A.C., Franco Martin, J., Duran Gonzalez, L.J. and Jimenez Martin, P.J. (2012) *Initiation into Basketvalues.* Madrid: MCV.

Webb, H. (1969) Professionalization of attitudes towards play among adolescents. In Kenyon, G.S. (ed.) *Aspects of Contemporary Sport Sociology.* Chicago, IL: The Athletic Institute, pp. 161–78.

Whitehead, J. and Gonçalves, C.E. (2013) How similar are sport values in different nations? Chapter 6, this book.

Whitehead, J., Lee, M.J. and Hatzigeorgiadis, A. (2003) Goal orientations as mediators of the influence of values on ethical attitudes in youth sport: Generalization of the model. *Journal of Sports Sciences*, 21(4), 364–5.

Appendices

Appendix 1
Cross-cultural use, validity, and modification of the YSVQ-2
ANTONIS HATZIGEORGIADIS AND JEAN WHITEHEAD

Appendix 2
Further use of the AMDYSQ and development of AMDYSQ-2
JEAN WHITEHEAD AND NIKOS NTOUMANIS

Appendix 3
Questionnaires for discussion groups

Appendix 4
The values and attitudes questionnaires, and their adminstration and scoring

Attitudes to Moral Decision-making in Youth Sport Questionnaire (AMDYSQ)
Attitudes to Moral Decision-making in Youth Sport Questionnaire 2 (AMDYSQ-2)
Youth Sport Values Questionnaire (YSVQ)
Youth Sport Values Questionnaire 2 (YSVQ-2)

Note:
Appendices 1 and 2 are for committed researchers. They provide new information about the psychometric properties of the values and attitude questionnaires.
Appendix 3 is for newcomers to value theory. It provides items for people to discuss to get a feeling for the ideas and issues.
Appendix 4 is for people who would like to carry out carefully controlled research with the questionnaires described in the book.

Appendix 1

Cross-cultural use, validation and modification of the YSVQ-2

Antonis Hatzigeorgiadis and Jean Whitehead

The YSVQ-2 was constructed as described by Lee *et al.* (2008) to measure *moral values*, *competence values*, and *status values*. These multi-item scales were used in that chapter to predict prosocial and antisocial attitudes, showing the value-expressive function of attitudes initially proposed by Katz (1960). However, the scales represent key reference points in the structure of human values proposed by Rokeach (1973) and extended by Schwartz (1992), hence they have wider potential application, for example in studying conflict between the values of fair play and winning (see Chapter 8 by Bardi and Schwartz). The moral and competence values represent Rokeach's interpersonal and intrapersonal categories, since our moral items are socio-moral and our competence values are self-referenced. The interpersonal moral and status values illustrate the opposing self-transcendent and self-enhancing poles of Schwartz. Coincidentally by adopting these landmarks from value theory our competence and status values have some correspondence with the task- and ego-oriented achievement goals that have dominated research in sport psychology in recent decades. In this appendix we report some cross-cultural use and validity of the YSVQ-2 and give guidance on its modification for international use.

Cross-cultural use

To our knowledge, the YSVQ-2 has been, or is being, used in eight nations outside the UK representing four continents (Portugal, Italy, Greece, Lithuania, Japan, Hong Kong, Kenya, and Brazil). Their ratings of moral, competence and status values are presented in Chapter 6 by Whitehead and Gonçalves (Figure 6.4), but in this appendix we focus instead on validity data and on modifying the instrument. In Kenya the young competitors completed the English version, but in other nations the questionnaire was translated locally.

Findings

In Kenya (Kanyiba, 2011) the YSVQ-2 was used for descriptive purposes and it was found that moral and competence values were endorsed more than status values, that status was valued more by males than females, and that moral values decreased with age. In Portugal (Gonçalves *et al.*, 2005) the research focused on the suitability of the model, as described later. Elsewhere the researchers have explored relationships of YSVQ-2 scales with other variables (Table A1.1).

Table A1.1 Source of national samples with YSVQ-2 data

Study and variables	Competence	Moral	Status
Whitehead *et al.* (2003) *UK data*		Path coefficients	
Sport commitment and conventions[a]	.63	.21	
Cheating and gamesmanship[a]		−.33	.43
Task orientation	.73		
Ego orientation			.67
Lee *et al.* (2008) *UK data*			
Sport commitment and conventions[*]	.41	.61	
Cheating and gamesmanship[*]		.52	.44
Task orientation	.72		
Ego orientation			.78
Šukys (2010) *Lithuanian data*		Regression	
Prosocial behaviour to opponent		.30*	
Prosocial behaviour to team mate	.35**	.34**	
Antisocial behaviour to team mate		−.29**	
Gymnopoulou and Vatali (2009) *Greek data*		Correlations	
Task orientation	.54**	.49**	.13*
Ego orientation	.29**		.64**
Gymnopoulou and Vatali (2010) *Greek data*			
Keeping winning in proportion	.36**	.58**	−.14**
Acceptance of cheating		−.45**	.35**
Acceptance of gamesmanship		−.28**	.42**
Lucidi *et al.* (2013) *Italian data*			
Keeping winning in proportion		.37**	−.30**
Acceptance of cheating		−.33**	.26**
Acceptance of gamesmanship		−.28**	.17**
Koumleli and Vatali (2011) *Greek data*			
Prosocial behaviour to opponent		.31**	
Prosocial behaviour to team mate		.40**	−.15*
Antisocial behaviour to opponent		−.24**	.34**
Antisocial behaviour to team mate		−.28**	.40**
Vatali (2011) *Greek data*			
Learning-oriented climate	.58**	.66**	−.31**
Performance-oriented climate			.58**
Chan *et al.* (2013) *Hong Kong data*			
Keeping winning in proportion	.34**	.34**	
Acceptance of cheating	−.30**	−.39**	.18*
Acceptance of gamesmanship	−.28*	−.41**	.20*
Fukami *et al.* (2012) *Japanese data*			
Sport commitment	.69**	.57**	.41**
Conventions	.25**	.36**	.16**
Cheating and gamesmanship[a]		−.15**	.18**
Šukys and Jansonienė (2012) *Lithuanian data*			
Moral disengagement		−.24**	

Note: [a] Composite factor for 2 scales

Cross-cultural validation

Researchers in Greece (Gymnopoulu and Vatali, 2009), Hong Kong (Chan *et al.*, 2013), and Kenya (Kanyiba, 2011), have provided data for comparative analysis with UK data (Chapter 5 Lee *et al.*, 2008). The UK and Greek samples include both team and individual sports but the Kenyan sample covers seven team sports and the Hong Kong sample covers one individual sport (golf). A comparison of data from these diverse samples on three continents should indicate the suitability of the YSVQ-2 for different cultural contexts.

Model fit

Using confirmatory factor analyses (CFA) the fit of the 13-item model was good in the UK. In other nations the fit was marginal. However, a multi-sample analysis provided reasonable support for the invariance of factor structure and factor loadings across the four nations, as the difference between the unconstrained and the constrained models was small (Table A1.2).

Table A1.2 Fit indices for the three-factor model in four nations

Model	Age	n	χ^2	d.f.	p	RMSEA	SRMR	CFI	NNFI
UK	12–15	434	107.45	62	.00	.04	.05	.97	.96
Greece	12–15	216	124.02	62	.00	.07	.09	.89	.86
Hong Kong	11–18	100	101.60	62	.00	.08	.10	.97	.96
Kenya	10–18	274	123.30	62	.00	.06	.08	.92	.90
Multi-nation unconstrained		1014	434.03	248	.00	.03	.07	.90	.88
Multi-nation constrained		1014	492.58	287	.00	.03	.14	.89	.88

Note: Robust ML solution; Satorra-Bentler scaled χ^2.

Factor loadings and factor correlations

The individual items may be perceived differently by participants in different nations, hence they relate differently to the factors as shown in Table A1.3. In the case of Greece, Hong Kong, and Kenya, removal of one low loading item (different for each country) produced a good fit. Factor correlations between moral and competence values are high, demonstrating that these values are compatible, rather than conflicting (Chapter 8). Correlations between competence and status values are much lower showing more differentiation between these values. Correlations between moral and status values are very low, showing little relationship between these values. Before recreational participants were removed from the original Greek school sample ($n = 346$), for correspondence with UK data, correlations between moral and status values were negative ($r = -0.12$).

Table A1.3 Factor loadings and inter-factor correlations for four nations

Factor and item	UK	Greece	Hong Kong	Kenya
I. Moral values				
I do what I am told	.63	.69	.65	.61
I show good sportsmanship	.78	.77	.84	.58
I help people when they need it	.76	.56	.86	.62
I always play properly	.59	.71	.77	.64
I try to be fair	.64	.66	.70	.60
II. Competence values				
I become a better player	.74	.89	.87	.72
I use my skills well	.76	.74	.81	.73
I set my own targets	.53	.45	.71	.56
I improve my performance	.75	.76	.83	.69
III. Status values				
I show that I am better than others	.71	.52	.66	.77
I am a leader in the group	.87	.65	.52	.42
I win or beat others	.67	.73	.67	.79
I look good	.71	.52	.69	.67
Factor correlations				
Moral and competence	.85	.78	.79	.83
Status and competence	.49	.42	.33	.40
Moral and status	.18	.07	.13	.20
Mean/SD				
Moral values	3.65/.92	4.13/1.01	3.57/1.05	4.00/.73
Competence values	3.66/.94	4.24/.96	3.63/1.09	4.17/.74
Status values	1.40/1.40	1.96/1.26	1.86/1.15	1.78/1.32

Note: Shaded items were removed to produce a good fit.

Guidance for modification and analysis of the YSVQ-2

In different cultures, items may have different meanings from those in the UK, or the translated wording of an item may give it a slightly different context. Competent back translation should minimise these problems (Brislin, 1970). Translators of the YSVQ-2 should also be aware of the wider context in which the proxy value items for the earlier YSVQ were initially selected and of alternative pilot items which provide complementary views of each value.

Context of the YSVQ value items

The 18 YSVQ values were drawn directly from spontaneous comments made by young sport competitors when discussing moral dilemmas in their sport. Each value was given an initial descriptor, and examples of the young competitors' comments appropriate for each value are given in Chapter 2 (Lee and Cockman, 1995). The adult value descriptors were then explored in focus group discussions with more young competitors to ensure the meaningfulness to them of each value. For example, the descriptor *contract maintenance* (keeping a contract) was not used with the participants but their responses showed that they understood the idea of maintaining the spirit of the game. A pool of about six items was compiled for each value from their statements and an initial proxy item was selected (e.g. 'I don't spoil the game or competition'). After further pilot tests a final proxy item was chosen that was usually shorter (e.g. 'I always play properly'; see Chapter 3; Lee *et al.*, 2000). Value descriptors and proxy items drawn from children are given in Table A1.4. This method had high ecological validity because care was taken to ensure that the items did not reflect adult values but were dawn directly from children.

Researchers have modified items effectively when appropriate. In Canada (MacLean and Hamm, 2008) the words 'get a buzz' were removed because their local meaning was linked to alcohol. In Italy (Borraccino, 2011) the item 'I do what I'm told' was replaced with 'I follow my coach's instructions', which was an alternative UK pilot item for the same value of obedience. In Portugal (Gonçalves *et al.*, 2005) the translation of the item 'I always play properly' meant 'I always play correctly'. This could be interpreted as playing with technical correctness, hence the item was recoded as a competence item rather than a moral one and this improved the fit. Such adjustments seem necessary to enhance the suitability of the instrument for different cultural and language characteristics, and subsequently for content and construct validity.

Some analytical considerations

Researchers who use self-report questionnaires have used different strategies in different circumstances to test for aspects of validity. Some have relied on the validation work of the test constructors and simply reported the reliability of the scales in their own sample using the Cronbach alpha statistic. Some have used exploratory factor analysis (EFA) to identify the common factors in their own sample. In the case of the YSVQ-2 researchers in Japan (Fukami *et al.*, 2012), Lithuania (Šukys, 2010), and Hong Kong (Chan *et al.*, 2013) used EFA to modify the model for their nations. However, EFA is dependent on the idiosyncrasies of a particular sample and the selection of other variables within the analysis. Confirmatory factor analysis is a better method because it specifies which items shall load on which factor and is free from measurement error in testing the fit of the specified model to the population data (see Chapter 5). The CFA approach was used in Brazil (Gonçalves *et al.*, 2012) and Italy (Borraccino, 2011).

In Portugal researchers administered a composite 26-item pilot questionnaire which included both YSVQ and YSVQ-2 items (Gonçalves *et al.*, 2005). Their EFA on this was inappropriate to identify moral, competence and status values because 8 unrelated YSVQ items were present and EFA varies with extraneous

Table A1.4 Development of Lee's proxy items from his values and their location within Schwartz value types

Value	Lee and Cockman (1955) Descriptor	Initial proxy item	Lee et al. (2000) Final proxy item	Schwartz value
Achievement (personal achievement)	Being personally or collectively successful in play	I put in the best performance I can	I improve my performance	Self direction
Caring (compassion)	Showing concern for other people	I am concerned about the people around me in my sport	I help people when they need it	Benevolence
Companionship	Being with friends with a similar interest in the game	I am there with my friends	I do things with my mates	None specific
Conformity	Conforming to the expectations of others in the team	I try to fit in with the group	I go along with everybody else	Conformity
Conscientious	Doing one's best at all times and not letting others down	I am reliable and give 100% when playing or competing	I don't let people down	Benevolence
Contract maintenance (keeping a contract)	Supporting the essence of agreeing to play the game, to play in the spirit of the game	I don't spoil the game or competition	I always play properly	Conformity
Enjoyment	Experiencing feelings of satisfaction and pleasure	I enjoy myself and have fun	I enjoy myself and have fun	Hedonism
Fairness (being fair)	Not allowing an unfair advantage in the contest/judgement	I am fair and don't cheat	I try to be fair	Universalism
Good game (excitement)	Enjoying the contest regardless of outcome, this usually embodies a balance between the contestants	I have a close game, race, or event	It is an exciting contest	Stimulation

Table A1.4 continued

Value	Lee and Cockman (1955) Descriptor	Lee et al. (2000) Initial proxy item	Lee et al. (2000) Final proxy item	Schwartz value
Health and fitness	Becoming healthy as a result of the activities, and becoming fit to enhance performance	I get fit and healthy through sport	I do sport to get fit	Achievement
Obedience	Avoiding punishment, being dropped, sent off or suspended	I do what I'm told	I do what I am told	Conformity
Public image	Gaining approval of others	I look good	I show a good image to others	Achievement
Sportsmanship	Being of good disposition, accepting bad luck with the good, demonstrating positive behaviours towards opponents, and accepting defeats	I am well mannered, sporting, and I am not a bad loser	I show good sportsmanship	Universalism Benevolence Conformity
Self-actualisation	Experiencing the activity for its own sake and the accompanying transcendent feelings	I get a buzz or feel really good when playing	I get a buzz or feel really good when playing	Self direction Hedonism
Showing skill	Being able to perform the skills of the game well	I do the skills or techniques well	I do the skills or techniques well	Self direction
Team cohesion	Doing something for someone else and for the sake of the team performance	I lift the team when things are difficult	I make sure we all stick together	Benevolence
Tolerance	Being able to get along with others despite interpersonal differences	I try and get on with the other people in my sport, even if I don't like them	I accept other people's weaknesses	Benevolence
Winning	Demonstrating superiority in the contest	I win or beat people	I can show that I am better than others	Power

Note: The classification of Lee's values into the basic values of Schwartz has been made by Anat Bardi.

variables. Subsequent CFA of the 13-item YSVQ-2 *within* this data set has shown a good fit with the removal of one item ($\chi^2 = 93.20$, d.f. = 51, $p < 0.00$, RMSEA = 0.04, SRMR= 0.05, CFI = 0.96, NNFI = 0.95). However, the correlation between moral and competence factors was $r = 0.98$ because males, in particular, did not discriminate between these values. Further analysis showed a fitting 9-item model ($\chi^2 = 42.68$, d.f. = 24, $p = 0.01$, RMSEA = 0.04, SRMR= 0.08, CFI = 0.96, NNFI = 0.94) with a lower correlation ($r = 0.84$). This deeper unpublished analysis facilitates further examination in Portugal of the relationships among values, attitudes and achievement orientations described in chapter 5. Such analyses may sometimes be needed. However, we recommend that researchers use CFA analyses on the 13 item model.

Conclusion

We consider that this material demonstrates that the YSVQ-2 is a psychometrically sound instrument for use around the world, and that its scales are sufficiently robust for intelligent local modification where necessary.

References

Bardi, A. and Schwartz, S.H. (2013) How does the value structure underlie value conflict? Chapter 8, this book.

Borraccino, A. (2011) I valori nello sport [Values in sport]. In R. Grimaldi, *Valori e modelli nello sport: Una ricerca nelle scuole del Piemonte con Stefania Belmondo*. Milan: FrancoAngeli.

Brislin, R. W. (1970) Back-translation for cross-cultural research. *Journal of Cross-Cultural Psychology*, 1, 185–216.

Chan, Y., Whitehead, J., Hatzigeorgiadis A. and Chow, B. (2013) Sport values and ethical attitudes in young Hong Kong golfers. Paper presented at the ISSP 13th World Congress of Sport Psychology, Beijing, China.

Fukami, K., Kondo, A., Ishidate, K., Fukami, M. and Mizouochi, F. (2012) Social attitudes in sport of high school students: verification of measurements-composition. *The Ohmon Research Bulletin of Physical Education, Nihon University*, 45(1), 1–8.

Gonçalves, C.E., Cardoso, L., Freitas, F., Lourenço, J. and Coelho e Silva, M. (2005) Valores no desporto de jovens: concepções, instrumentos e limitações [Values in youth sport: concepts, instruments and limits]. *Boletim da Sociedade Portuguesa de Educação Física*, 30–31, 93–110.

Gonçalves, M.P., Oliveira, L.C. and Moura, M.A.R. (2012) Validation of the Youth Sport Values Questionnaire-2 in Brazil. Unpublished preliminary data.

Gymnopoulou, V. and Vatali, D. (2009) Relationships among goal orientations and values in adolescent students. In *Proceedings of 10th Thematic Congress of Northern Greece Physical Education Teachers Association*. Thessaloniki: Northern Greece Physical Education Teachers Association, p. 53.

Gymnopoulou, V. and Vatali, D. (2010) Relationships among values and moral attitudes in adolescent students. In *Proceedings of 10th Thematic Congress of Northern Greece Physical Education Teachers Association*. Thessaloniki: Northern Greece Physical Education Teachers Association, pp. 130–1.

Kanyiba Nyaga, L.R. (2011) Valued outcomes in youth sport programs in Kenya: Towards the government's Vision 2030. Doctoral dissertation, Springfield College, MA.

Katz, D. (1960) The functional study of attitudes. *Public Opinion Quarterly*, 24, 163–204.

Koumleli, X. and Vatali, D. (2011) Relationship among values and prosocial and antisocial behaviour in high school students. In *Proceedings of 10th Thematic Congress of Northern Greece Physical Education Teachers Association*. Thessaloniki: Northern Greece Physical Education Teachers Association, p. 92.

Lee, M.J. and Cockman, M. (1995) Values in children's sport: Spontaneously expressed values among young athletes. *International Review for the Sociology of Sport*, 30, 337–52.

Lee, M.J, Whitehead, J. and Balchin, N. (2000) The measurement of values in youth sport: Development of the Youth Sport Values Questionnaire. *Journal of Sport and Exercise Psychology*, 22, 307–26.

Lee, M.J, Whitehead, J., Ntoumanis, N. and Hatzigeorgiadis, A. (2008) Relationships among values, achievement orientations, and attitudes in youth sport. *Journal of Sport and Exercise Psychology*, 30(5), 588–610.

Lucidi, F., Mallia, L., Nicolais, G. and Zelli, A. (2012) Unpublished data on Italian tennis players, University of Rome.

Maclean, J. and Hamm, (2008) Values and sport participation: Comparing participant groups, age, and gender. *Journal of Sport Behavior*, 31(4), 352–67.

Rokeach, M. (1973) *The Nature of Human Values*. New York: The Free Press.

Schwartz, S.H. (1992) Universals in the content and structure of values: theoretical advances and empirical tests in 20 countries. In M.P. Zanna, *Advances in Experimental Social Psychology*, 25, 1–65. New York: Academic Press.

Šukys, S. (2010) Adaptation and validation of the Prosocial and Antisocial Behavior in Sport Scale and Youth Sport Scale for Lithuanians. *Education, Physical Training, Sport*, 78(3), 97–104.

Šukys, S. and Jansonienė, A.J. (2012) Relationship between athletes' values and moral disengagement in sport, and differences across gender, level and years of involvement. *Education, Physical Training, Sport*, 84(1), 55–61.

Vatali, D. (2011) Relationship among values and motivational climate in physical education students. Paper presented at the 3rd International Conference of the Psychological Society of Northern Greece.

Whitehead, J. and Gonçalves, C.E. (2013) How similar are sport values in different nations? Chapter 6, this book.

Whitehead, J., Lee, M. and Hatzigeorgiadis, A. (2003) Goal orientations as mediators of the influence of values on ethical attitudes in youth sport: generalization of the model. *Journal of Sports Sciences*, 21(4), 364–5.

Appendix 2

Further use of AMDYSQ and the development of AMDYSQ-2

Jean Whitehead and Nikos Ntoumanis

The Attitudes to Moral Decision-making in Sport Questionnaires (AMDYSQ) was constructed as described in Chapter 4 (Lee *et al.*, 2007) to measure attitudes to cheating, gamesmanship, and keeping winning in proportion (KWIP). The cheating scale drew on Reddiford's (1998) cheating dimensions and the games-manship scale focused on upsetting an opponent psychologically. In this appendix we present new data on the concurrent validity of AMDYSQ and describe the construction and cross-validation of AMDYSQ-2.

Concurrent validity

In Chapter 4, the concurrent validity of AMDYSQ was demonstrated by correlations with four MSOS (Multidimensional Sportsmanship Orientation) scales (Vallerand *et al.*, 1996). Subsequently AMDYSQ scales have been shown to relate logically to sport values (moral, competence, status), components of achievement goal theory (goal orientations, perceptions of the motivational climate), components of a negative approach to performance (moral disengagement, negative affect, general aggression), parental psychological control (dependency and achievement), and to hubristic pride, obsessive passion and socially prescribed perfectionism (Table A2.1). The structure of AMDYSQ was invariant across the UK and Hong Kong ($\chi^2 = 111.62$, d.f. = 69, $p < 0.00$, RMSEA = 0.05, SRMR = 0.06, CFI = 0.98, NNFI = 0.98).

Construction of AMDSYSQ-2

The cheating and gamesmanship scales were subsequently used as described in Chapter 5 (Lee *et al.*, 2008) when they were combined into a factor for antisocial attitudes. Within that study the composition of all scales was improved through administration of a 24-item pilot questionnaire which included nine new items and indicators for measurement models were drawn from the revised instrument. However, an AMDYSQ-2 was not reported then because (a) the study focused on hypothesis testing rather than questionnaire construction, (b) the scale for keeping winning in proportion was not part of that study, and (c) the potential AMDYSQ-2 had not been cross-validated in a second sample.

Table A2.1 Significant relations of AMDYSQ scales with other variables

Study and variables	Cheating	Gamesmanship	Winning
[a]Whitehead *et al.* (2003) *UK data*		Path coefficients	
Moral values (path to antisocial attitudes)	−.33**	−.33**	–
Status values (path to antisocial attitudes)	.43**	.43**	–
[a]Lee *et al.* (2008) *UK data*			
Moral values (path to antisocial attitudes)	−.52**	−.52**	–
Status values (path to antisocial attitudes)	.44**	.44**	–
Whitehead (2007) *UK data*		Regression	
Moral values		−.27**	–
Competence values	−.24**		–
Status values	.37**	.28**	–
Task orientation	−.26**	−.19*	–
Ego orientation	.27**	.28**	–
Mastery climate	−.18*		–
Performance climate	.35**	.37**	–
Ntoumanis *et al.* (2011) *UK data*			
Peer created task climate Level1	−.23*	−.19*	–
Peer created task climate × time Level1	.19*	.18*	–
Peer created ego climate Level 1		.22**	–
Peer created ego climate Level 2		.21**	–
Peer created ego climate Level 3		.72**	–
Coach created ego climate Level 2	.22**	.24**	–
Coach created ego climate × time Level 1	.21*	.29**	–
[a]Bureau *et al.* (2013) *UK data*		Correlations	
Hubristic pride (*r* with immoral behaviour)	.52**	.52**	–
Obsessive passion (*r* with immoral behaviour)	.32**	.32**	–
Chan *et al.* (2013) *Hong Kong data*			
Moral values	−.39**	−.41**	.34**
Competence values	−.30**	−.28**	.34**
Status values	.18*	.20*	
Lucidi *et al.* (2013) *Italian data*			
Moral values	−.33**	−.28**	.37**
Status values	.26**	.17**	−.30**
Task orientation	.24**	.23**	−.22**
Ego orientation	−.21**	−.18**	.34**
Gymnopoulou and Vatali (2010) *Greek data*			
Moral values	−.45**	−.28**	.58**
Competence values			.36**
Status values	.35**	.42**	−.14**
Charlton and Hill (2010) *UK data*			
Socially prescribed perfectionism	.41**	.26*	
[b]Zengaro *et al.* (2009) *Italian data*			
Prosocial behaviour scale	−.14*	−.19*	.28**
Moral disengagement	.40**	.35**	−.15**
[b]Zengaro (2010) *Italian data*			
Moral disengagement	.39**	.25**	−.15**
Negative affect	.18**	.12*	
Aggression	.28**	.25**	−.13*

Table A2.1 continued

Study and variables	Cheating	Gamesmanship	Winning
[b]Zengaro *et al.* (2011) *USA data*			
Moral disengagement	.52**	.27**	−.38**
Aggression	.22*	.30**	
[b]Zengaro *et al.* (2012) *Chinese data*			
Moral disengagement	.45**	.40**	−.19**
Aggression	.29**	.26**	−.10**
Negative affect	.20**	.16**	−.12**
Costa *et al.* (2013) *Italian data*			
[c]Mother's psychological control – dependency		.21*	
[c]Mother's psychological control – achievement		.23**	
[c]Father's psychological control – achievement			−.22*
[d]Father's psychological control – dependency	.19*		
[d]Mother's psychological control – dependency	.23**		
Wagnsson *et al.* (2012) *Swedish data*			
Father's worry conducive climate	.21**	–	–
Mother' worry conducive climate	.26**	–	–
Mother's learning and enjoyment climate	−.23**	–	–

Notes: [a] Path coefficient to the composite factor named. [b] AMDYSQ scales were also used as a composite factor indicating acceptance of sport aggression. [c] Male athletes. [d] Female athletes.

In the construction of AMDYSQ-2 the 24 items were analysed using the scores of 344 participants aged 11 to 16 years (males: $n = 178$, females: $n = 166$) who participated in a pilot test for Study 2 in Chapter 5 and had no missing scores. An EFA extracted four factors including two winning factors, one dominated by the item 'Winning and losing are part of life', and the other by a new item, 'I think fairness is more important than winning'. We selected the second factor because it is more appropriate for research relating to moral attitudes and fair play in youth sport. The three items on this factor and the six highest loading items for cheating and for gamesmanship were submitted to confirmatory factor analysis of a 15-item three-factor model. A good fit is shown in Table A2.2 for the overall sample, males, females, and a multi-sample analysis to confirm the invariance of the scales across gender. This table also includes factor correlations. Factor loadings for exploratory and confirmatory analyses are given with descriptive statistics in Table A2.3.

Cross-validation of AMDYSQ-2

A cross-validation sample for AMDYSQ-2 was drawn from 408 participants aged 11 to 17 years who attended schools in South West England and participated in the study described in Chapter 11. Recreational participants were removed, as

Table A2.2 Fit indices and factor correlations for the three-factor models in the construction and cross-validation of AMDYSQ-2

Model	Items	n	χ^2	d.f.	p	RMSEA	SRMR	CFI	NNFI	Correlations		
										CrG	CrW	GrW
Construction												
All	15	344	147.87	87	.00	.05	.05	.97	.96	.74	-.68	-.72
Male	15	178	113.89	87	.03	.04	.06	.94	.93	.69	-.60	-.68
Female	15	166	105.23	87	.09	.04	.05	.96	.95	.79	-.73	-.69
Multisample	15	344	214.51	207	.35	.02	.08/.07	.95	.93			
Cross-validation												
All	15	293	147.81	87	.00	.05	.05	.96	.95	.61	-.64	-.40
Male	15	142	123.40	87	.01	.05	.07	.97	.99	.54	-.65	-.40
Female	15	149	109.82	87	.05	.04	.08	.99	.99	.67	-.61	-.38
Multisample	15	291	245.27	207	.04	.04	.08/.09	.99	.99			

Notes: LISREL analyses. The multisample analysis imposed constraints for factor loadings, and factor variances and covariances. RMSEA: Root Means Square Error of Approximation; SRMR: Standardized Root Mean Residual; CFI: Comparative Fit Index; NNFI: Non-Normed Fit Index. SRMR is given for males before females. Correlations. CrG: cheating and gamesmanship; CrW: cheating and winning; GrW: gamesmanship and winning.

were seven participants with non-varying responses. Fit indices for the 15-item models were all acceptable and factor correlations were lower than in the construction of AMDYSQ-2 (Table A2.2).

Table A2.3 Descriptive statistics and factor loadings for the AMDYSQ-2 items

Factor and item	Construction					Cross-validation			
	Mean	SD	EFA	CFA15	CFA9	Mean	SD	CFA15	CFA9
I. Gamesmanship	2.75					2.69			
I sometimes try to wind up the opposition[a]	2.90	1.25	.68	.81	.80	2.90	1.25	.85	.81
It's not against the rules to 'psyche' people out so it's OK to do[a]	2.99	1.31	.74	.78		2.79	1.16	.75	
It's a good idea to upset your opponents	2.20	1.19	.57	.77	.76	2.16	1.05	.81	.84
If I don't want another person to do well, then I put them off a bit	2.68	1.22	.58	.76	.80	2.43	1.10	.79	.81
Sometimes I waste time to unsettle the opposition[a]	2.51	1.19	.56	.69		2.63	1.13	.67	
You can unsettle your opponent as long as you don't break the rules	3.23	1.25	.71	.67		3.23	1.22	.74	
II. Cheating	2.28					2.06			
I cheat if I can get away with it	2.34	1.18	.76	.88	.90	2.12	1.07	.87	.81
Sometimes I cheat to gain an advantage	2.25	1.11	.65	.85		2.11	1.01	.88	
It's OK to cheat if nobody knows[a]	2.26	1.19	.65	.84		1.99	1.19	.90	
Sometimes I have to cheat	2.22	1.14	.77	.73	.74	2.03	1.08	.75	.78
I would cheat if I thought it would help me win[a]	2.20	1.24	.70	.71	.73	1.88	1.01	.75	.81
If other people are cheating, I think I can too[a]	2.43	1.28	.47	.70		2.22	1.14	.68	

Table A2.3 continued

Factor and item	Construction					Cross-validation			
	Mean	SD	EFA	CFA15	CFA9	Mean	SD	CFA15	CFA9
III. Keeping winning in proportion	3.79					3.67			
I think fairness is more important than winning	3.67	1.22	.67	.72	.72	3.43	1.11	.81	.72
You have to think about other people, not just winning	3.75	1.06	.61	.69	.69	3.55	1.04	.52	.58
It's OK to lose sometimes because in life you don't win everything[a]	4.14	1.01	.48	.61	.61	4.04	1.10	.61	.63

Notes: [a]AMDYSQ item. Fit for CFA9 χ^2 = 30.84, d.f. = 24, p = 0.16, RMSEA = 0.03, SRMR = 0.05, CFI = 0.98, NNFI = 0.97.

Discussion

Compared with AMDYSQ, the 15-item AMDYSQ-2 model has a conceptually improved KWIP scale, in which two items are replaced to focus on the importance of fairness and consideration of others over winning. It also adds three items to both the cheating and gamesmanship scales, thus providing gender invariance over a greater diversity of items than the 9-item AMDYSQ. Means (range from 2.06 to 3.67) are closer than in AMDYSQ (range from 1.69 to 4.37) and factor correlations are higher ($-0.40 < r < 0.61$) than in AMDYSQ ($-0.12 < r < 0.55$).

Note that Table A2.3 includes factor loadings for a nine-item model formed from the indicators for cheating and gamesmanship used by Lee and colleagues (Chapter 5), and the new KWIP scale. That model is more parsimonious and had a good fit. However, we consider the 15-item model superior because the 9-item model would exclude conceptually important items. Specifically, the cheating items 'Sometimes I cheat to gain an advantage' and 'It's OK to cheat if nobody knows' represent two major dimensions of Reddiford's (1998) conceptualisation of cheating, and the gamesmanship item 'It's not against the rules to "psych" people out so it's OK to do' provides clarification for younger competitors. Gamesmanship is a more sophisticated concept than cheating and develops slowly with experience. We conclude that the 15-item AMDYSQ-2 provides improved assessment of attitudes to cheating, gamesmanship, and keeping wining in proportion and is conceptually appropriate to explore central issues in youth sport psychology.

References

Bureau, J., Vallerand, R.J., Ntoumanis, N. and Lafreniere, M.K. (2013) On passion and moral behavior in achievement settings: the mediating role of pride. *Motivation and Emotion*, 37, 121–33.

Chan, Y., Whitehead, J., Hatzigeorgiadis, A. and Chow, B. (2013) Sport values and ethical attitudes in young Hong Kong golfers. Paper presented at the ISSP13th World Congress of Sport Psychology, Beijing, China.

Charlton, B. and Hill, A. (2010) The relationship between multidimensional perfectionism and attitudes towards moral decision making in youth rugby players. Unpublished BSc dissertation, York St John University, UK.

Costa, S., Oliva, P., Cuzzocrea, F. and Larcan, R. (2013) Parental psychological control and moral attitudes in sport. Paper presented at the ISSP 13th World Congress of Sport Psychology, Beijing, China.

Freeman, P., Leslie, A., Leger, H. and Williams, C. (2013) How important are the values of significant others? Chapter 11, this book.

Gymnopoulou, V. and Vatali, D. (2010) Relationships among values and moral attitudes in adolescent students. In Proceedings of 10th Thematic Congress of Northern Greece Physical Education Teachers Association. Thessaloniki: Northern Greece Physical Education Teachers Association, pp. 130–1.

Lee, M.J., Whitehead, J. and Ntoumanis, N. (2007) Development of the Attitudes to Moral Decision-making in Youth Sport Questionnaire (AMDYSQ). *Psychology of Sport and Exercise*, 8, 369–92.

Lee, M.J., Whitehead, J., Ntoumanis, N. and Hatzigeorgiadis, A. (2008) Relationships among values, achievement orientations, and attitudes in youth sport. *Journal of Sport and Exercise Psychology*, 30, 585–610.

Lucidi, F., Mallia, L., Zelli, A., Nicolais, G. and Baldacci, A. (2013) Cheating and games-manship in youth Italian players: from attitude to behaviour. Paper presented at the ISSP 13th World Congress of Sport Psychology, Beijing, China.

Ntoumanis, N., Taylor, I. and Thøgersen-Ntoumani, C. (2011) A longitudinal examination of coach and peer motivational climates in youth sport: Implications for moral attitudes, well-being, and behavioural investment. *Developmental Psychology*, 48, 213–23.

Reddiford, G. (1998) Cheating and self-deception in sport. In M.J. McNamee and S.J. Parry (eds) *Ethics and Sport*. London: E. & F.N. Spon, pp. 225–39.

Vallerand, R. J., Deshaies, P., Cuierrier, J.-P., Brière, N.M. and Pelletier, L.G. (1996) Toward a multi-dimensional definition of sportsmanship. *Journal of Applied Sport Psychology*, 8, 89–101.

Wagnsson, S., Gustafsson, H. and Augustsson, H.C. (2012) The relation between perceived parent created motivation climate and elite youth soccer player's moral deci-sions in sports: the importance of mothers. Paper presented at the International Convention on Science, Education and Medicine in Sport, Glasgow, 19–24 July.

Whitehead, J. (2007) New dimensions in understanding ethical attitudes of young competi-tors. In Gonçalves, C.E., Cumming, S.P., C e Silva, M.J. and Malina, R.M. (eds) *Sport and Education*. Coimbra: University of Coimbra, pp. 256–73.

Whitehead, J., Lee, M. and Hatzigeorgiadis, A. (2003) Goal orientations as mediators of the influence of values on ethical attitudes in youth sport: generalization of the model. *Journal of Sports Sciences*, 21(4), 364–5.

Zengaro, S. (2010) Biofunctional embodiment of moral development: The impact of affect, moral cognition, gender, and experience in playing sport on acceptance of aggression in sports by Italian adolescents. Unpublished doctoral dissertation, University of Alabama, Tuscaloosa, AL.

Zengaro, F., Zengaro, S. and Malfi, M. (2009) Acceptance of aggression and moral decision-making in Italian adolescents. Paper presented at the meeting of the European Committee on Sports History, Pisa, Italy.

Zengaro, S., Iran-Nejad, A. and Zengaro, F. (2011) Adolescent attitudes toward the acceptance of sports aggression: Comparing a multi-source model across cultures. Paper presented at the Meeting of the American Educational Research Association, New Orleans, LA.

Zengaro, S., Zengaro, F., Song, C. and Zhang, J. (2012) A cross-cultural investigation of the acceptance of sports aggression. Paper presented at the meeting of the American Psychological Association, Orlando, FL.

Appendix 3

Questionnaires for discussion groups

Some exercises for coaches developed by Martin Lee

Your coaching values

Look at the reasons for coaching children that are given below and place them in order of importance first for you and, second, for your club.

Reason	You	Club
Being able to continue to have fun in a game you enjoyed	.....	.....
Finding a really talented performer for top basketball	.....	.....
Giving children the opportunity to learn new skills	.....	.....
Giving opportunities to belong to a group	.....	.....
Helping children to understand fair play	.....	.....
Helping your own child	.....	.....
Providing children with the opportunity to have some fun	.....	.....
Providing opportunities for children to make new friends	.....	.....
To promote your national team	.....	.....
Winning competitions for your club	.....	.....

How much are you in agreement with the club where you coach? (Circle one)

Not at all   Not very much   Quite a lot   Completely

Children's playing values

Now, talk to the children you coach, and place in order of the importance that you think they would give, the different reasons for doing sport in the following list

Reason	Ranking of importance
Having fun	.....
Learning new skill and getting better at old ones	.....
Being recognised for how good they are	.....
Being with friends	.....
Belonging to the group	.....
Facing new challenges	.....
Winning tournaments	.....

A Rokeach-based questionnaire for discussion groups

Abridged from Lee (1993: 30–2)

In recent years I have asked coaches and students about their values in sport and in life. Using the same technique as Milton Rokeach (1973) and adapting his value labels for sport, I have produced a short questionnaire to help coaches explore their value systems.

Instructions

Rank each of the values listed in order of importance to you both in column (a) and column (b). In (a) rank them on how important they are in your life in general; in (b) rank them on how important they are to you in sport. Identify which values in each list you think are intrapersonal and interpersonal.

Sports Value Survey

Terminal values	(a)	(b)	Instrumental values	(a)	(b)
Accomplishment	___	___	Accepting	___	___
Equality	___	___	Ambitious	___	___
Freedom	___	___	Capable	___	___
Friendship	___	___	Considerate	___	___
Justice	___	___	Disciplined	___	___
Pleasure	___	___	Forgiving	___	___
Self-respect	___	___	Honest	___	___
Social recognition	___	___	Independent	___	___

Source: adapted from Rokeach (1973)

Now ask yourself three questions:

1 Are you consistent in sport and life in general?
2 How do your values affect your coaching?
3 Which values are strongest in your system:
   (i) Attainment or social?
   (ii) Competence or moral?

Classification of human values according to dimension and focus

Focus	Value dimension	
	Terminal	Instrumental
Intrapersonal	Attainment	Competence
Interpersonal	Social	Moral

You may find, as have many of my students, that there are differences between what they value, and consequently how they behave, in life generally and in sports. As a result many of them have begun to look again at what they believe to be most important.

However, among coaches I have found that there is more agreement between their instrumental values in life and sport; they set their priorities about conduct in much the same way in both situations. But their goals, terminal values, in sport tend to be personal while in life they value social goals more strongly.

References

Lee, M. (1993) Why are you coaching children? in Lee, M. (ed.) *Coaching Children in Sport: Principles and Practice*. London: E. & F.N. Spon, pp. 27–38.

Rokeach, M. (1973) *The Nature of Human Values*. New York: The Free Press.

Appendix 4

The values and attitude questionnaires and their administration and scoring

Introduction

These are self-report questionnaires. Participants rate a list of questionnaire items by circling a number for each one to give their opinion about it. However, the results will be valid only if participants answer honestly and independently. Precautions are needed to encourage honest answers.

a) **Administrative conditions.** Use controlled conditions where participants cannot be influenced by others in the room, and there are no distractions. Tell participants that the questionnaires are not a test and that there are no right or wrong answers because everyone thinks differently. Assure them that their participation is voluntary, they can withdraw at any time, their scores will be anonymous, and their data will not be shared with anyone outside the research team. Seek the approval of an ethics committee for your project.

b) **Instructions written on the questionnaires.** The questionnaires have simple titles to use when administering them to young competitors. Give them only a brief account of the nature of your research. Do not indicate what results you may expect as this will bias their answers. Clarify the instructions on the questionnaires and encourage participants to ask questions at any time if they do not understand.

There are additional safeguards for the values questionnaires. Because values are all desirable qualities there is a tendency for participants to give too many high ratings. Instructions on the questionnaires ask participants to read through the list to first identify the two items that are most and least important to them, then to rate the other items in relation to these two. This is called anchoring the scales.

Further guidance can be used to spread the scores. Participants may be told that the top rating is for a 'value of supreme importance in guiding what I do in sport' and there are not usually more than two or three such values. They may be asked to distinguish as much as possible between the values by using all the numbers.

c) *Analysing the results.* There is a scoring key at the end of each questionnaire, which should be deleted before administering it. The participants should not know which items are on which scales because this can bias their responses. The YSVQ includes two non-scoring items. These say opposite things and are used only to detect participants who strongly agree with all items. Screen your data file and eliminate participants who give the same answer to each question or have almost no variability in their answers.

What do the research questionnaires measure?

The Attitude Questionnaires

1. **AMDYSQ (Attitudes to Moral Decision-Making in Youth Sport Questionnaire)** is a short 9-item questionnaire which has three scales to measure attitudes to *Keeping Winning in Proportion* (KWIP), *Acceptance of Gamesmanship* (AG) and *Acceptance of Cheating* (AC). Each scale comprises 3 items which should be averaged to produce the *mean score* for the scale. This will be between 1 and 5. Generally youth sport competitors have higher means for KWIP than AG, with AC having the lowest means. Within any group the scores of the individual members normally show that AG and AC correlate positively with each other, and that each of these scales correlates negatively with KWIP.

2. **AMDYSQ-2.** This is a revised 15-item version of AMDYSQ which measures the same scales and is described in Appendix 2. The new 3-item KWIP scale focuses more clearly on the attitude that fairness is more important than winning, and there are longer 6-item scales for AG and AC. There is a short form if your time is limited but it has some disadvantages (see Appendix 2). A unique feature of the two AMDYSQ questionnaires is the measure of gamesmanship which is not, to our knowledge, assessed by other questionnaires.

The Values Questionnaires

3. **YSVQ (Youth Sport Values Questionnaire).** This questionnaire measures the *relative importance of 18 distinctly different youth sport values*. There are no scales in this instrument because each item was selected to be different from the others in order to cover the greatest range of values. i.e. *enjoyment* and *health and fitness* can't be put in a common scale. The questionnaire provides scores to rank the priorities of the 18 values and thus show the hierarchical *value system* of a person or group. Youth sport competitors typically rank enjoyment first, followed by personal achievement and a group of socio-moral values including sportsmanship, contract maintenance and fair play – with winning ranked at the bottom. The value systems of different groups can be compared.

4. **YSVQ-2.** This 13-item questionnaire has three scales to measure *moral, competence* and *status* values with multi-item scales of 4 or 5 items. *Mean scores* are obtained by averaging the item scores for each scale. Generally youth sport competitors have slightly higher means for *competence* than *moral* values with *status* values considerably lower. *Competence* values correlate more highly with *moral* values than with *status* values and the correlation between *moral* and *status* values is lowest of all. This questionnaire will give a better measure of a more restricted range of values, e.g. it excludes enjoyment. These three values were selected as the first candidates for higher order measurement to address research questions posed in Chapters 5 and 8. Future research should develop other multi-item scales.

Further information

1. **Psychometric detail**
   In the abridged articles in Chapters 2 to 5 some psychometric information was removed to enhance readability. For this, consult the original articles. Details about the construction of the questionnaires has been submitted to PsycTESTS, a database of the American Psychological Association together with appropriate supplementary information. For example, the original articles offered further information 'on request' to readers through footnotes. We provide a composite questionnaire, the YSVQ-C, containing both the YSVQ and YSVQ-2, and a clarification of how a related version has been wrongly analysed and interpreted by others. Further relevant information, e.g. translations, will be submitted as it becomes available.

2. **Age differences**
   The questionnaires have been developed with the 12–16 year age group. Some constructs will not be understood by younger age groups. For example, gamesmanship measures upsetting an opponent psychologically without breaking the rules. It is a more subtle concept than cheating and it takes time to develop. These two factors may not be differentiated by young or inexperienced players.

3. **Qualitative and quantitative measures**
   The development of every questionnaire began with qualitative methods. These give a much richer source of data but cannot be applied to a large population. Consider the role of qualitative methods to supplement your enquiries with quantitative questionnaires.

AMDYSQ

How I play sport

Here is a list of things that young people have said about the way they play sport. Please **CIRCLE** one number for each item to show how well it describes how you play in your **main sport**. There are no right or wrong answers. This is what the numbers mean:

> 1= **Strongly Disagree (SD)**
> 2= **Disagree**   **(D)**
> 3= **Neutral/Uncertain (N)**
> 4= **Agree**   **(A)**
> 5= **Strongly Agree**   **(SA)**

Please answer the following questions in relation to your **main sport**:

		SD	D	N	A	SA
1.	I would cheat if I thought it would help me win	1	2	3	4	5
2.	Sometimes I waste time to unsettle the opposition	1	2	3	4	5
3.	It's OK to lose sometimes because in life you don't win everything	1	2	3	4	5
4.	It is not against the rules to 'psyche' people out so it is OK to do	1	2	3	4	5
5.	If other people are cheating, I think I can too	1	2	3	4	5
6.	I sometimes try to wind up the opposition	1	2	3	4	5
7.	Winning and losing are a part of life	1	2	3	4	5
8.	It's OK to cheat if nobody knows	1	2	3	4	5
9.	If you win properly, it feels better than if you did it dishonestly	1	2	3	4	5

PLEASE CHECK THAT YOU ANSWERED **ALL** THE QUESTIONS AND
THAT YOU GAVE ONLY **ONE** ANSWER FOR EACH QUESTION
THANK YOU FOR YOUR HELP

Scoring key for administrators (delete before administering the questionnaire)

Acceptance of cheating: 1, 5, 8
Acceptance of gamesmanship: 2, 4, 6
Keeping winning in proportion: 3, 7, 9

AMDYSQ-2

How I play sport

Here is a list of things that young people have said about the way they play sport. Please **CIRCLE** one of the numbers beside each item to show how well it describes how you play in your **main sport**. There are no right or wrong answers. This is what the numbers mean:

1= **Strongly Disagree (SD)**
2= **Disagree**   (D)
3= **Neutral**   (N)
4= **Agree**   (A)
5= **Strongly Agree** (SA)

Please answer the following questions in relation to your **main sport**:

		SD	D	N	A	SA
1.	You can unsettle your opponents as long as you don't break the rules	1	2	3	4	5
2.	I would cheat if I thought it would help me win	1	2	3	4	5
3.	If I don't want another person to do well, then I put them off a bit	1	2	3	4	5
4.	I think fairness is more important than winning	1	2	3	4	5
5.	If other people are cheating, I think I can too	1	2	3	4	5
6.	Sometimes I waste time to unsettle the opposition	1	2	3	4	5
7.	It's OK to lose sometimes because in life you don't win everything	1	2	3	4	5
8.	I cheat if I can get away with it	1	2	3	4	5
9.	It's a good idea to upset your opponents	1	2	3	4	5
10.	Sometimes I have to cheat	1	2	2	4	5
11.	It's OK to cheat if nobody knows	1	2	3	4	5
12.	It is not against the rules to 'psyche' people out so it is OK to do	1	2	3	4	5
13.	I sometimes try to wind up the opposition	1	2	3	4	5
14.	You have to think about the other people and not just winning	1	2	3	4	5
15.	Sometimes I cheat to gain an advantage	1	2	3	4	5

PLEASE CHECK THAT YOU ANSWERED **ALL** THE QUESTIONS AND
THAT YOU GAVE ONLY **ONE** ANSWER FOR EACH QUESTION
THANK YOU FOR YOUR HELP

Scoring key for adminstrators (delete before administering the questionnaire)

The complete questionnaire	*The short form*
Acceptance of cheating: 2, 5, 8, 10, 11, 15	*2, 8, 10*
Acceptance of gamesmanship: 1, 3, 6, 9, 12, 13	*3, 9, 13*
Keeping winning in proportion: 4, 7, 14	*4, 7, 14*

YSVQ

What is important to me in sport

Please **CIRCLE** one of the numbers beside each item to show how important it is to you when competing in your **main sport**. This is what the numbers mean:

-1 = This idea **is the opposite of what I believe**.
0 = This idea is **not important** to me.
1 = This idea is **slightly important** to me.
2 = This idea is **quite important** to me.
3 = This idea is **important** to me.
4 = This idea is **very important** to me.
5 = This idea is **extremely important** to me.

BEFORE YOU BEGIN please read through the list to find which idea is **most** important to you and which idea is **least** important. Mark those ideas first, then go through the list again and mark the other ideas.

When I do sport it is important to me that....

		the opp	not imptnt	slight imptnt	quite imptnt	imptnt	very imptnt	extra imptnt
1.	I don't let people down	-1	0	1	2	3	4	5
2.	I get a buzz or feel really good when I am playing	-1	0	1	2	3	4	5
3.	I show a good image to others	-1	0	1	2	3	4	5
4.	I go along with everybody else	-1	0	1	2	3	4	5
5.	I do things with my mates (friends)	-1	0	1	2	3	4	5
6.	I can wear what I like	-1	0	1	2	3	4	5
7.	I try to be fair	-1	0	1	2	3	4	5
8.	I improve my performance	-1	0	1	2	3	4	5
9.	I do what I am told	-1	0	1	2	3	4	5
10.	I do sport to get fit	-1	0	1	2	3	4	5
11.	It is an exciting contest	-1	0	1	2	3	4	5
12.	I show good sportsmanship	-1	0	1	2	3	4	5
13.	I do the skills or techniques well	-1	0	1	2	3	4	5
14.	I accept other people's weaknesses	-1	0	1	2	3	4	5
15.	I enjoy myself and have fun	-1	0	1	2	3	4	5
16.	I wear the right kit for it	-1	0	1	2	3	4	5
17.	I make sure we all stick together	-1	0	1	2	3	4	5
18.	I show that I am better than others	-1	0	1	2	3	4	5
19.	I help people when they need it	-1	0	1	2	3	4	5
20.	I always play properly	-1	0	1	2	3	4	5

PLEASE CHECK THAT YOU ANSWERED **ALL** THE QUESTIONS AND
THAT YOU GAVE ONLY **ONE** ANSWER FOR EACH QUESTION
THANK YOU FOR YOUR HELP

Scoring key for administrators (delete before administering the questionnaire)
Items 6 and 16 are non-scoring and may be eliminated.
There are no scales within this questionnaire. Each item is independent.

YSVQ-2

What is important to me in sport

Please **CIRCLE** one of the numbers beside each item to show how important it is to you in your **main sport**. This is what the numbers mean:

-1 = This idea **is the opposite of what I believe.**
0 = This idea is **not important** to me.
1 = This idea is **slightly important** to me.
2 = This idea is **quite important** to me.
3 = This idea is **important** to me.
4 = This idea is **very important** to me.
5 = This idea is **extremely important** to me.

BEFORE YOU BEGIN please read through the list to find which idea is **most** important to you and which idea is **least** important. Mark those ideas first, then go through the list again and mark the other ideas.

When I do sport it is important to me that....

		the opp	not imptnt	slight imptnt	quite imptnt	imptnt	very imptnt	extra imptnt
1.	I show that I am better than others	-1	0	1	2	3	4	5
2.	I try to be fair	-1	0	1	2	3	4	5
3.	I win or beat others	-1	0	1	2	3	4	5
4.	I improve my performance	-1	0	1	2	3	4	5
5.	I do what I am told	-1	0	1	2	3	4	5
6.	I show good sportsmanship	-1	0	1	2	3	4	5
7.	I am a leader in the group	-1	0	1	2	3	4	5
8.	I become a better player	-1	0	1	2	3	4	5
9.	I look good	-1	0	1	2	3	4	5
10.	I always play properly	-1	0	1	2	3	4	5
11.	I use my skills well	-1	0	1	2	3	4	5
12.	I help people when they need it	-1	0	1	2	3	4	5
13.	I set my own targets	-1	0	1	2	3	4	5

PLEASE CHECK THAT YOU ANSWERED **ALL** THE QUESTIONS AND
THAT YOU GAVE ONLY **ONE** ANSWER FOR EACH QUESTION
THANK YOU FOR YOUR HELP

Scoring key for adminstrators (delete before administering the questionnaire)

Moral values: 2, 5, 6, 10, 12
Competence values: 4, 8, 11, 13
Status values: 1, 3, 7, 9

Glossary

Achievement goal orientation A dispositional orientation which relates to a particular view of success that is dependent on how ability is construed and evaluated (Nicholls, 1989).

Attitude 'learned pre-disposition to respond in a consistently favorable or unfavorable manner with respect to a given object' (Fishbein and Ajzen, 1975: 5).

Cheating 'infractions of the rules in order to gain some unfair advantage in which there is a degree of successful deception' (Lee *et al.*, 2007: 372)

Gamesmanship 'actions that do not actually violate the rules of the sport but that do appear to violate the spirit of the contest...Potter...described... strategies to upset opponents and win without actually cheating' (Lee *et al.*, 2007: 372).

We use the term *gamesmanship* to apply equally to both genders. We consider that the gender-neutral term 'gamespersonship' would be widely misinterpreted to mean someone who plays games. Outside the UK *gamesmanship* and *sportsmanship* have been confounded. Similarly we use *sportsmanship* as a generic term.

Motivational climate Environmental structures and cues that make different achievement goals salient to participants (Ames 1992).

Value 'an enduring belief that a specific mode of conduct or end state of existence is personally or socially preferable to an opposite or converse mode of conduct or end state of existence' (Rokeach, 1973: 5).

Value structure Correlational relationships among basic values, showing motivational conflicts and compatibilities (Schwartz, 1992)

Value system 'an enduring organization of beliefs concerning preferable modes of conduct or end states of existence arranged along a continuum of relative importance' (Rokeach, 1973: 5).

References

Ames, C. (1992) Achievement goals, motivational climate, and motivational processes. In G.C. Roberts (ed.) *Motivation in Sport and Exercise*. Champaign, IL: Human Kinetics, pp. 161–76.

Fishbein, M. and Ajzen, I. (1975) *Belief, Attitude, Intention, and Behavior: An Introduction to Theory and Research*. Reading, MA: Addison-Wesley.

Lee, M.J. (1995) Relationships between values and motives in sport. Paper presented at the 9th European Congress in Sport Psychology, Brussels, Belgium, 4–9 July.

Lee, M.J., Whitehead, J., and Ntoumanis, N. (2007) Development of the Attitudes to Moral Decisions in Youth Sport Questionnaire (AMDYSQ). *Psychology of Sport and Exercise*, 8(3), 369–92.

Nicholls, J.G. (1989) *The Competitive Ethos and Democratic Education*. Cambridge, MA: Harvard University Press.

Rokeach, M. (1973) *The Nature of Human Values*. New York: Free Press.

Schwartz, S. (1992) Universals in the content and structure of values: Theoretical advances and empirical tests in 20 countries. In M. P. Zanna (ed.) *Advances in Experimental Social Psychology*, 25, 1–65. London: Academic Press.

Index